HABERMAS AND CONTEMPORARY SOCIETY

John F. Sitton

HABERMAS AND CONTEMPORARY SOCIETY
© John F. Sitton, 2003

First published 2003 by PALGRAVE MACMILLAN™
175 Fifth Avenue, New York, N.Y. 10010 and
Houndmills, Basingstoke, Hampshire, England RG21 6XS.
Companies and representatives throughout the world.

PALGRAVE MACMILLAN is the global academic imprint of the Palgrave Macmillan division of St. Martin's Press, LLC and of Palgrave Macmillan Ltd. Macmillan® is a registered trademark in the United States, United Kingdom and other countries. Palgrave is a registered trademark in the European Union and other countries.

ISBN 1–4039–6192–1 hardback
ISBN 1–4039–6193–X paperback

Library of Congress Cataloging-in-Publication Data
Sitton, John F., 1952–
    Habermas and contemporary society/John F. Sitton.
      p. cm.
    Includes bibliographical references.
    ISBN 1–4039–6192–1—ISBN 1–4039–6193–X (pbk.)
      1. Frankfurt school of sociology. 2. Habermas, Jérgen. 3. Critical theory.
I. Title.

HM467.S58 2003
301—dc21   2002044970

A catalogue record for this book is available from the British Library.

Design by Newgen Imaging Systems (P) Ltd., Chennai, India.

First edition: August 2003
10 9 8 7 6 5 4 3 2 1

Printed in the United States of America.

For Irene, Junior, and Liz,
and for our late brother Chuck

CONTENTS

ACKNOWLEDGMENTS

The preliminary research for this book was accomplished during a sabbatical granted by Indiana University of Pennsylvania for the Fall of 1994. I would like to thank the Indiana University of Pennsylvania Sabbatical Committee for its encouragement.

Parts of chapters 5, 7, and 8 were previously published as "Disembodied Capitalism: Habermas's Conception of the Economy," *Sociological Forum* Volume 13, Number 1 (March 1998): pp. 61–83. I thank the University Senate Grant Committee for a summer grant in 1995 that supported the work for the article.

Finally, other parts of chapters 5, 7, and 8 were also aided by a different summer grant in 1996 from the University Senate Grant Committee. Again, without the diligent and time-consuming efforts by these university committees, such work would not be possible.

PREFACE

The astrophysicist Stephen Hawking once related a dismal joke making the rounds among his colleagues: The reason we have not been contacted by more advanced life from other planets is that when civilizations reach our level of technological sophistication, they inevitably destroy themselves.

For all of its bravado, contemporary capitalism is at an impasse. It continues to form powerful forces of production yet is apparently incapable of applying these forces so as to satisfy the basic needs of the world's population. There is economic growth, but also mass poverty and environmental destruction. Even in the developed world, productivity grows in odd conjunction with a determined attack on standards of living and entitlements, mass unemployment, and a vicious scapegoating to explain the general experience of decline. One hundred and fifty years after Marx's *Manifesto*, contemporary capitalism does indeed appear to be a "sorceror...who is no longer able to control the powers of the nether world whom he has called up by his spells."

The traditional socialist remedies for this impasse are also suspect. Socialism has always promised rational control and application of socially generated wealth but the historical form of socialism—primarily public control of production—has demonstrated its own shortcomings, especially a disregard for the rule of law. Neither contemporary capitalism nor socialism as historically experienced lives up to its promises; neither has been able to establish freedom and the satisfaction of needs.

A third option has been in place in the advanced industrial countries since World War II: an interventionist state that actively stimulates economic growth and skims part of the profits to fund various programs of social security, an arrangement Jürgen Habermas and others call the "welfare state compromise." However, this welfare state has now been under intensifying attack for over two decades. Although barely yesterday progressives were arguing that the welfare state does not go far enough, today they are reduced to attempting to blunt conservative initiatives.

Somewhat surprisingly, Habermas continues to place himself in the socialist, even Marxian socialist, tradition. On several occasions Habermas has insisted that his social theory is a continuation of Marxian theory in contemporary circumstances, describing Marxism as a tradition that "I've quite fiercely decided to defend as a still-meaningful enterprise."[1] He has even humorously referred to himself as "the last Marxist."[2] However, he believes that the traditional socialist approach to the problems of capitalism has exhausted its possibilities. Habermas also recognizes the ambivalent consequences of the welfare state compromise, regarding it as at the same time necessary but disempowering, and therefore dangerous to a healthy political community. Instead, he outlines an alternative political project based on an intriguing analysis of the strengths and limitations of contemporary capitalism.

Although this analysis could well stimulate new arguments and strategies, Habermas's theory is largely addressed to specialists in social theory and political theory. The consequence is that there is an enormous literature on Habermas but it largely remains the province of experts. This is truly unfortunate. It is also somewhat ironic in that Habermas argues repeatedly and vigorously that one of the central problems of contemporary society is precisely that relevant perspectives remain "encapsulated in expert cultures."

A major part of the problem is that Habermas's work is extraordinarily wide-ranging. He has contributed to and advanced discussions in the fields of social theory, linguistics, moral philosophy, and legal theory. In the process he has produced an original analysis of contemporary capitalism and its conflicts. In his central work of social theory, the two-volume *The Theory of Communicative Action*, Habermas has also given interesting readings of major social theorists such as Karl Marx, Max Weber, George Herbert Mead, Emile Durkheim, and Talcott Parsons.

The obverse of this situation is that Habermas's work is confusingly diverse and demandingly abstract. This results from developing his own theory through commentaries on and critical appropriation of the theories of others. Habermas himself has called *The Theory of Communicative Action* "hopelessly abstract" and "a monster." All too often his overall picture of contemporary capitalist society—its structure, dynamic, and likelihood of crisis—is lost in the detailed examination of some interesting point or other. It is hard to appreciate the forest while one is pondering all these trees.

The purpose of this book is to introduce Habermas's social theory to a larger audience by attempting to grasp that broad picture, tracing the overall contours of his argument. The focus is especially on Habermas's substantive view of contemporary society and the relation between that and his political proposals. It will therefore downplay methodological points as much as possible. This will clarify how Habermas conceives the major domestic political development of recent decades, the crumbling of the welfare state compromise. It will also show how his work is related to recent initiatives in political theory, such as the interest in "civil society" and the increasing doubts about the utility of seeking direct political power.

Habermas is the premier representative of the second generation of critical theorists known as the Frankfurt School. The first generation, which included Max Horkheimer, Theodor Adorno, and Herbert Marcuse, moved away from the Marxian emphasis on the dynamic of the capitalist economy by expanding their analyses to consider broader processes of the "rationalization" of social life. Stimulated by the work of Max Weber, the Frankfurt School focused attention on the dangerous predominance of "instrumental reason" in contemporary society. As the phrase suggests, the employment of reason in modern society is overwhelmingly informed by a project of controlling the natural world. The danger, as the critical theorists saw it, was that this modern project would be (and, in fact, has been) extended to subduing and manipulating social life in a variety of ways. Many earlier critical theorists believed (as do some today) that our language itself is predisposed to further this project, raising the specter of an "administered world" populated by monads who have lost their capacity to live or even conceive a more emancipated and humane social life.

For this reason some critical theorists sought out nonlinguistic aspects of human existence in which resistance to these developments and a glimpse of an alternative could be found. To this end they speculated on the possible "redemptive" power of art or tried to tease out some basis for revolt in allegedly primordial human instincts, the latter investigations inspired by Freudian theory. It is fair to say, at least at this remove, that these earlier efforts do not appear very persuasive. Habermas, on the other hand, constructs a social theory that to a considerable extent escapes the theoretical cul-de-sacs of his predecessors.

Proceeding from certain themes of Weber, Habermas argues that the modernization of social life depends on a prior rationalization of cultural life. In the course of cultural development specific cultural areas become independent of each other—natural science, moral and legal argumentation, and artistic expression—as each pursues the "inner logic" of its own subject area. The shearing off of these cultural areas from each other is often experienced as the destruction of reason itself in that traditional beliefs and practices lose their unquestionable character.

Habermas proposes that rather than the end of reason these cultural developments signify the emergence of alternative rational attitudes toward the world. Modern understanding is based on acknowledging different dimensions of rationality or "voices of reason" that are specific to natural science, morals, and subjective expression and that are irreducible to one another. An example might be in regard to the natural world: One can approach it as merely a set of useful facts to be exploited for human purposes ("cognitive-rationality"), or one can seek to formulate an ethical relation to, for example, the treatment of animals ("moral–practical rationality"), or one can view nature from a third approach of aesthetic appreciation and fulfillment ("aesthetic–expressive rationality"). None of these "attitudes" toward the world can be conflated with nor legitimately subsume the others. The prior unity of reason based on God, nature, or metaphysical principles, by means of which one could try to make sense of and order various cultural and social practices, has dissolved.

On the other hand, the differentiation of cultural spheres opens up possibilities for new knowledge, "learning processes," that can be utilized in confronting social and political problems. However, contemporary capitalist society promotes one type of rationality above all, an instrumental approach to the world that assimilates all human phenomena to "things" in the natural world. Habermas's central contention is that, due to the expansion of a state-managed capitalism, arenas of social life dominated by an instrumental attitude ultimately encroach on social relations that can only be sustained in other ways, specifically by "reaching understanding" with each other. Consequently Habermas outlines a political project that might shore up processes of mutual understanding so as to resist further expansion of the "monetary–bureaucratic complex" and create a more balanced social life in which all the dimensions of reason are given their due. This would encourage innovative ways of addressing the searing social and political conflicts that contemporary capitalism, regardless of its technological prowess, has proven itself quite incapable of resolving.

Rather than anticipate the argument any further here, I will simply briefly mention the topics of the chapters. First, since Habermas's theory of cultural rationalization is consciously indebted to Max Weber, chapter 1 considers Weber's "diagnosis of the times" and how his analysis helped frame Habermas's own approach. Habermas's specific appropriation of Weber is partly but crucially informed by the limitations of earlier attempts to rethink critical theory in light of Weber's theses on rationalization. Chapter 2 presents an overview of the themes of these previous critical theorists, specifically Georg Lukács, Horkheimer and Adorno, and Marcuse. Much of Habermas's own social theory relies on his extension of the concept of rationality and his central idea of "communicative action" as the process of people's reaching understanding with one another, the subject of chapter 3. Chapter 4 then examines what Habermas means by "societal rationalization." This leads to Habermas's all-important theoretical distinction between society conceived as a "lifeworld" and society conceived as a "system." This distinction grounds Habermas's conceptualization of contemporary capitalism and its conflicts. Chapter 5 explains Habermas's conception of the origins of social conflict in contemporary society and his alternative political proposals for alleviating these.

Needless to say, such a wide-ranging and innovative social and political theory is bound to underplay certain, nevertheless important, topics and provoke serious criticisms. In chapter 6 I briefly examine three such areas of criticism, a postmodern repudiation of the emphasis on consensus in the linguistic practices central to social life, confusions stemming from the underdevelopment of the idea of aesthetic rationality, and multiple criticisms of Habermas's treatment (or neglect) of gender. In the next chapter, on a fairly abstract level I explore what I believe to be the central weakness of Habermas's social theory, the relation between system and lifeworld, and how this produces an overly restricted conception of possible and necessary political action today. Finally, the concluding chapter examines Habermas's more specific arguments on contemporary political affairs, revealing the ways in which Habermas's theory guides and limits his political understanding. In doing so we can gain a provisional appraisal—all theoretical arguments are inescapably provisional—of twenty-first-century possibilities for, to borrow a phrase from Anthony Giddens, "reason without revolution."[3]

Habermas explores new paths along which a balanced and emancipated social life might be pursued. In so doing he outlines a more "procedural" socialism that can help us face the challenges of the twenty-first century while avoiding the now obvious failings of socialism of the twentieth century. Whatever ambiguities and limitations there may be to his social and political arguments, Habermas's theoretical achievements cannot be ignored by anyone who puzzles over a world that proliferates tremendous productive forces, and hungry, frightened children who cry themselves to sleep at night.

CHAPTER 1

WEBER AND MODERNITY

In trying to understand Habermas's theory of contemporary society it is best to begin with the early twentieth-century sociologist Max Weber. Habermas argues that certain analyses by Weber—which Habermas calls Weber's "diagnosis of the times"—help uncover the origins of contemporary cultural and social disarray. For this reason, the overarching framework of Habermas's most detailed work in social theory, *The Theory of Communicative Action*, is a reconsideration of Weber's diagnosis in light of later social theories and present political dilemmas.

Weber is especially known for *The Protestant Ethic and the Spirit of Capitalism*, his study of the religious origins of the capitalist way of life, as well as for his analysis of the principles behind the organizational efficiency of bureaucracy. He argues that modern social life resulted from the confluence of several forces of cultural and social "rationalization," a transformation that was most fully actualized in Europe and the United States. Similarly, the guiding thread of Habermas's theory is that both the material successes and the various social conflicts that are endemic to early twenty-first-century society can be traced back to the problematic path of this rationalization. In order to understand Habermas's theory of contemporary society, it is therefore useful to begin with those arguments of Weber on which Habermas focuses attention.

WEBER ON RATIONALITY

Weber states that modern society is characterized by the dominance of rational action. This is so from the standpoint of several meanings of "rationality": systematic thought using precise concepts; analysis of means for their effectiveness in obtaining a goal; methodical action; and rejection of traditional beliefs in favor of independent reasoning about a situation.[1] At the beginning of *The Protestant Ethic and the Spirit of Capitalism* Weber gives numerous examples of European social and cultural practices that embody some of these dimensions of rationality. Natural science based on methodical experimentation is of course the most prominent and Weber also mentions the extensive development of mathematics and of chemistry-based medicine. A similar rationalization is seen in the formulation of a systematic theology based on the dual heritage of Christianity and ancient Greek thought. In the political sphere, Weber points to the establishment of a constitutional state, a rigorous articulation of legal concepts, and the dominant role of "officials." In the sphere of culture, the persistent exploration of new artistic and architectural possibilities (e.g., perspective and the arch) and musical development based on notation and culminating in the symphony can also be conceived as examples of rationalization. Economic activity is rationalized with the emergence of organizations for the systematic pursuit of profit through regularized exchange (rather than through force or political manipulations). The economic activity is based on the establishment of a pool of "free labor" (not bound to the land, a particular occupation, or through other forms of servitude), the legal separation of business property from one's personal property, and bookkeeping that allows a clear calculation of the contribution to gain by the individual economic factors. Finally, many of these developments were supported by the enduring European institution for the pursuit of knowledge, the university.

The core of Weber's conception of rationalization, then, is the increase in a methodical and systematic approach to various spheres of social activity. Although there were precursors in many cultures, according to Weber only Western ("Occidental") society fully pursued the possibilities of rationalizing this broad variety of fields of human endeavor. In fact, the above examples bring to mind the project of the eighteenth-century Enlightenment "encyclopedists" who aspired to apply independent reasoning to the full range of human experience and activity. The primary puzzle that Weber wants to investigate is precisely why this and not another society took the lead. He concludes that the impetus for the rationalization of social action was a prior cultural rationalization, especially the elaboration of a particular worldview in Western religious development.

In explicit contrast to Marx, Weber insists on the independent causal importance of ideas and images of the world. Ideas are historically important in two different ways. First, the motives of individuals are not reducible to a narrow desire for material improvement. Rather, Weber argues that people are powerfully motivated by certain "ideal interests," for example, an interest in spiritual salvation, as well as by more mundane "material interests." Second, although these multiple interests are certainly the driving force of history, they do not of themselves determine the direction of history. At any particular time more or less coherent interpretations of how the world "is"—that is, worldviews, often expressed by the German word *Weltanschauungen*—shape the paths along which interests are pursued. "Not ideas, but material and ideal interests, directly govern men's conduct. Yet very frequently the 'world images' that have been created by 'ideas' have, like switchmen, determined the tracks along which action has been pushed by the dynamic of interest."[2] Furthermore, in an argument that is central to Habermas's own theory, Weber states that the autonomy of ideas in history is reinforced by the fact that ideas are subject to the independent requirement of "logical or teleological 'consistency.'"[3] Although this demand may be muted from time to time, it can never be ignored for long if the world is to make sense.

Therefore ideas cannot be discounted as the mere self-serving ideology of social classes or other groups. However, Weber is not a complete "idealist," seeking to explain historical developments solely on the basis of religious or other ideas. He argues that religious ideas can unfold differently depending on a number of factors other than the logical possibilities contained in the specific religious doctrine. The interests of the ruling strata at crucial times in the history of a religion play a part as do the interests of the "carrier strata," the social groups most engaged by a doctrinal innovation. Weber further argues that the urban culture of Europe played a role in weakening other, potentially resistant, community bonds, especially kinship. He even refers to the "practical rationalism" of all civic strata that may have facilitated the reception of certain doctrines.[4]

This last suggests that there may be certain "elective affinities" between ideas and social groups.[5] However, cultural and social rationalization as a whole is much more contingent than a history of ideas, religious or otherwise, would show. A complete historical analysis would have to detail the complex interplay between ideas and the historically specific interest situation of different social groups. That is not Weber's immediate task. Instead, he tries to show how the contours of religious change can be understood as cultural rationalization and the way in which one particular religious doctrine contributed to the development of capitalism.

Weber is also using his well-known analytical tool of "ideal types"; that is, he is presenting positions in "their most consistent and logical forms," a pure form that is "seldom to be found in history." This "artificial simplicity" reveals the rational core of cultural ideals and social practices, necessary if we are to make clear distinctions at all. To be sure, this procedure courts the danger of over-emphasizing the consistency of religious beliefs. However, some such simplification is necessary and historians, consciously or not, must also presuppose ideal types.[6] Historical specificity and the interplay of causal factors can be explored only after this conceptual and typological spadework is done. It is only then that one can formulate broad generalizations for the concrete historical developments.

Weber does not argue that all cultural and social areas were rationalized at the same time or proceeded from the same source. A good example is the rationalization of law stemming from the systematization of legal concepts by the Romans. Not only did this occur centuries before the methodical approach to science, art, or economic life, but it also seems to have had its roots in particular Roman religious practices. Weber states that for the Romans, precise observance of religious rituals appears to have been more important than salvation. Roman religion especially concentrated on articulating the acceptability of new practices or institutions from the standpoint of sacred law. Therefore, religious disputes took on the flavor of a debate among "lawyers." "In this way, sacred law became the mother of rational juristic thinking."

Therefore we cannot deduce the growth of rational practices in any particular cultural field from some all-embracing wave of rationalization peculiar to Western history. Nevertheless Weber argues that religious developments were crucial for cultural and social rationalization. This does not deny the fact that different areas of social life can be rationalized in different ways, and, very importantly, that the rationalization of one social or cultural area may appear wholly irrational from the standpoint of another area.[7] As we will see, the latter is an argument of great significance for Habermas's own social theory.

THE RATIONALIZATION OF RELIGION

There is hardly a more powerful and universal human desire than to try to make sense of the world. Even schizophrenics pursue it, although in ways that the rest of us cannot share. Weber says that it is precisely this search for a comprehensible construction, confrontation with the apparent "irrationality of the world," that drives all "religious evolution." The demand "that the world order in its totality is, could, and should somehow be a meaningful 'cosmos'" pushes religious belief in the direction of rationalization. Theology is grounded on the assumption that the world is meaningful and develops to the extent that it attempts to make this meaning "intellectually conceivable."[8]

According to Weber, the immediate irrationality one confronts in the world is the inequality of rewards and punishments, the issue that Weber calls "theodicy." (The root of the word is *dike*, the Greek word usually translated as "justice.") Although it arises in other contexts, this is an especially pressing issue for religions predicated on the existence of an omnipotent and benevolent god. "The age-old problem of theodicy consists of the very question of how it is that a power which is said to be at once omnipotent and kind could have created such an irrational world of undeserved suffering, unpunished injustice, and hopeless stupidity."[9] Systematic theology is stimulated by intellectually grappling with the seemingly incomprehensible and arbitrary distribution of misery in the world.

Unless convincing explanations are found, some may reject the belief in god (or at least in a benevolent god) altogether, as does Dr. Rieux in Albert Camus's *The Plague*. After seeing a young boy endure an excruciating death from the plague, Dr. Rieux remarks to a priest, "Until my dying day, I shall refuse to love a scheme of things in which children are put to torture." On more than one occasion Weber mentions a contemporary survey of German workers that revealed that more of them rejected religious belief because of the injustice in the world than because of the arguments of natural science.

In earlier societies, various individual calamities were considered a sign of "secret guilt" from actions which provoked the wrath of the gods. One engaged the services of magicians to uncover the causes of suffering. As Weber remarks, the obverse of explanations of this kind is that they legitimate the good fortune of others. "The fortunate is seldom satisfied with the fact of being fortunate. Beyond this, he needs to know that he has a *right* to his good fortune."[10] Almost any commentary today on the distribution of wealth in the United States reinforces this insight.

The question of theodicy becomes particularly keen with the emergence of the "salvation religions." According to Weber, these were the key step in furthering the rationalization of religious belief and practice. Weber gives a number of political and sociological reasons for the emergence of the salvation religions, which we need not go into. The most relevant aspect is the rise of the conception of an ethical god who is influenced by one's "obedience to religious law," rather than the various appeasements demanded by magical spirits or more anthropomorphic gods. Also important is the rise of a priesthood that is concerned with working out procedures through which souls can be saved. Furthermore, prophets play a role in the development of these religions in that their revelations often encourage a break with tradition.[11]

Weber argues that a theology of redemption especially relies on the work of intellectuals to create a "systematic and rationalized image of the world." This systematization partly results from increased conflict within the religion. When the religion is based on holy books it is more difficult for priests to control religious interpretation, resulting in challenges by independent prophets and mystics who may be actively hostile to the established priests. Therefore, salvation religions are in greater need of doctrine, and the more doctrine, the more need for "rational apologetics."[12]

Furthermore, the salvation religions have an important effect on religious practice. Prophets demonstrate their charisma ("gift of grace") much the same way as magicians, their "historical precursor[s]," through magical powers (miracles) and visions. However, their distinctiveness lies in the fact that they hold out the possibility of a path to alleviate suffering of all believers through a methodical mode of living. "For the substance of the prophecy or of the savior's commandment is to direct a way of life to the pursuit of a sacred value. Thus understood, the prophecy or commandment means, at least relatively, to systematize and rationalize the way of life, either in particular points or totally."[13] This new "habitude" of the holy differs from the previous beliefs of mere temporary contact with the divine through contemplation, use of intoxicants, trials, or other activities believed to stimulate mystical experiences.

The demands of theodicy, of an intellectually satisfying explanation for the "incongruity between destiny and merit," are thereby intensified with the rise of salvation religions. The insistence that the world make sense generates theology, and theology begets a search for a more systematic, clearer image of the world, by which we can orient our lives. Weber states boldly that there have really only been three coherent answers to the problem of theodicy: the doctrines of "Indian Kharma," "Zoroastrian dualism," and "predestination."[14] The first is the belief in reincarnation, that is, the transmigration of souls. It explains the distribution of suffering by asserting that the nature of one's present life is determined by one's actions in previous lives, as one's next life will be determined by actions in this one. The second is a belief in a fundamental dualism of forces of good ("light") and forces of evil ("darkness") that contend for supremacy in the world. It therefore responds to the question of theodicy by surrendering the idea of an omnipotent god. One of its best known variants—the name of which has become an adjective in English—is Manicheanism. The third is the Calvinist doctrine that is the origin of "the Protestant ethic" on which Weber focuses his attention because of its importance for rationalizing social action. Rationalized, methodical conduct in pursuit of salvation does not necessarily result in social rationalization. It can lead to sustained contemplation, the life of a monk, or to the regimen of yoga. In Protestant Calvinism it led to an "active, inner-worldly asceticism" that sought to tame wickedness through work in the world, in contrast to the active, other-worldly asceticism of, for example, Buddhism.

Weber draws a helpful contrast here between paths of salvation, which emphasize becoming a "vessel" of the divine as opposed to those in which adherents seek to become a "tool" of the divine. The primary goal of the former is to be inhabited by the divine and leads in the general direction of mysticism. This category could be applied today to many fundamentalist denominations in the United States that engage in practices like speaking in tongues, rolling on the floor, being rendered unconscious ("slain by the spirit," according to Catholic "Charismatics"), or other expressions of religious ecstasy. Faith healing is akin to these but actually appears to go all the way back to magical beliefs.

In contrast, the spiritual goal of being a *tool* of the divine emphasizes an active engagement in the world in accord with God's commandments. A methodical way of life ordered in this fashion is deemed necessary to attain (or assure oneself that one has already attained) a state of grace.[15] Weber famously proposes that this ideal interest generated a mode of conduct in everyday life that encouraged the rationalization of Western society, especially by forging a personality type that was conducive to capitalism.

THE PROTESTANT ETHIC

The peculiarity that Weber wishes to explain remains: Why did the multifarious tendencies toward rational, methodical action come together exclusively in Western culture? Weber's discussions of this topic are more or less scattered among texts concerned with other immediate objects. To the extent that Weber gives an answer it seems to center on the creation of a special personality type that engages the world in a methodical, calculating, and unremitting way. As the analysis above suggests, for Weber this personality type coalesces from the demands required by one of the alternative paths leading toward religious salvation. The clearest, and historically most fateful, expression of ascetic, inner-worldly action for spiritual goals is the Calvinist doctrine of predestination and the concept of the "calling" that emerged from it.[16]

In the sixteenth century Jean Calvin articulated the Protestant doctrine of "predestination" as a response to the problem of the ethical order of the world. Calvinist Protestantism is historically associated in the United States with the Puritans. Predestination means that from the beginning, God has chosen some to be saved and others to be damned. We cannot ultimately comprehend God's decision in this matter; there is an unbridgeable gulf between God and man. We cannot know his thoughts and he is not subject to mere human conceptions of justice. He chose the "elect" for his own reasons. In fact, to inquire after those reasons is an act of presumption and a challenge to God's majesty. This was the response of God to Job's questioning of the disasters that befell him, a book of the Bible held in high regard by the Puritans. (Hobbes named his masterpiece in political theory *Leviathan* from the Book of Job: God uses the example of his creation "leviathan" to "humble the children of pride.") As Weber puts it, citing an analogy of Calvinists, for the damned to complain about their fate would be the same as animals complaining because they had not been made human beings.[17]

In sum, the doctrine of predestination answers the problem of theodicy by declaring that, given our conception of God, it is unanswerable in principle. We only know what God wills through what he has revealed in the Bible and by reflecting on the orderly construction of the world, which both the Bible and "natural intuition" tell us is for use by mankind. However, the world is not to be used for mankind's own purposes but for "the greater glory of God." "God does not exist for men, but men for the sake of God."[18] From the Bible we know that it is manifestly God's will that people obey his commandments, which Luther had already interpreted partly to mean that individuals should perform the social role in which God had placed them. Calvin was to increase the religious charge of this endorsement of inner-worldly action.

As stated earlier, Weber is particularly interested in the way in which the desire for salvation led to a methodical approach to everyday life. The doctrine of predestination would at first appear unsuited for this in that, if one's fate is fixed, a likely response would be to deny the relevance of any action in the world, leading to fatalism. Calvin's argument seems to be that if God's will is truly free and transcendent, then it must not·be conditioned or influenced in any fashion by the actions of individuals. "Good works" therefore cannot alter God's decision as to the elect, nor is God's grace "revocable." As Weber remarks, this is the culmination of "the elimination of magic from the world, which had begun with the old Hebrew prophets and, in conjunction with Hellenistic scientific thought, had repudiated all magical means to salvation as superstition and sin."[19] This raises the question of how this doctrine could stimulate any interest in the world, much less lead to a rationalization of day-to-day conduct.

Weber explains that under the worldview of predestination an individual's desire to know whether she or he was one of the elect or not must have been intense, especially in an age in which the highest concern of the individual was "eternal salvation." It is hard for most moderns to appreciate the depths of this passion.[20] Furthermore, Calvinists argued that it was a religious duty to push aside all doubts about one's election, "since lack of self-confidence is the result of insufficient faith, hence of imperfect grace." It was then recommended that the most effective way to eliminate these doubts, to become a "self-confident saint," was through complete engagement in the world through one's "calling."

Weber considers the idea of the "calling" to be the central concept linking the doctrine of predestination with the rationalization of everyday life. "For everyone without exception [including the wealthy] God's Providence has prepared a calling, which he should profess and in which he should labor. And this calling is not, as it was for the Lutheran, a fate to which he must submit and which he must make the best of, but God's commandment to the individual to work for the divine glory."[21] In the context of Calvin's conception of predestination, diligent work at one's calling becomes more than the mere fulfillment of earthly obligations or an attempt to please God. It is God himself working in the world through the individual. Although success in one's calling (good works) could not alter one's fate, it was a "sign" of election and therefore a way of reaching conviction that one is *assured* salvation, "the highest good toward which this religion strove."

In the elaboration of Calvinist teachings, following a calling came to mean work in a specialized occupation. Since success in one's occupation was taken to be a sign of election, the unceasing accumulation of wealth was not only freed from traditional constraints but was even given a religious sanction. Material goods were not to be privately enjoyed, of course; wealth was regarded as part of the glorification of God and the producers of wealth should consider themselves as only "trustees" of God's treasure. The late nineteenth-century Calvinist Andrew Carnegie recommended precisely this as the appropriate attitude of the wealthy toward their wealth.[22]

Work at one's calling also protected one against idleness and temptations by the pleasures of this world. A life oriented by the idea of predestination and the calling thereby loses its "planless and unsystematic character" in working for the greater glory of God as his tool or instrument in this world. Weber remarks that it is not for nothing that one of the Calvinist revivals took the title of "Methodists."[23]

CONSEQUENCES OF RELIGIOUS RATIONALIZATION

According to Weber, there were three broad consequences of the long process of the rationalization of religious ideas. The first is what Weber, borrowing a phrase from Friedrich Schiller, calls the "disenchantment of the world." At least tendentially, the salvation religions eliminated the interventions of magical forces into everyday life. This, coupled with other historical contributions to Western civilization such as Greek speculative thought, culminated in the reconceptualization of the world as a "causal mechanism" following its own inherent laws. This worldview does not mean that ordinary individuals necessarily know better how their world operates. Instead it is the widespread belief that the conditions within which humans find themselves are *in principle* knowable and capable of control. "Hence, it means that principally there are no mysterious incalculable forces that come into play, but rather that one can, in principle, master all things by calculation."[24] The conception of the world as a chain of causes, none of the links of which are permanently hidden from mankind, led to a fundamental division of the world. "The unity of the primitive image of the world, in which everything was concrete magic, has tended to split into rational cognition and mastery of nature, on the one hand, and into 'mystic' experiences, on the other."[25] This pushes religion into "the realm of the irrational," that is, as the simply "given" presuppositions of certain social practices. In this way the demands of theodicy contributed to a progressive rationalization, which, over thousands of years and flowing into other intellectual forces, ended up emptying the world of meaning except as an arena in which God's ultimately incomprehensible demands must be pursued. It led to a world "robbed of gods."

Second, the rationalization of religious belief and practice created a methodical approach to everyday life. Although this was originally oriented to the pursuit of religious ends, this sustained, sober accounting of one's actions contributed to the development of a capitalist economic system. Weber takes pains to clarify that capitalism is not simply "greed." He states that greed has always motivated people in different historical epochs and societies. For Weber, capitalism is the mode of economic gain based on the methodical calculation of profit (rather than mere windfalls or booty) through regularized exchange (as opposed to political power or force) and the establishment of organizations for this purpose. Capitalism, properly so-called, therefore requires an orientation to the world, even a personality type, that rationally weighs the marginal gain from various exchange activities. It is under this definition that Weber argues that the separation of business property from personal property, the development of bookkeeping techniques, and the establishment of labor freed from feudal and other restrictions were crucial for capitalism. These allowed this strict and unstinting evaluation of productive processes and exchange relations.

The overwhelming need to know that one is saved and the Calvinist revaluation of the calling as the answer to this need created the requisite personality type. The calling is therefore the vehicle through which cultural rationalization of a certain kind is transformed into a rationalization of society. It is, as Weber put it, an example of how "ideas become effective forces in history."[26] The specific "carrier" strata are always important for determining the direction of the transformation of social action in accord with innovative cultural developments.[27]

However, once going, an economic system can displace religious motivations. The principled *origin* of a state of affairs and the rules under which it functions *once established* are not necessarily the same. Weber argues that the very material success of the approach to life of the Calvinists led to temptations that weakened religious motivations.[28] The religious significance of the accumulation of material goods was gradually replaced by "sober economic virtue" and a utilitarian attitude toward economic affairs. Capitalism can dispense with religious motivations because of the sheer demands of the struggle for existence in an economically competitive environment.

> The Puritan wanted to work in a calling; we are forced to do so. For when asceticism was carried out of monastic cells into everyday life, and began to dominate worldly morality, it did its part in building the

tremendous cosmos of the modern economic order. This order is now bound to the technical and economic conditions of machine production which today determine the lives of all the individuals who are born into this mechanism, not only those directly concerned with economic acquisition, with irresistable force.[29]

The "care" for material goods has now become an "iron cage," an "inexorable power." Paradoxically, a variety of Christian asceticism led to a civilization dominated more than any in history by material goods and the means for obtaining them.

Although, as above, Weber often suggests that we are compelled by our insertion into this "cosmos," he also argues that we still perceive the life pursuit of a specialized vocation as some kind of "duty," although the religious basis that would make sense of this duty has dissolved. "[T]he idea of duty in one's calling prowls about in our lives like the ghost of dead religious beliefs."[30] Duty thus appears to be like the practice of "taboo" in certain societies. As explained by Alasdair MacIntyre, the statement that something is "taboo" seems to carry its own unarticulated reasons for why certain actions are not allowed. However, if someone from outside the culture should ask why something is taboo, the answer amounts to a restatement that it is taboo. This is not to say that action oriented by duty or taboo is meaningless. Even though the presuppositions of an action may not be rationally justifiable, especially to those who do not share the actor's "ultimate values," it can still be meaningful action.[31]

The final consequence of the religious development reconstructed above is that the resulting process of cultural and social rationalization fragmented modern social life in multiple ways. The long process of intellectualization and the formation of the capitalist cosmos ultimately resulted in differing and sometimes competing areas of social action. Weber especially focuses on tensions between ethical conceptions and other practical arenas. He argues that an ethic of "brotherliness" is central to all salvation religions, a brotherliness that emerges from recognizing the common suffering and common frailties of human beings. This regard for others tendentially flows beyond all existing associations and social identities into a quasi-mystical "acosmic benevolence," even to the point of loving thine enemies.

Weber argues that this ethic of brotherliness has always clashed with other social practices. In the still "enchanted" world of earlier societies, the conflicting demands of social life were represented as struggles of gods among themselves. Similarly, in Indian society these conflicts were handled by being assigned as duties of discrete castes.

However, these longstanding tensions are intensified "the more the values of the world have been rationalized and sublimated in terms of their own laws." For us, these differing "life orders" appear as governed by "impersonal forces," or at least as following a logic of action that is inconsistent with other orders.[32]

For example, especially obvious in the global economy today, an economic order that is free to follow its own internal dynamic negates the idea of a social order governed by brotherliness.

> A rational economy is a functional organization oriented to money-prices which originate in the interest-struggles of men in the *market*. Calculation is not possible without estimation in money prices and hence without market struggles. Money is the most abstract and "impersonal" element that exists in human life. The more the world of the modern capitalist economy follows its own immanent laws, the less accessible it is to any imaginable relationship with a religious ethic of brotherliness.[33]

The argument is quite familiar to us. For an economy to be rational, the monetary value of a good must be determined by the demand for the good in the market, in Weber's phrase, by "market struggles." The only nonarbitrary way of assigning a value to a particular good or service is by what the market will bear. Only this automatic monetary evaluation of goods and services allows an accurate calculation of the costs of production of a good and the costs of satisfaction of consumer needs. In contrast, political interventions, such as subsidizing bread or housing, alter pricing and disrupt the presumptively rational weighing of individual needs versus available resources. Furthermore, the political setting of prices makes calculation more difficult because the political decisions of what prices are assigned to which goods may change. Calculation requires an economy that follows its own inner laws, letting the chips fall where they may.

The cold logic of a capitalist economy is clearly at odds with brotherly love. However, Weber argues that, due to their particular religious interpretations, the Puritans actually escaped the tension between the life order of the economic sphere and the demands of a salvation religion holding out redemption from suffering for all. The doctrine of predestination actually repudiates the notion that all can be saved. Although the Puritan was part of a community of believers, the individual would have to recognize that even members of her or his own congregation may possibly not be part of the elect. These were irretrievably damned; "even Christ had died only for the elect."

As Weber mentions, the Calvinist search for salvation is in this respect powerfully isolating.[34] The most the individual Puritan could do was try to individually attain a sense of certainty of salvation by methodically applying himself or herself to a vocation. Calvinist doctrine thereby freed economic activity from ethical constraints issuing from a strong sense of community, of a shared destiny. Not only did it "put a halo" around individual economic activity, but Weber argues that it also means that "Puritanism renounced the universalism of love" and, on this basis, should perhaps not be considered a true salvation religion at all.[35]

Political practice is a second arena of social action that conflicts with an ethic of brotherliness founded on the promise of salvation religions. According to Weber, the successful pursuit of political goals, domestically as well as in international affairs, ultimately rests on effective power, not ethics. The acquisition and maintenance of power—especially the capacity to bring force to bear if necessary—follows its own "external and internal laws," traditionally expressed by the phrase "reasons of state." Weber argues that the political association may even come into direct competition with "religious ethics" for the loyalty of the citizenry, most pointedly in time of war.[36] Furthermore, in carrying out their official duties in the rational organization of a public bureaucracy, individuals acting properly act in an "impersonal" manner, "without hate and therefore without love."

Weber famously explored the contending demands of ethics and politics in the 1918 lecture "Politics as a Vocation," a subject that was particularly pressing in Germany at the end of World War I. Therein he contrasts the mutually exclusive orientations of what he calls the "ethic of ultimate ends" versus an "ethic of responsibility." The former only concerns itself with uncompromising, right action; from its perspective, the moral quality of an act resides in acting with the right intention. An ethic of responsibility, on the other hand, evaluates acts by their consequences.[37]

Although Weber and others have remarked that there were many precursors to Machiavelli, we generally attach Machiavelli's name to the disturbing calculus of employing morally dubious or even abhorrent means in order to achieve certain political ends. That immoral means may be necessary to accomplish crucial political ends—for example, bombing civilians in wartime—strikes us as revealing a distinctive logic of political affairs. Once one becomes involved in politics, it is no longer possible to simply say, "Do right and let God take care of the rest." As Machiavelli argues in *The Prince*, and as

Weber reaffirms, the hard fact is that good may require evil means. The obverse is also true: ethical acts will sometimes result in evil consequences. The failure of Machiavelli's employer, the Florentine leader Piero Soderini, to act ruthlessly enough led to the destruction of the Republic of Florence by the Medicis. The good will suffer in a world filled with those who are not good, and so will their communities. It is not for nothing that Machiavelli once said of himself (and in a different place of his fellow Florentines), "I love my fatherland more than my soul." Weber adds that he who is concerned with his soul had better not become involved in politics.[38]

Even earlier, Thucydides indicated this distinctive logic of politics in the dialogue of the Athenians with the inhabitants of the island of Melos. The Melians desired to stay neutral in the war between Athens and Sparta, but the Athenians, representatives of what is still considered the great model of democracy, insisted that the Melians join the Athenian side or be destroyed. When the Melians complained of the injustice of this demand, the Athenians responded that they did not invent these rules and that if the Melians were in their place, the Melians would act the same. The Athenians summarized the rules that govern political affairs as, "the strong do what they will, and the weak suffer what they must." (The Melians still refused and were destroyed.)

The contending viewpoints of the ethic of ultimate ends and the ethic of responsibility lead to differing evaluations of basic moral virtues. For example, each asserts opposing conceptions of what is honorable behavior. For the political actor, "turning the other cheek" is not only politically ineffective but the ethic of slaves. Each viewpoint differs on the virtue of truthfulness and whether pride is or is not a virtue at all. Neither side can comprehend the perspective of the other, as was well-expressed by Socrates in articulating his own version of an ethic of ultimate ends when refusing to escape from prison. "So one ought not to return a wrong or an injury to any person, whatever the provocation is.... I know that there are and always will be few people who think like this; and consequently between those who think so and those who do not there can be no agreement on principle; they must always feel contempt when they observe one another's decisions."[39] Weber does allow, in the end, that an ethic of ultimate ends that is truly and boldly followed regardless of consequences may contain some majesty, as our example of Socrates shows.

In sum, Weber states that the "religious ethic of brotherliness" is in tension with any "purposive-rational conduct that follows its own laws." This causes some individuals to give up on all "purposive rational action" because involvement in the world will necessarily entail becoming entangled with "diabolic powers." Those who reach this position generally retreat to what they take to be the morally superior standpoint of simply condemning the world as it is, and confine their actions to at most keeping the perspective of absolute morality alive. That is, they resign themselves, often unconsciously, to political impotence.[40]

Besides the classical conflicts between ethics and economic and political action, Weber argues that modern life is fragmented in other ways. The rationalized social practices of economics and politics have provoked the establishment of other life orders organized around alternative values, especially art and eroticism. These spheres of social action are pursued as compensations for the "routines of everyday life" but they also come into competition with religion insofar as people seek a kind of inner-worldly salvation that does not require religious inspiration.

In regard to the first, with the increasing "intellectualism and rationalization of life," art, like economics and politics, develops an "inherent logic" elaborating a distinct set of values. "[A]rt becomes a cosmos of more and more consciously grasped independent values which exist in their own right."[41] In response to the desiccated, narrow routines of workaday life, art serves a "redemptory function," a promise of the free expression of individuals's "innermost selves." Weber has in mind not only the creative refuge of the visual arts but also the sublime experience of music, which, as many religions have long suspected, is in competition with religion in that it offers an alternative to an ecstatic religious experience. Contemporary attacks on the seductiveness of rock music, from evangelical Christians to the political theorist Allan Bloom, reinforce this point. As Weber remarks, however, this competition has not stood in the way of religions allying themselves with this power of music in seeking to expand their own audience.

With the rationalization of society "eroticism" has also increased as compensation for everyday existence. Weber contends that the separation of modern life from "the organic cycle of peasant life" has culturally charged the "naturally given." "Eroticism was raised into the sphere of conscious enjoyment," rather than sexual relations simply accepted as part of the natural rhythms of generations. In opposition to the methodical practice of a vocation, and similarly to art, the erotic presents the possibility of authenticity and the experience of individuality. "[E]roticism appeared to be like a gate into the most irrational and thereby real kernel of life, as compared with the mechanisms of rationalization."

Weber specifically mentions extramarital affairs as creating this feeling of escape, of freedom from the gray on gray of office and home. An important part of the attraction is that in a romantic affair one experiences the unification with one unique one, for whom the first is the irreplaceable other unique one. One is coveted as the individual she or he is and the situation, although definitely carrying the flavor of the irrational, beyond calculation and consequences, feels overwhelmingly *real*. It is not surprising that for those drawn to this compensatory life order, passion itself may be celebrated as a "type of beauty."[42]

Therefore, in multiple ways, capitalist society, by its very rationalization of life conduct, intensifies certain already present tensions between differing life orders. Modern social life is actually filled with simmering conflicts between "various life-spheres, governed by different laws." The apparent emptiness of the methodical life it forces on individuals born into it also provokes reaction formations as individuals seek redemption in life orders the principles and values of which are far from the routines of everyday life. At the end of *The Protestant Ethic and the Spirit of Capitalism* Weber summarizes the vaunted development of contemporary society with a few phrases from Goethe: "Specialists without spirit, sensualists without heart; this nullity imagines that it has attained a level of civilization never before achieved."[43]

The emergence of areas of social life that are governed by contending principles seems to deprive an ethics of brotherhood of any secure roots. But beyond this, the more the inner logic of the orienting values of these life orders is elaborated, the more confusing our culture becomes. The unity that, for example, Keats expressed of ancient Greek culture—"Beauty is truth, truth beauty; that is all ye know on earth and all ye need to know"—is irretrievably shattered. In modern culture there are sharp distinctions between the good, the true, and the beautiful. The "gods of the various orders and values" are simply locked in interminable struggle with each other.

In "Science as a Vocation" Weber gives many examples of the incommensurability of these value spheres with each other and the dilemmas this poses for cultural life. The common thread of the argument is that any particular cultural practice cannot ground the presuppositions of its own practice. As suggested before, science gives no meaning; it therefore cannot tell us how we should live nor even convincingly say why what it explores is "worth being known." Similarly, as the debate around euthanasia shows, medicine instructs us on what we can do to live but it cannot answer "when life is worth living."

This is equally true of other value spheres. Aesthetics assumes that works of art should exist but its partisans are not able to compellingly demonstrate this to those who do not share the presupposition. The "cultural and historical sciences" can analyze and display the variety of human practices in their fields but they cannot articulate criteria, which would allow us to judge which cultural practices should be preferred above others. Similarly, theology presupposes revelation and holiness but has little to offer those who want supporting evidence for this presumption.[44]

Since these values are incommensurable, Weber argues that an individual must simply choose on the basis of whatever "ultimate ends" she or he finds meaningful: "[A]s long as life remains immanent and is interpreted in its own terms, it knows only of an unceasing struggle of these gods with one another. Or speaking directly, the ultimately possible attitudes toward life are irreconcilable, and hence their struggle can never be brought to a final conclusion. Thus it is necessary to make a decisive choice."[45] Individuals must choose who is "god" and who is the "devil" with the awareness that however they choose, they will unavoidably offend some other god. Still, Weber suggests that one can make a meaningful choice if one tries to remain "faithful to yourself."[46]

In light of Weber's survey of this archipelago of life orders and the values around which they are organized, some have concluded that Weber should be described as an existentialist, although perhaps a reluctant one.[47] Individuals in modern society are placed in a situation in which they are required to make a radical choice of life paths. However, Weber does suggest that "science" (in the broad sense of rigorous inquiry) can help inform individual choices by clarifying the situation, thereby aiding individuals in giving "an account" of their own practices. Revealingly, Weber argues that science can be considered a kind of "moral" service in that this clarification can at least promote "responsibility" and "integrity."[48]

We should remind ourselves again that Weber is utilizing ideal types. From the standpoint of a rational reconstruction of the various life orders and related cultural spheres of values, conflict is apparently inevitable. However, Weber repeatedly holds out the possibility of reconciliation partly because the logical implications of a practice or sphere of value are not always followed to the end in reality. Nevertheless, the fact that rationally consistent cultural positions *would* come into conflict with each other is a significant social fact, revealing a fundamental incoherence in our social life.

WEBER AND HABERMAS

Habermas argues that Weber's diagnosis of the times is still as current as when Weber presented it.[49] Weber's account of cultural and social rationalization is the starting point for Habermas's own social theory in three important respects. First, although Weber was specifically commenting on the dominance of contemporary social life by material things, a life that would have seemed "contemptible" or even "perverse" to individuals in a precapitalist age,[50] Habermas interprets the "iron cage" as a loss of freedom due to the emergence of narrowly rational organizational frameworks such as the capitalist economy and bureaucracies. Second, in regard to the "loss of meaning" thesis, Habermas follows Weber in tracing this to the emergence of logically independent value spheres and the life orders that "crystallize" around them, but also to disruptions of social life caused by the expansion of economic and bureaucratic networks.

Third, Habermas takes from Weber the idea that cultural development is analytically separate from and sometimes necessarily prior to social change. Both Habermas and Weber reject "functionalist" arguments, that is, that the existence of social or cultural phenomena can be explained simply on the grounds that they are useful for maintaining society. The conditions for the emergence of social structures or practices are logically distinct from the benefits that the structure or practice in question might bring. New social relations do not emerge just because it would be useful for them to do so. For both Habermas and Weber, social development draws on previously and independently emergent "ideal interests" and "worldviews" (Weber) or "cognitive potentials" (Habermas). Just as a species's future evolution is limited by its existing physical chemistry and biological structure, so are future social directions of the human species limited by its previous cultural development. This is what it means to have a history: present possibilities depend on what has previously been done, on "circumstances inherited and transmitted from the past" (Marx). Social and political departures are simply not possible under just any circumstances whatsoever.

However, neither are Weber and Habermas cultural determinists. Cultural developments only establish the range of possible social changes. Which cultural potentials will be realized depends on the actions and conflicts of social groups and on historical opportunities created by events. This is also what it means to have a history, rather than a set of eternal principles that would always work out the same way no matter how many times the simulation is run.

Nevertheless, although Weber's work provokes interesting lines of analysis of cultural development, his arguments regarding cultural and social rationalization beg many questions. For example, in a situation of such cultural disarray in which one must simply choose what are one's ultimate ends, which criteria account for Weber's apparently *universalist* endorsement of the values of "self-clarification," "responsibility," and "integrity"? Also, although Weber insists that he is not judging the rational practices that are peculiar to the West nor evaluating different cultures, the above remarks on "specialists without spirit" certainly appear to be an evaluation.

Partly because of questions such as these, Habermas proceeds far beyond Weber's own conclusions. However, Habermas explicitly constructs his own theory as a "second attempt to appropriate Weber in the spirit of Western Marxism."[51] His argument can therefore be placed in better perspective by first looking at what he considers to be the limitations of the prior attempt of critical theorists to utilize Weber's arguments on social rationalization for comprehending the derailment of the Marxian locomotive of history.

CHAPTER 2

WEBER AND WESTERN MARXISM

With only slight exaggeration, Frank Parkin once stated that "Inside every neo-Marxist there seems to be a Weberian struggling to get out."[1] Indeed, many in the Marxian tradition have turned to the analyses of Weber in order to remedy the perceived weaknesses of Marxian social theory. Although Weber was a political conservative, he is not the "anti-Marx" that he is sometimes portrayed to be. Weber himself stated that his exploration of the religious roots of capitalist culture was intended not to displace "materialist" explanations but to complement them.[2] Repaying the favor, a number of thinkers who helped constitute what is known as "Western Marxism"—especially Georg Lukács, Max Horkheimer and Theodor Adorno, and Herbert Marcuse—drew on Weberian insights in order to deepen the analysis of contemporary capitalism and, in the case of Horkheimer and Adorno, in order to understand the defeat of Marxian hopes by the middle of the twentieth century.

To borrow a phrase from G. A. Cohen, Marx argued that the "coherence" of history lies in the tendency of the productive forces of mankind to increase. The forces of production—technology, labor skills, raw materials, and especially, as Cohen notes, "productively useful science"—are promoted by historically specific relations of production, that is, a dominant property form and other social relations that stem from it.[3] At a certain point the existing relations of production, instead of furthering the development of the productive forces, begin to "fetter" these forces, creating a stagnation that can only be alleviated by installing a new property form more appropriate for economic development. Fettering therefore creates the objective possibility of social revolution, under capitalism a revolution carried out by the class whose exploitation is crucial to capitalist production, the proletariat. To overcome the restraints of capitalism on the development and employment of the productive capacities of humanity, private property must be abolished and replaced by common property that will allow the rational use of the means of production to directly satisfy needs.

In previous class societies such as the slave-based society of ancient Rome or under feudalism it was obvious that the wealth of society was created by the exploited class, respectively, slaves or serfs. Under capitalism it is also true that wealth comes from the labor of an exploited class but this is hidden from the workers in a number of ways. A key topic for Marxian theory is therefore how the consciousness of the working class *as* a class is obstructed or encouraged, a topic pursued by a Marxian theorist who was associated with Weber's intellectual circle, Georg Lukács.[4]

LUKÁCS: RATIONALIZATION AS REIFICATION

In his essay "Reification and the Consciousness of the Proletariat," Lukács attempted to explain the effects of capitalist social relations on the consciousness of the working class by combining the idea of "reification" expressed by Marx in *Capital* with Weber's notion of rationalization. The most important premise of Marx's critique of capitalism is that the goods and services produced in society are actually created by society as a whole, a collective social product. Under capitalism the fact that production is thoroughly social is difficult to see because this collective labor is coordinated by the exchange of commodities among individual owners occupying different positions in society's division of labor, rather than directly coordinated by the associated producers, which would be the case under common ownership of property.

Lukács argued that the "mediation" of inherently social production by exchange relations among individuals has important consequences for how individuals perceive and interact with the world. First, objectively, the coordination of social labor through the exchange of commodities makes the relation of producers to one another appear as a relation between the "things" exchanged rather than a mere dividing up of productive tasks among society's members. Further, the laws of the market that emerge to govern the exchange of commodities create an overarching web of social relations that compel individuals to act in specific ways, Weber's "iron cage." As Lukács puts it, these economic laws confront individuals "as invisible forces that generate their own power."[5] This situation reminded Marx of the way in which earlier societies often attributed magical powers to a certain totem or other object, to a "fetish." Therefore he referred to this process under capitalism as "commodity fetishism." Since Lukács, the manner in which collective social powers are actually manifested as a relation between things bought and sold, resulting in this alienated web of social relations, has been referred to by the clumsy but irreplaceable word "reification," the "thing-ification" of social life.

According to Lukács, the dominance of commodity exchange under capitalism has a powerful effect on the consciousness of individuals, especially the working class. Under capitalism the vast majority does not own productive property—land, workshops, stock—the proceeds of which they can exchange for things they need. The only thing they have to exchange is their ability to labor, which they must therefore turn into a commodity. The commodification of labor means that individuals must regard their personal capacities as objects of sale: "[The commodity relation] stamps its imprint upon the whole consciousness of man; his qualities and abilities are no longer an organic part of his personality, they are things which he can 'own' or 'dispose of' like the various objects of the external world."[6] Although Lukács does not, it is worth noting that this self-understanding of human beings is already in evidence in the works of Thomas Hobbes and John Locke in the seventeenth century, a perspective later called by C. B. Macpherson "possessive individualism." Arguably, the political theories of Hobbes and Locke can in this respect be seen as a reflection of emergent capitalist society.

For Lukács, the consequence is that human beings are regarded and regard themselves as objects in the world. Human activity is transformed into "performances" that serve the economic system. On this analysis, Lukács reinterpreted Weber's processes of social and cultural rationalization as part and parcel of the increasing dominance of commodity exchange for regulating social life. As Marx argued, for commodity exchange to become generalized, products of different individuals must be regarded as in some way equal, so that they can be exchanged in specific quantities. As we will explore more fully later, Marx argued that what allows commodities to be reduced to a relation of units to each other is how much socially necessary labor the individual item represents. For exchange to proceed we must abstract from all the individual qualities of the products of specialized labor in order to bring them into a quantitative relation to each other. For Lukács this "abstraction" is the fundamental form of oppression of the proletariat.

> The quantification of objects, their subordination to abstract mental categories makes its appearance in the life of the worker immediately as a process of abstraction of which he is the victim, and which cuts him off from his labor-power, forcing him to sell it on the market as a commodity, belonging to him. And by selling this, his only commodity, he integrates it (and himself: for his commodity is inseparable from his physical existence) into a specialized process that has been rationalized and mechanized, a process that he discovers already existing, complete and able to function without him and in which he is no more than a cipher reduced to an abstract quantity, a mechanized and rationalized tool.[7]

Specialization, abstraction, quantification, calculability: for Lukács, it is the conditions of commodity production that actually ground the increasing rationalization of social life. The consciousness of the capitalist is also affected, but for the worker this "split in his being" is a "slavery without limits."

Capitalist exchange relations therefore create an understanding of the world in which everything is considered an "object," even the subjectivity of human labor. This objectifying or reifying consciousness is only fundamentally shaken by economic crises which, for the proletarian, make understanding society "a matter of life and death."[8] Understanding can have this effect, Lukács argues, because the worker's emerging awareness of herself or himself as a commodity is "practical," not merely "contemplative." What he means is that this sort of knowledge changes the very object of knowledge, the seller of labor-power, and in so doing the deeper reality of the society in which they labor is also laid bare.

> The specific nature of this kind of commodity had consisted in the fact that beneath the cloak of the thing lay a relation between men, that beneath the quantifying crust there was a qualitative, living core. Now that this core is revealed it becomes possible to recognize the fetish character *of every commodity* based on the commodity character of labor-power: in every case we find its core, the relation between men, entering into the evolution of society.[9]

The consciousness of the proletariat is therefore revolutionary consciousness, awareness that things are not as they appear to be nor is this reified existence the only possible one.

Therefore, for Lukács the rationalization of capitalist society reaches its limits when through the dehumanization of the working life and the devastations of periodic economic crises the worker recognizes that social production is just that, *social* production merely privately appropriated in accord with the class interest inscribed in capitalist property relations. Thus is revealed what the quantifying abstractions of capitalist rationalization must necessarily obscure: the pulse of capitalist production. This consciousness is grounded in the fact, alleged by Lukács but not really supported, that for all the brutalization of the worker "his humanity and his soul are not changed into commodities."[10] However Lukács, the Leninist, further argues that the class consciousness of the proletariat only reaches fruition and becomes a political force through the Communist Party, the "*autonomous form*" of proletarian class consciousness serving the interests of the revolution."[11]

HORKHEIMER AND ADORNO: RATIONALIZATION AS INSTRUMENTAL REASON

Utilizing Lukács's insights, Horkheimer and Adorno constructed their own Weberian synthesis in response to a very different set of political experiences. As Habermas recounts it, "Critical Theory was initially developed in Horkheimer's circle to think through political disappointments at the absence of revolution in the West, the development of Stalinism in Soviet Russia, and the victory of fascism in Germany. It was supposed to explain mistaken Marxist prognoses, but without breaking with Marxist intentions."[12] Writing during World War II, Horkheimer and Adorno set out to understand "why mankind, instead of entering into a truly human condition, is sinking into a new kind of barbarism."[13] Bureaucratized state socialism appeared to confirm Weber's position that, given the ineluctable growth of a purely instrumental kind of rationality, a society based on common ownership would still be rigid, oppressive, and soulless, perhaps even more so in that it gives free rein to an alienating bureaucracy.[14] On other fronts, the rise of fascism and the deradicalization of the labor movement in other capitalist countries showed the first generation of the Frankfurt School that capitalism has powers of integration beyond those previously imagined. The critical analysis of capitalist society was therefore in need of drastic revision.

Lukács argued that universalized commodity relations created an objective social structure that confronted individuals as an alien force. He also argued that the commodification of labor-power in particular required that individuals regard everything, including their own human capacities, as something objective, something alienable from themselves. In Lukács's view, it was this that encouraged the rise, detailed by Weber, of a type of rationality that focused on calculation of efficient means to given ends. Horkheimer and Adorno, on the other hand, argue that this instrumentalizing reason is ultimately rooted in self-preservation, in a species that historically seeks to preserve itself by dominating nature.[15] Nevertheless, although self-preservation as a human drive is primordial, "in the first man's calculating contemplation of the world as a prey," Horkheimer and Adorno agree with Lukács that this form of reasoning is only "given full rein in the free market economy."[16]

In *Eclipse of Reason* Horkheimer contrasts the older philosophical quest of what he calls "objective reason" to contemporary "subjective reason." The idea of objective reason is that the world as a whole, including human existence, can and does express an intelligible order. The task of philosophy is to comprehend the truth of this order, a truth that would show the proper place of human beings in the cosmos. He writes, "Great philosophical systems, such as those of Plato and Aristotle, scholasticism, and German idealism were founded on an objective theory of reason. It aimed at evolving a comprehensive system, or hierarchy, of all beings, including man and his aims. The degree of reasonableness of a man's life could be determined according to its harmony with this totality."[17] In different places Horkheimer and Adorno mention several causes of the increasing marginalization of the above view of the world: bloody conflicts stemming from differing religious beliefs encouraging the political neutralization of religious belief by making it purely subjective, the rise of natural science that regards nature as merely a toolbox and source of raw materials, and the legitimation of self-interest as a ground for political action.[18] All of this culminated in the Enlightenment.

The ideal manifested in the Enlightenment was that reason applied to all human activities would emancipate human beings from imprisoning illusions and unnecessary oppression. Horkheimer states that the original project of the Enlightenment especially intended to replace contentious religious beliefs as the anchor of the absolute with a conception of an objective order based on reason; however, the consequence was that under the bright sun of reason, the idea of a meaningful natural order evaporated. In the struggle against traditional authorities and received wisdom a subject-centered conception of reason became dominant. With this, reason becomes calculation, a mere assessment of means to any ends: "The system the Enlightenment has in mind is the form of knowledge which copes most proficiently with the facts and supports the individual most effectively in the mastery of nature. Its principles are the principles of self-preservation."[19]

With the rise of "subjective reason," nature is completely instrumentalized and deprived of all meaning. Man becomes the measure of all things. A number of important consequences follow this victory. In *Dialectic of Enlightenment* Horkheimer and Adorno focus attention on how humans, in trying to dominate external nature in the interests of self-preservation, must also learn to dominate their own internal desires. In their view, one must learn to "master oneself" as a requirement for pursuing projects in the world. Invoking the figure of Odysseus, bound to the mast so he can hear the sirens's song without destroying himself, Horkheimer and Adorno argue that this self-mastery is the very ground of our sense of "self-hood." Horkheimer gives this a Freudian thrust in *Eclipse of Reason*, agreeing with Freud that civilization requires a mastery of instincts, that is, that it is built on denial of expression of immediate impulses of human beings, a denial especially imposed through socialization of the individual in the family.[20]

Echoing both Lukács and Weber, Horkheimer and Adorno argue that the rationalization of modern society intensifies this elementary need for self-mastery and control.

> Just as all life today tends increasingly to be subjected to rationalization and planning, so the life of each individual, including his most hidden impulses, which formerly constituted his private domain, must now take the demands of rationalization and planning into account: the individual's self-preservation presupposes his adjustment to the requirements for the preservation of the system. He no longer has room to evade the system.[21]

In industrial society self-preservation comes to mean accommodation to existing social relations. Mass consumption capitalism encourages this by preforming what we are supposed to think and feel.

> Through the countless agencies of mass production and its culture the conventionalized modes of behavior are impressed on the individual as the only natural, respectable, and rational ones. He defines himself only as a thing, as a static element, as success or failure. His yardstick is self-preservation, successful or unsuccessful approximation to the objectivity of his function and the models established for it.[22]

Things now become the measure of man. The extent to which a merely subjective or "instrumental" reason structures social life, the self one intends to preserve must actually be denied satisfaction. People are reduced to "mere objects of the administered life ... against which they believe there is nothing they can do."[23]

Self-preservation as a goal is therefore ultimately self-defeating. When self-preservation becomes posed as an absolute end it destroys other dimensions that make a specifically *human* life possible: "[A]ll the aims for which he keeps himself alive—social progress, the intensification of all his material and spiritual powers, even consciousness itself—are nullified..."[24] The instrumentalization of reason thereby results in the instrumentalization of human beings themselves, the emptying of their content as ends. Consequently, as Nietzsche did on other grounds, Horkheimer and Adorno conclude that the path of Western civilization leads ultimately to the denial of all values, to "nihilism."[25]

The establishment of instrumental reason has another important consequence. Bereft of a concept of an overarching natural order, which goals are pursued becomes purely subjective, leading to a thoroughgoing relativism. Referring to "the black writers of the bourgeoisie," those such as the Marquis de Sade who openly acknowledged that subjective, calculating reason can be applied to any ends whatsoever, Horkheimer and Adorno state starkly that this means "the impossibility of deriving from reason any fundamental argument against murder."[26] From this conception of reason it is also hard to see how one can construct a critical view of society. "Since ends are no longer determined in the light of reason, it is also impossible to say that one economic or political system, no matter how cruel and despotic, is less reasonable than another."[27] As Hegel once put it, relativism results in "a night in which all cats are gray."

However, just as Lukács proposed that something resists, so Horkheimer argues that as domination of nature intensifies, the point of continued domination is lost and this encourages the growth of a sort of rebellious nature.

> The repression of desires that society achieves through the ego becomes even more unreasonable not only for the population as a whole but for each individual. The more loudly the idea of rationality is proclaimed and acknowledged, the stronger is the growth in the minds of people of conscious or unconscious resentment against civilization and its agency within the individual, the ego.[28]

Sullenly, most people adjust and submit. However, under other circumstances this creates one of the supports for fascism. Horkheimer explains that the power of fascism came especially from finding ways to harness this resentment for its own purposes.[29]

In *Eclipse of Reason* Horkheimer mentions another basis of possible resistance, arguing that although the instrumental interest in "controlling nature" has always been important, "society could not completely repress the idea of something transcending the subjectivity of self-interest, to which the self could not help aspiring."[30] This suggests a ground for resurrecting the philosophical project of absolute reason, comprehensive philosophies such as those of Plato and Saint Thomas Aquinas, in which the various orders of being are designated a place. Certainly in recent times there have been a number of political and moral philosophers who have pursued this possibility. Besides the neo-Thomism of Alasdair MacIntyre, perhaps the best-known attempt was the earlier one by the conservative political theorist Leo Strauss, continued by his successors today. In *Natural Right and History* Strauss complains of the disorienting effects that result from modern social science rejecting as "unscientific" any conception of "natural right." Sounding very much like Horkheimer and Adorno, although from virtually the opposite side of the political spectrum, Strauss states that "Such a science is instrumental and nothing but instrumental: it is born to be the handmaid of any powers or any interests that be." Strauss concludes that "The contemporary rejection of natural right leads to nihilism—nay, it is identical with nihilism."[31] The severing of human purposes from any conception of a larger order is "madness." "We are then in the position of beings who are sane and sober when engaged in trivial business and who gamble like madmen when confronted with serious issues—retail sanity and wholesale madness."[32] Finally, like Horkheimer and Adorno, Strauss argues that the modern conception of nature is a chief culprit in the alienation of human beings from a place in the cosmos.

However, for his part, Horkheimer casts serious doubt on whether such a philosophical orientation is plausible today, drawing attention to the fact that these various restorative projects are often inspired by their *usefulness*. "Their revival, therefore, is completely artificial: it serves the purpose of filling a gap. The philosophies of the absolute are offered as an excellent instrument to save us from chaos."[33] The very fact that these philosophical revivals are recommended as *practically* useful demonstrates once again the overall dominance of an instrumental reason: "The absolute becomes itself a means, objective reason a scheme for subjective purposes, general as they may be."

Horkheimer and Adorno stated that their purpose in writing the *Dialectic of Enlightenment* was to "prepare the way for a positive notion of enlightenment which will release it from entanglement in blind domination." To this end, they tried to feel their way toward some kind of "reconciliation" between human beings and nature, to overcome the antagonisms generated by a reason that turns everything into an object of potential domination, especially of outer and inner nature. However, they suspected that language itself had been subverted by a reason that insists on seeing everything as a discrete object, cut off from a history and from relations with other things.[34] A theory that is *critical* of what exists is thereby deprived of its ground in reasoned discussion itself. The dilemma, as Habermas presents it, is that they suspect that something has been destroyed but, since reason has been disabled, they cannot really say what it is. Horkheimer and Adorno are reduced to simply pointing to the capacity they call "mimesis."

> Imitation designates a relation between persons in which the one accommodates to the other, identifies with the other, empathizes with the other. There is an allusion here to a relation in which the surrender of the one to the example of the other does not mean a loss of self but a gain and an enrichment. Because the mimetic capacity escapes the conceptual framework of cognitive-instrumentally determined subject–object relations, it counts as the sheer opposite of reason, as impulse.[35]

However, Habermas argues that this idea, necessarily, is more a gesture toward reconciliation than a theory, a recommendation for a kind of "mindfulness" of nature, or perhaps only a "yearning lament."[36]

In the end, Horkheimer sought a path by reconsidering philosophy as potentially revealing a glimpse of a reconciled world. He conceived this as an attempt to comprehend "truth" in the primordial sense of everything having its proper name and place, "enabl[ing] thought to withstand if not to overcome the demoralizing and mutilating effects of formalized reason."[37] However, this fell short of a "program of action."[38] Adorno, on the other hand, specifically turned to great works of art in which, in Habermas's phrase, "the mimetic capacity," this promise of reconciliation between man and the world, "gains objective shape."[39] Distinctively, Marcuse utilized Freud to probe more deeply the possibility of an instinctual revolt.

MARCUSE AND "REBELLIOUS SUBJECTIVITY"

Contemplating the experience of the twentieth century, Horkheimer and Adorno profoundly doubted that socialism still promised a different civilization.[40] Like capitalism, its project too is forged as the domination of nature. However, Horkheimer continued to place this domination in a societal context, suggesting that it is still the social structure that constrains alternative ways of living.

> It is not technology or the motive of self-preservation that in itself accounts for the decline of the individual; it is not production *per se*, but the forms in which it takes place—the interrelationships of human beings within the specific framework of industrialism. Human toil and research and invention is a response to the challenge of necessity. The pattern becomes absurd only when people make toil, research, and invention into idols. Such an ideology tends to supplant the humanistic foundation of the very civilization it seeks to glorify.[41]

Writing during the ferment of the 1960s, Marcuse vigorously pursued this line of argument.

Marcuse, the most politically influential member of the Frankfurt School, developed a variation on some of the arguments of Horkheimer and Adorno, a variation to which Habermas on occasion has paid particular attention. As Habermas puts it, "Marcuse did not, in contrast to Adorno, only encircle the ineffable; he made appeals to future alternatives."[42] In his rather pessimistic work *One-Dimensional Man* (1964), Marcuse accepts and elaborates Horkheimer and Adorno's assessment of the imminence of the "administered life." However, as the movements of the 1960s gathered steam, Marcuse proposed possibilities for overcoming the impasse of an instrumentalized reason.

Hardly an idle utopian, Marcuse had a keen awareness of the powerful forces sustaining the existing order. In *An Essay on Liberation*, written shortly before the dramatic radical takeover of Paris in May and June 1968 by students and others, Marcuse contends that mass consumption capitalism has developed a profound hold on the very definition of happiness for the majority. Reformulating Freudian theory to give it a sharper political point, Marcuse argues that "The so-called consumer economy and the politics of corporate capitalism have created a second nature of man which ties him libidinally and aggressively to the commodity form."[43] Marcuse meant "second nature" quite seriously, arguing that commodity capitalism has actually affected the "biological" array of fundamental desires. Admittedly using the word "biological" loosely, Marcuse proposes that manufactured needs are *still* important needs. "[I]nclinations, behavior patterns, and aspirations become vital needs which, if not satisfied, would cause dysfunction of the organism."[44] Even the neurotic who compulsively washes her or his hands truly *needs* to wash as long as the person remains neurotic. Being restrained from doing so would cause intense discomfort, even though another might argue that it is not "really" a need. Something similar has arisen in the commodity culture of contemporary capitalism.

> The second nature of man thus militates against any change that would disrupt and perhaps even abolish this dependence of man on a market ever more densely filled with merchandise—abolish his existence as a consumer consuming himself in buying and selling. The needs generated by this system are thus eminently stabilizing, conservative needs: the counterrevolution anchored in the instinctual structure.[45]

Because this system of "introjected needs" is, as Horkheimer and Adorno argued, a system of domination of human nature, Marcuse refers to "voluntary servitude" and "cruel affluence."[46]

Marcuse's objection is, again, the same as that of Horkheimer and Adorno: Due to the development of the productive forces, this fundamentally inhumane domination of inner nature is no longer necessary. Unlike them, however, Marcuse proposes a number of reasons for why this fettering of human possibility may be increasingly recognized and challenged. In observing the generalized revolt of the 1960s, Marcuse points to the apparent emergence of a "new sensibility" that rebels against the performances required by capitalism and is informed especially by aesthetic concerns. This new sensibility holds the promise of altering the fundamental needs of human beings toward a rejection of ugliness, toward a new appreciation of play, and for a demand for the free expression of self that would be incompatible with the requirements of consumer capitalism.

Marcuse appeals to Freud's theory of human instinctual structure to provide hope unavailable to Horkheimer and Adorno. In his later work Freud postulated that two intertwined "instincts" (or "drives"; to some extent it is a matter of translation[47]) profoundly shape human action, the life instinct (Eros) and the death instinct (Thanatos). The life instinct strives to create "greater unities," especially through sexuality and the pleasure that entails. The death instinct, on the other hand, seeks the kind of "pleasure" that is found in the cessation of pain, in finding peace, or, as Freud calls it, the "Nirvana Principle."[48] Both instincts try to find satisfaction, although the path for doing so is constrained by "reality" as interpreted and imposed by the ego.[49]

Marcuse extends Freud by arguing that the "reality principle" has a historical dimension, that the real possibilities of satisfying instincts change with the growth of the productive forces.

> [T]echnical progress has reached a stage in which reality no longer need be defined by the debilitating competition for social survival and

advancement. The more these technical capacities outgrow the framework of exploitation within which they continue to be confined and abused, the more they propel the drives and aspirations of men to a point at which the necessities of life cease to demand the aggressive performances of "earning a living," and the "non-necessary" becomes a vital need.[50]

Given the tremendous increase in the productive forces, contemporary capitalism now signifies "surplus repression."[51]

Although the precise connections are unclear, Marcuse suggests that it is this pressure of the instincts for satisfaction under new historical conditions that prepares the soil for the growth of a new sensibility.[52] The new sensibility leads to the development of "nonmaterial needs" among some members of society, needs that conflict with the imposed requirements of capitalism.

> This transformation appears in the fight against the fragmentation of work, the necessity and productivity of stupid performances and stupid merchandise, against the acquisitive bourgeois individual, against servitude in the guise of technology, deprivation in the guise of the good life, against pollution as a way of life. Moral and aesthetic needs become basic, vital needs and drive toward new relationships between the sexes, between the generations, between men and women and nature.[53]

With this Marcuse forges a link with traditional Marxian theory, that capitalism has produced needs that it cannot satisfy and therefore push beyond it. Although capitalism does not "fetter" production it still establishes the possibility, even need, of a qualitatively new kind of living based on a different relation to nature and other human beings. "It is still true that capitalism grows through growing *impoverishment*, and that impoverishment will be a basic factor of revolution—although in new historical forms."[54]

Marcuse argues that this new sensibility is still a minority development within advanced capitalism, mentioning the "nonconformist young intelligentsia" and others alienated from the existing order, urban minorities, and marginalized workers in underdeveloped countries.[55] The traditional working class is too enthralled by existing needs and their satisfaction. Those who define themselves through the existing needs will consider those who reject them to be at least unreasonable and probably subversive, undermining the order that provides the benefits of technology. In response Marcuse argues that happiness cannot be defined purely subjectively. As the ancients believed, the happy life must be understood as having an objective aspect, that beyond merely personal feelings of satisfaction, some lives are better than others.[56] He also argues that we must try to conceive a new science and technology that is not subverted by commodity production and the unrestrained domination of the natural world. Only this can redeem the original promise of socialism as a truly different and higher level of civilization.

HABERMAS AND CRITICAL THEORY

On several occasions Habermas indicates his appreciation of Marcuse, recently noting that the ups and downs of Marcuse's political influence have obscured his real theoretical contributions.[57] Habermas's admiration appears to be based partly on Marcuse's discomfort with resigning himself to political inaction, with quietly residing at what Lukács, in a jab at the Frankfurt School, called "the Grand Hotel Abyss."[58] However, although sympathetic to the "rebirth of rebellious subjectivity," Habermas criticizes the undertheorized character of Marcuse's Freudian notion of a basic instinctual structure. He also rejects the very possibility of a new science and technology that would not dominate nature.[59] Habermas's own rejection of defeatism follows a different path.

In developing his theory of advanced capitalism, Habermas had first to come to terms with the godfather of modern critical theory, Karl Marx. Especially in the works *Toward a Rational Society* and *Legitimation Crisis* Habermas argues that contemporary capitalism renders inapplicable central assumptions of classical Marxism. The most important reason is that the rise of an interventionist state in the wake of the Great Depression and the aftermath of World War II means that, unlike in the nineteenth century, the dynamic of the economy is no longer autonomous. Active political intervention in stimulating and guiding economic growth shows that "politics" can no longer be considered merely a superstructural phenomenon.[60] Second, one of the ways in which the state intervenes is by actively supporting the development of science and technology, partly as a consequence of military spending.[61] According to Habermas, this destroys the labor theory of value on which Marxian economic crisis theory depends. Science and technology have now become the "leading productive force[s]." In fact, "scientific–technical progress has become an independent source of surplus value," displacing the labor theory of value and the theory of exploitation based on it.[62] For both these reasons, the idea of the relations of production autonomously determining the growth of the productive forces only applies to the bygone era of "liberal capitalism."[63] Habermas, like Marcuse, strengthens this position by arguing that in the *Grundrisse* Marx himself mentions that science is a source of economic value and in places anticipates the possibility of science becoming the *primary* determinant of value.[64]

Because of the extensive welfare policies of the interventionist state, in these works Habermas also argues that the significance of social class has declined in contemporary capitalism, that class conflict has become "latent."[65] Conflicts continue because economic growth and distribution are indeed uneven; "disparities" exist that provoke regional, ethnic, and racial conflict. However, since science and technology are now an independent source of economic value, the dispossessed of the cities are not exploited because society no longer lives off of their labor. The excluded of inner cities and other areas are simply that: marginalized. The ramifications of their protests are correspondingly weak. Habermas alleges the same about developing countries: Their economic exploitation is no longer crucial to economic development, although an *economic* interest in other parts of the world has been replaced by continuing (and oppressive) *military* interests.[66]

Instead of the crisis tendencies identified by classical Marxism, Habermas contends that two other serious difficulties challenge capitalism: legitimation of the existing order and motivation of society's members. Capitalist economic relations and the distributional consequences of these relations were formerly legitimated as merely the outcome of the freely entered market exchanges of equal individuals. Political power was legitimated by its role in maintaining these market relations, which allegedly embodied freedom and equality. However, through its interventions the state now obviously makes specific decisions to advance certain economic sectors and not others, certain geographical regions and not others, certain societal interests and not others. The state can therefore no longer hide behind the defense that it is solely maintaining allegedly outcome-neutral exchange relations. Therefore, as with precapitalist regimes, the need for legitimation of the state reappears, but now without the possibility of appealing to divine sanctions or tradition that sustained the legitimacy of precapitalist states.

The interventionist state responds to its legitimacy problem with what Habermas and others call the "substitute program": the provision of at least a minimal social welfare net, maintenance of continued economic growth and a rising standard of living, and promotion of the idea that individual success is governed by educational achieve-ment. A well-functioning substitute program steers individuals toward the private satisfactions of career, family, and friends, depoliti-cizing the masses and encouraging "adaptive" behavior on the part of the citizenry.[67] However, in a bow toward Marcuse and others who have seen intimations of a new sensibility, Habermas argues that there do appear to be needs that cannot be satisfied through the old rewards, posing the danger of a "motivation crisis." Like Marcuse, he points to the student movement's questioning of whether the "virtues and sacrifices" required by commodity society "have become superfluous," that is, whether the "dictates of professional careers, the ethics of status competition, and ... possessive individualism" should still dictate individual lives. A "crumbling achievement ideology" challenges adaptive behavior, encouraging a motivation crisis, an argument Habermas pursues in *Legitimation Crisis*.[68] The question of emancipation now boils down to how alternative paths of devel-opment are chosen, and this requires "removing restrictions on com-munication" in society such that the people can indeed choose.[69]

For two decades, in the essay collections *Toward a Rational Society, Theory and Practice*, and *Communication and the Evolution of Society*, Habermas explored the topics of reconstructing Marx's his-torical materialism, the significance for a theory of social evolution of Piaget and Kohlberg's portrayal of the stages of cognitive and moral development, and various other theoretical and philosophical issues of contemporary society. In his most methodical work to that point, *Legitimation Crisis*, he confronted and rejected theories that postu-lated insuperable economic or planning crises of contemporary capi-talism and explored, as above, how the most serious crisis tendencies actually stem from difficulties in legitimating existing political and social arrangements.

As Habermas states it, in these earlier efforts he often felt that the substantive theory was getting lost in the details. He was also having trouble presenting his ideas in a satisfactory way, so he followed the advice of Thomas McCarthy to "make a new start."[70] What followed can reasonably be considered to be his authoritative statements of social theory and political theory, respectively, the two volume *The Theory of Communicative Action* and *Between Facts and Norms*.

In the former, it is Habermas's criticisms of Horkheimer and Adorno's argument that set the stage for his own mature theory. A central task of critical theory must be to formulate the basis of critique itself. To condemn something begs the question as to which criteria the critic is appealing. In a charge he is to repeatedly make against postmodernist thinkers, Habermas insists that the reflections of Horkheimer and Adorno lead to a dead end because their critique of reason deprives them of the basis for any *reasoned* critical theory. Habermas argues that they end up committing a "performative contradiction." They cannot state ("perform") their criticism without partly contradicting the criticism itself: "[T]his description of the self-destruction of the critical capacity is paradoxical, because in the moment of description it still has to make use of the critique that has been declared dead."[71] Although Horkheimer and Adorno were aware of this problem, their all too thorough critique of reason had deprived them of the tools for responding to it.[72]

Specifically, by arguing that power—domination of nature—is an inescapable aspect of existing rationality, Horkheimer and Adorno deprive themselves of any rational grounds for criticizing power itself. Habermas argues that from this position creating a normative foundation for criticism presents "two options." The first is that of Nietzsche, who accepts the fusion of power and validity, and in boldly asserting the struggle for power presents the world as once again an arena for the mythological struggle of independent powers against each other, in Weber's phrase, the "struggle between gods and demons."[73] Habermas rejects this on the grounds that the distinction between validity and power, what is true or right instead of what merely prevails, is crucial to "any theoretical approach" and is the basis on which modern understanding claims its superiority over myth.[74]

The second normative option is to simply circle around in a self-aware performative contradiction, tending toward skepticism. Habermas argues that this is the position ultimately accepted by Horkheimer and Adorno. Since growth of the forces of production is no longer "explosive," crisis produces only a fragmented consciousness. The "black writers" of the bourgeoisie demonstrated, against the wishes of the defenders of the dominant order themselves, that the ideals of the bourgeois could no longer guide; therefore Horkheimer and Adorno simply saw "no way out."[75] As stated, "mimesis" is, and given the corruption of reason must remain, a "gesture" rather than an argument. Habermas's theory of communicative rationality is an attempt to articulate an alternative.

Habermas believes that Horkheimer and Adorno find themselves in this bind because they identify "reason" with the analysis and control of nature associated with natural science. This necessarily deprives reason of criteria by which to analyze a different kind of action in the world, for example, moral action.[76] Because of this, Horkheimer and

Adorno "do not do justice to the rational content of cultural modernity." Their notion of reason cannot appreciate the way in which modernity, in Habermas's favored phrase, "frees the logic of different cultural spheres." That is, Horkheimer and Adorno's identification of reason with *instrumental* rationality does not allow them to comprehend the important advance represented by "constitutional government," nor is it adequate for fully analyzing modern aesthetic experience.

In order to articulate a more differentiated conception of reason that can restore the normative grounding of critical theory, Habermas starts anew from Weber. Habermas argues that the cultural developments described by Weber have differentiated "reason" itself. Consequently, three discrete types of rationality have emerged and one of those—"instrumental rationality"—is privileged in capitalist society, presenting challenges to the coherence of social life. Habermas advances this thesis by first asking in a much more philosophically rigorous way what constitutes "rational action." His answer reveals that there are distinct claims to "validity" inhering in different types of statements, leading to Habermas's conception of the "three worlds" of human activity. By elaborating a conception of modern understanding as "decentered," Habermas expands our definition of what constitutes rational action and brings the three spheres of the good, the true, and the beautiful under something of a common framework.

Habermas's own theory of rationality then opens doors for rethinking what "societal rationalization" means. He argues that rationalization transforms social life such that, in order to capture it in theory, we must develop a dualistic conception of society as both a "lifeworld" and as a "system." This doubled perspective sheds new light on the experiences of the loss of freedom and loss of meaning. It also allows us to reconsider the possible anchoring of moral community in contemporary social life, replacing Weber's rather pessimistic conclusions regarding the corrosion of an ethic of brotherliness.

Finally, Habermas's theoretical path leads to a diagnosis of the sustained and multifaceted discontent with the welfare state and to new political proposals that he contends must serve as an alternative to the traditional socialist agenda. This political project seeks to accommodate the efficiencies of the market and bureaucracy while sensitizing these forces to the community-disrupting actions that both often entail. Habermas's political argument has in this way contributed to the wide-ranging discussion of an expanded role for a public sphere (or "civil society") that affects decision making without taking it over. Whether this is a plausible vision is something we need to address, but we must begin with how Habermas understands rationality, from which his social and political theory unfolds.

CHAPTER 3

RATIONALITY AND
COMMUNICATIVE ACTION

Habermas agrees with Weber that the ultimate consequence of religious and cultural rationalization is that modern culture fragments into different value spheres following their own inner logics of elaboration. He also agrees that this particular rationalization of culture and society is responsible for widespread feelings that modern life has become confusing and oppressive. In our day this contributes to a number of reactions, from religious fundamentalism to "postmodern" suspicions of rationality itself.

However, Habermas contends that the fragmentation of culture is not the destruction of reason but its differentiation into distinct "voices." This differentiation is disorienting but it also opens up possibilities for knowledge that are closed off to more traditional views. Furthermore, the autonomous value spheres of contemporary understanding need not be irredeemably antagonistic toward the perspectives of each other. Although reason can no longer be convincingly unified on the level of a comprehensive worldview, the different aspects of rationality can be brought into communication with each other through the elaboration of a philosophical theory of argumentation, on the one hand, and through the interplay of these varied perspectives in a more open everyday life on the other. Habermas thereby seeks to defend reason against skeptics. Contrary to Weber, ineluctable struggle is not our fate.

In his portrayal of the different dimensions of rationality, Habermas brings forth the promise that the currently dominant kind of social rationalization is not the only possible kind. He argues that contemporary society is actually only "selectively" rationalized. Certain types of rational action are encouraged in contemporary society and other types are stunted. It is this *selective* rationalization that leads to loss of meaning and loss of freedom, not rationalization itself. By posing the question of rationality in a new way Habermas boldly intends to defend the Enlightenment project against those who have concluded that the application of reason in human affairs is futile, dangerous, or both.

WHAT IS RATIONAL ACTION?

It is quite intimidating to ask what "rationality" means. However, since we use the word meaningfully in conversation, we must have criteria to which we are implicitly appealing when we say that this or that is "rational" but something else is not. To explore what rationality means is to clarify and critically examine the criteria that govern our everyday usage of the term. This is essentially Habermas's approach.

In much of the philosophy of the last century, the study of language has displaced the study of "consciousness." Language appears to be the necessary manifestation of consciousness—"consciousness concrete" as Marx once put it—and is more amenable to rigorous study than the necessarily ambiguous realm of consciousness. Drawing on speech act theory, one branch of this "linguistic turn" of contemporary philosophy, Habermas tries to reconstruct the idea of what rational belief or action is from the ordinary intuitions guiding our use of the term. His project therefore requires "mak[ing] explicit . . . the pretheoretical grasp of rules on the part of competently speaking, acting, and knowing subjects."[1]

In the first instance, we typically say an action is rational if it selects effective means to accomplish some goal. The image that comes to mind is that of a person attempting to successfully intervene in the world, to alter it in some way with least effort and cost. Rationality is at least, as Weber indicated, bound to the idea of efficiency. Habermas states that this dimension of rationality—"instrumental" rationality—exerts an especially powerful influence over modern thought. However he also insists that human interest in responding to demands of the environment has always encouraged regard for "economy of effort and efficacy of means."[2]

Nevertheless, Habermas contends that the image of a solitary actor intervening in the world limits our understanding of rationality in a number of ways. Mere success of the action is not sufficient to establish rationality. The success could be accidental, like "choosing" a winning lottery number. Or the action could be mere stimulus–response behavior like that of simpler organisms. Although Habermas says that the latter could be interpreted as rational, this is only to speak figuratively because the action is not actually guided by an intention.[3]

A second problem with the model of a solitary actor is that rationality in this case is conceived exclusively as an evaluation of a means to an end. The end itself is merely given—as economists say, "exogenous"—and by definition ultimately not subject to *rational* challenge or defense. In this model at some point one's choices of goals must be conceded as merely arbitrary.

Habermas points out that Weber himself expanded the discussion by judging the rationality of action on three levels. First, as stated above, rational action requires choosing appropriate means to achieve goals. However, one must also choose *goals* that will actually advance the values one holds; one's choice of goals must not be constrained by what is merely customary. One's actions are "substantively rational" only if one consistently chooses goals according to one's convictions. Finally, values themselves contribute to comprehensive rational action to the extent that they can be "generalized into principles," which can be applied across various life circumstances, resulting in what Weber called a "methodical-rational conduct of life." In Weber's account, Calvinism embodied all these levels of rationality: choice of means, choice of goals, acting on principle.

"Value-rationality" is being able to order life in this fashion. Anything short of this would leave a person bouncing from one arbitrary goal to another like a ball in a pinball machine. A *random* selection of goals is an absurd life, even if the discrete means are rational in the sense of effectiveness.[4] It is true that Weber believed that the choice between principled value systems, for example, a life oriented toward aesthetic values versus a life oriented by moral values, cannot ultimately be grounded. However, this does not deny the *substantive* rationality of an internally coherent, methodically pursued life.

Habermas rejects the arbitrariness of choice of principles and the inescapable conflict of value spheres that follow from Weber's position. Instead he argues that if we approach the actor from another perspective we can develop an alternative view of rational action that avoids these limitations. Even a solitary actor silently intervening in the world reveals through her or his action an implicitly held view of "how the world is." A person who acts purposively is implying that the world is such that she or he can bring about the intended goal. In evaluating the probable success of the action, an observer can challenge the implied claim of how the world is. A puzzled observer could engage the actor in conversation in regard to the reasons for the action, that is, make explicit the implied claims. The rationality of the action would then be assessed according to the plausibility of the claims about the world in view of this communication community of two.

Habermas states that the rationality of a belief or action inheres precisely in the plausibility of the reasons that can be marshalled for the claim that the world is such. For a person's action to be rational, she or he must be able to defend the action and the implied beliefs about the state of the world by giving reasons for proceeding as she or he does. Moreover, it is only if reasons are offered in discussion that "failures can be explained."[5] It is criticizability that makes learning possible. From this line of argument Habermas concludes that the key aspect of calling an action rational is that it can be criticized and defended with reasons.

In contrast to the image of the solitary actor, Habermas's conception of rationality is immediately intersubjective in that the core of rationality is the justification to others of one's beliefs or actions. Habermas's shift of perspective draws on the ancient conception of *logos*, generally meaning "reasoned speech" but more specifically implying being able to give an account of one's actions or beliefs. Rationality is now seen as grounded in the intersubjective process of reaching agreement through the give and take of reasoned discussion.

However, more than this is taking place. Through reasoned discussion we are actually "assuring" each other that we belong to a *common* world. That is, without access to the reasoning of others, in an important sense it is not clear that we truly inhabit the same "world." Habermas proposes that it is only through a process of reasoned discussion that a common world is "constituted."[6] Unlike other approaches to rationality as successful intervention *in* the world, Habermas inquires as to how belief in this presumed common world is sustained. Instead of focusing on the instrumental rationality of a solitary actor, exploring the conditions under which the common-ness of our world is reproduced unfolds a more comprehensive notion of rationality which Habermas calls "communicative rationality."[7]

Although this raises several additional questions, such as what is to count as a "reason" and what makes a discussion reasonable, rather than mutually reinforcing ignorance, Habermas's position is compelling. It can be noted that those who would reject this conception will have to give reasons for doing so. Even postmodern critics of reason must give reasons for their skepticism if their beliefs are to be taken seriously, or even understood.

COMMUNICATIVE RATIONALITY

Habermas argues that when a dispute arises that must be resolved by reaching understanding with each other, individuals attempt to collectively establish what their situation is, that is, they collaboratively "define" or "interpret" the situation. They develop a common understanding by giving reasons for their differing perspectives on what is "the case." Understanding is precisely this capacity to evaluate the offered reasons; as Habermas states repeatedly, "we understand a speech act when we know what makes it acceptable."[8] Beliefs and actions inherently claim to be valid. As he puts it, these "validity claims," when challenged, must be "redeemed" through reasons and argument. We understand practices of different cultures when we grasp the reasons why people engage in those practices. Equally so, different cultures understand our practices when they understand our reasons.

This emphasis on justification of one's beliefs or actions to a communication community opens new doors. By focusing on rationality as actions or beliefs potentially defensible by reasons, we expand the applicability of the concept far beyond the issue of "facts" about the "objective world" of things, beyond the question of efficiency of interventions into this world.[9] When challenged we also defend the morality of actions by giving reasons, by appealing to justified moral principles or by trying to justify the principles themselves if they are contested. Therefore "normatively regulated actions" are also potentially open to reasoned discussion.

Furthermore, we can see that even evaluations typically described as "subjective" can be critically appraised through reasoned discussion. To employ Habermas's example, a conversation with friends over whether a work of art or a film is "good" is conducted by offering reasons for one's assessment. In this case, the object is to try to get others to see the work of art or film in a certain light, altering the very standards by which they evaluate the work. "[I]n aesthetic criticism grounds or reasons serve to guide perception and to make the authenticity of a work so evident that this aesthetic experience can itself become a rational motive for accepting the corresponding standards of value."[10] In brief, reasoned discussion here opens up a new way of seeing. As the main character of *The Horse's Mouth*, Scully Jimson, says about his first experience of a great work of art, "it skinned my eyes for me." Through this process one's aesthetic evaluation can become more than simply something in the eye of the individual beholder.

Finally, Habermas argues that even expressions of desire or need can be subject to discussion based on reasons. Using examples such as envy or the desire for a vacation, Habermas states that these can be potentially defended through a discussion that establishes that others in a similar situation would have similar desires or preferences. The discussion thereby grounds the self-expression insofar as it causes the discussants to acknowledge "their own reactions to similar situations."[11] Evaluative and expressive statements are deemed even more rational if the participants are capable of reflecting on the standards they are utilizing in making their evaluations. "We call a person rational who interprets the nature of his desires and feelings in the light of culturally established standards of value"—this is what makes them recognizable—"but especially if he can adopt a reflective attitude to the very value standards through which desires and feelings are interpreted."[12]

If we approach rationality in the way Habermas indicates, with the phrase "communicative rationality," we can conceive of different "worlds" within which disputes take place and that are constructed through such discussion. The first world over which there can be rational argument is the "objective world," "the totality of states of affairs that are connected by natural laws and which exist or can come into existence or be brought about through interventions, at a given time."[13] The referent of this objective world is "facts" and contested claims of "truth" about these facts.

However, two other "world relations" are revealed through the above arguments about the range of possible rational discussion of contested validity claims. Besides the objective world of facts, we also participate in a "social world" constituted by presumably "legitimately regulated interpersonal relationships."[14] As the referent of the objective world is states of affairs, so the referent of the social world is "norms." The objective world is the realm of instrumental action, or, if it involves more than one actor, strategic action. The social world, on the other hand, is comprised of individuals bound together by acknowledged obligations and is the realm of "normatively guided interaction."[15]

Finally, there is a subjective world, the existence of which is revealed to an audience by the expression of desires, needs, and evaluations. The existence of this world is "attributed" to an actor by an audience. This is the realm of "dramaturgical action" or self-expression. The subject has "privileged access" to these experiences which she or he discloses to an audience in the first person. "Subjective experiences" are the referent.[16] Norms and subjective experiences are not subject to "truth," as are facts. However, these expressions do present validity claims that are "analogous to truth."[17] The claims are, respectively, normative rightness and truthfulness, or sincerity of expression.

It is very important to refrain from assimilating valid norms and authentic self-expressions to "things" in the objective world.[18] Their conditions of validity cannot be decided by the same criteria and methods for plausibly asserting the existence of things. The testing of the validity of norms requires application of the principle of "generalizable interests," about which we will say more later. Similarly, expressions of subjectivity are not things. Only the individual has access to her or his own feelings, desires, and valuations, so authenticity must be inferred by an audience being able to appreciate the stated feelings, desires, and valuations and also by observing whether a person's actions are in accord with the professed feelings: that one practices what one preaches. Many who confuse norms and expressions of subjectivity with "things" end up rejecting the possibility of rationally judging the validity of norms and self-expression because they cannot be examined like objects in the objective world.

Habermas elaborates this discussion in his contribution to a theory of speech acts that he calls "formal" or "universal pragmatics," that is, what is taking place when we communicate with each other. In all speech acts three different validity claims are present: truth in regard to facts, normative rightness, and sincerity. All speech acts can be critically appraised on these three grounds: true/untrue, right/not right, sincere/insincere. Habermas uses the example of a professor who tells a student to go get her or him a glass of water. The student could challenge the request because there is no water nearby (factually mistaken), on grounds that the request suggests that the student is the professor's servant (normatively wrong), or on the premise that the professor does not really want water but is merely testing the student to see what the student might do when faced with such a request (insincere statement).[19]

With the above argument Habermas indicates a correspondence between three different validity claims that are aspects of speech and three different worlds that are constituted through speech acts: an objective world of what is factually the case, a social world of justifiable moral principles that are binding on the participants, and a subjective world of sincere expression of one's desires and evaluations. The concepts of validity claims and corresponding worlds link up with and deepen Weber's discussion of the modern establishment of different "value spheres." For Habermas, three value spheres are constituted through the distinction and analysis of one type of validity claim to the exclusion of the others, resulting in the value spheres of natural science, laws and morals, and aesthetics. (Immanuel Kant is responsible for originally codifying these spheres in his three great critiques of pure reason, practical reason, and judgment.) Furthermore, the analysis of how the different validity claims implicit in speech acts constitute different worlds of action allows us to distinguish among three kinds of rational action: "cognitive–instrumental rationality" in analyzing facts and objects, "moral–practical rationality" in justifying rules for living together, and "aesthetic–expressive rationality" in exploring the possibilities of subjective experience. Reason has not disintegrated. It has become differentiated into three forms that correspond to different realms of human activity.

Habermas's approach to rationality shows why the different value spheres and their internal logics are not as completely unbridgeable as Weber believed. Modern cultural developments lead to a form of understanding that is "decentered" in that various realms of validity separate from each other. However, Habermas insists that since all of these areas are associated with certain validity claims, all are in principle defended through reasons. "Communicative reason finds its criteria in the argumentative procedures for directly or indirectly redeeming claims to propositional truth, normative rightness, subjective truthfulness, and aesthetic harmony."[20] Rationality has become "procedural"; it is socially and culturally grounded in the competence and inclination of actors to distinguish, challenge, and defend actions or beliefs on the basis of validity claims. Habermas argues that an analysis of argumentation can articulate the principles governing the contest of validity claims in all three worlds.

Habermas calls "the modern form of understanding" decentered because of the distinction of various realms of validity from each other and the distinct world relations that are constructed with this "scaffolding." In contrast, magical or mythical conceptions conflate differing realms of validity, such as attributing meaning to causal relationships in the natural world. The demythologization of worldviews is precisely the process of distinguishing realms of validity from each other, resulting in the decentered rationality of moderns. This decentering is furthered by the emergence of "expert cultures" that focus on the logical elaboration of one realm of validity by ignoring the others, for example, the elaboration of certain aesthetic principles that stray further and further from the everyday conception of the purpose of art as the production of the beautiful.[21] This freeing of the inner logics of cultural validity spheres fragments reason into specialities that devalue traditional understandings, with social consequences that Weber intimated and Habermas explores in his social theory.

There is an immediate problem with the above account. Habermas has been criticized for insufficiently acknowledging the ways in which different languages can limit the kinds of expressions that can be made. Since there is no direct, unmediated contact with what exists—all contact is mediated through language—in important respects Habermas must accede to Peter Winch's argument that, in Ludwig Wittgenstein's phrase, "the limits of my language mean the limits of my world."[22] Language *as a whole* therefore has a broader "constitutive" function than Habermas incorporates in his theory.

Habermas has clarified his argument under criticisms such as these. He now speaks of three "inner-worldly" functions of language: "presentation of factual matters, the creation of interpersonal relations and the expression of subjective experiences." He also admits a fourth function of language, its "world-disclosing" function.[23] Language "opens up a grammatically prestructured space," governing how things in the world can appear. A specific language therefore limits how we can consider topics under the three inner-worldly validity claims.

However these considerations intensify the problem of relativism. It would appear that people raised in different language communities have essentially incommensurable ways of experiencing the world and therefore cannot ultimately understand each other. From this perspective, the modern form of understanding is merely one particular way of interacting with the world. As Winch argues, to experience other cultures is to contemplate "different possibilities of making sense of human life."[24] None of these ways is superior to any other. Our judgments on these alternative forms of understanding must always be limited by our language and therefore relative.

Different cultures simply reason differently and there are no non–culture-bound criteria by which one culture could be accorded more rational than another. In this respect, all cultures are, as Ranke put it, "equally close to God." This is usually accompanied today by the more or less overt suspicion that any claim of the superiority of Western rationality is a form of cultural imperialism, that through history these claims have been and are justifications for the oppression of "inferior" cultures.

Habermas responds in two ways to these arguments about the relativity of rationality. First, in regard to the incommensurability of alternative ways of comprehending the world, he admits that we cannot know in advance that attempts at cross-cultural understanding will indeed be successful. It depends on our ability to, in Hans-Georg

Gadamer's famous phrase, "fuse horizons" of our world and the world we are trying to understand. Second, in regard to the advantages of the decentered modern understanding, Habermas criticizes the mythological worldview as "totalizing." In this form of understanding the natural world is comprehended through the framework of social relations and, obversely, social relations are regarded as part of the natural order of things. A major consequence is that there is little distance between what is *valid* and what is merely *given*: The interpretation of the world cannot be seen *as* an interpretation and is thereby innoculated against criticism. In contrast, many commentators on rationality have indicated at least this as a mark of the superior rationality of modern understanding, that a certain distancing from one's own interpretation can be achieved in modern thought that is closed off by the very structuring of traditionalist understandings.[25]

The worldviews of traditional societies simply leave little space for critical evaluation of existing practices. When dissonance of some sort does threaten, it is covered by the sheer assertion of "taboo." However, a distancing from one's own practices is necessary for learning to take place. If what is valid is confused with what is socially current, any change in beliefs would have to appear as discontinuous leaps. A capacity to reflect on what one holds as true or proper is an irreplaceable aspect of rationality of belief and, as Bryan R. Wilson suggests, some cultures have more experience with this than others.[26]

Charles Taylor points out another dimension of this topic that should be obvious but is rarely discussed. Modern cultures are technologically superior due to their approach to nature. Technological superiority is not everything, but it is something. The conception of the natural world constructed by modern scientists has deprived us of what Taylor calls an "attunement" with the world, a fact lamented, as mentioned, by Leo Strauss who suggests that we cannot perceive the natural moral order partly because of this. However, leaving aside nuclear weapons, being able to increase food sources or keep children from dying of disease are accomplishments that cannot be ignored, even by nonmodern societies.[27]

Habermas further develops his own position by drawing on the theories of cognitive psychology of Piaget. In his studies of children, Piaget attempted to reconstruct stages of learning and concluded that cognitive development is in the direction of greater "decentration" of thought in two respects. In her or his encounters with "external reality," the child learns to distinguish her or his own subjective world from the external world and further distinguishes the objective and social aspects of the external world.[28]

Habermas argues that there is an analogous development in cultural knowledge. In modern understanding, "reasons" current in premodern societies are disempowered by the new differentiated categories of understanding. Modern cultural differentiation, like Piagetian decentration, alters the *kinds* of reasons that are now acceptable. Not only new "contents," but a new *level* of learning is opened up, freeing the elaboration of the inner logics of different cultural fields. The superiority of this new stage of learning is established if "the learner can *explain*, in the light of his second interpretation, why his first interpretation is false."[29] As MacIntyre argues on a different issue, the master of a craft becomes a master partly by developing such that his or her standards of what *is* a good work are altered.[30]

Habermas does not really give clear examples of how new forms of understanding displace previous kinds of reasons for action and belief but we can extrapolate. Not speaking a dead person's name for fear of angering his or her spirit is a reason guiding action. However, given a different conception of the natural world, a disenchanted view, we can not only reject this type of reason but we can explain why it is wrong: It confuses the natural world with social relations.

For all this, on these difficult and important topics Habermas's position is necessarily incomplete. The reason is, as he readily concedes, this conception of cognitive and cultural development cannot be established by philosophical argument alone. The attempts to delineate stages and levels of learning must be based on reconstructions of how actors actually attain certain competences and what we understand by "competences." At most, on these issues philosophy can generate hypotheses that organize investigations that can be tested as empirical theories.[31] Here, as elsewhere, Habermas's primary goal is to help formulate lines of future research and create the theoretical framework that indicates why this research program is promising.

Nevertheless, the elaboration of a decentered mode of understanding expands the concept of rationality beyond the immediate notion of instrumental intervention into an objective world. This theoretical move allows Habermas to formulate his most innovative and central contribution to social theory, the concept of "communicative action," an idea that is occluded when one focuses only on instrumental rationality. It also yields the crucial distinction in Habermas's social analysis, that between "instrumental" or "strategic action" and communicative action.

COMMUNICATIVE ACTION AND SOCIAL LIFE

In social life, in order to accomplish one's goals, one must generally rely on the coordination of one's actions with the actions of others, so that at least they not obstruct you. Habermas argues that there are two fundamentally different ways of coordinating action in society: "influence" and "consent."[32] Action coordinated through influence occurs when one or more of the actors employs inducements other than reasons: threats of force, money, playing on emotional attachments, manipulative rhetoric, and the like. In this case, reasons are actually disempowered; words become weapons. Influence is a kind of strategic action: Achieving the goal is foremost. Everything else is simply a means to be used in a purely calculating manner. The actor treats others' resistance as facts to be changed, obstacles to be overcome, thereby assimilating social relations—including moral relations—to "things" in the objective world rather than relations maintained through intersubjective agreement.[33] Strategic action is of course the only comprehensible kind for those who believe that instrumental rationality is the sum of reason.

The expanded conception of rationality that focuses on the redemption of validity claims opens up an additional way of conceiving the maintenance of social order. Strategic action coordinates through "influence"; communicative action relies on coordination through "consent," that is, through the existence or generation of "common knowledge" of facts, norms, or subjective experiences. In contrast to immediately goal-directed strategic action, communicative action is necessary where the existence of common knowledge is crucial to the success of the individual's goals. We can act together when we share assumptions about what is the case or what is or is not legitimate in the situation. This sharing both binds us together and is the basis for the formation of convictions based on reasons.

Habermas's contrast between communicative action and strategic action is developed in a technical analysis of speech acts. Following Austin, he separates the "illocutionary" dimension of speech from its "perlocutionary" dimension. To be brief, the illocutionary aspect is the act of saying something; perlocutions are trying to get something to occur by saying something. Habermas has clarified his position by saying that illocutions "in the broader sense" means reaching understanding in the sense of accepting validity claims in a way that "effects coordination," not merely understanding the statement.[34] The details are not important for us here.[35] The important social point that Habermas derives from the distinction is that there are two alternative kinds of speech acts, one seeking agreement based on reasons (validity claims) and one that merely seeks to causally affect others.[36]

Contrary to the impression he sometimes gives, Habermas acknowledges that both ways of utilizing speech are actually goal oriented ("teleological" or "purposive"); the difference is in how the pursuit of the goal takes place. In communicative action, a middle term is inserted for goal attainment, that of reaching understanding.[37] He insists that the original use of language is actually that of reaching understanding with each other. The strategic use of arguments and language to manipulate individuals is logically secondary. One could not manipulate individuals unless they first comprehend what you are saying, and not merely in the sense of a well-formed sentence. The statement must have a plausible surface meaning that makes sense in context even if only to further hidden strategic ends. The original mode of language use, on which perlocutions are "parasitic," is agreement which leads to convictions.[38] He also argues that participants have an intuitive sense of when they are engaging in one rather than the other.

"Common knowledge" is more than mere opinions held in common. These opinions must be grounded in reasons that can be engaged if social coordination weakens. "I call knowledge *common* if it constitutes *consent* whereas consent relies on the intersubjective recognition of criticizable validity claims."[39] Habermas requires this strong definition of consent for the plausible creation of common convictions. The latter can only be based on the promise that validity claims can, in principle, be challenged and redeemed at any time (in contrast, for example to the "awe" inspired by the sacred or similar authority). Only a mutual orientation to validity claims can make agreements binding on participants in future coordinated action. The openness to challenge based on reasons maintains a presumption of validity, producing convictions that obligate and thereby sustain social order.

Habermas's position rests partly on the idea that understanding a statement actually requires taking a stand on the cogency of the reasons that could be offered in defending the statement. To understand, one must grapple with the proffered reasons in the first person, as a participant.[40] If one merely holds back evaluation and lists the reasons given, that is to say, takes the third person, one does not truly understand. Understanding means weighing and coming to a preliminary conclusion about the reasons given. An unavoidable claim to universal validity seems to reside in all speech in that understanding necessarily requires this *evaluation* of the profferred reasons. To understand is to apply one's *own* standards of what constitutes a "good reason," but one cannot help presuming that one's standards could be defended against all audiences. In this way understanding produces convictions rather than a mere record of alternative perspectives, and is therefore motivating.

Habermas's portrayal of the process of reaching understanding with one another immediately elicits two kinds of objections. First, interests must always enter into any communication. Therefore, any conception of a realm of discourse free from strategic considerations is hopelessly utopian and practically irrelevant. Second, even if discourse were not permeated by strategic interests, even if participants were engaged in a sincere effort to determine the truth of the matter, the fact that all reasoning is situated in a particular time and place necessarily limits what the participants will find reasonable. Historically relative agreement is all that is possible.

Habermas responds to both these criticisms by articulating a central concept in his work, the notion of "idealizations."[41] Habermas argues that certain idealizations are built into language use itself as part of the social practice of reaching understanding. They are not "objective" in the sense of standing apart from existing social relations, serving as an external moral yardstick for evaluating discussion. Rather, idealizations are *unavoidable* presuppositions of our action when we are trying to understand each other. These presuppositions organize our discussions, and therefore aspects of our social life, in fundamental ways. For example, the presupposition of an "objective world" structures disputes dealing with factual matters. For all the philosophical disputes over "truth" and "reality," these concepts unavoidably underpin common sense discussion, even of professional philosophers when they drive to work. Another presupposition is that "identical meanings" of expressions are being employed. Thomas McCarthy adds that one must also presume that one's discourse partners are accountable, that is, that they are actually competent to engage in discussion.[42]

The major presupposition or idealization is that the participants in discussion are actually oriented to validity claims, that is, sincerely attempting to decide what are the facts of the case or what is morally appropriate.[43] Habermas readily admits that, stated paradoxically, the necessary presupposition may actually be false. Although assumptions of an unreserved attempt at mutual understanding make sense of our attempts at justifying our decisions and positions, the participants may actually be engaging in strategic action. However, we must act *as if* the presuppositions are true or we would not discuss matters at all—there would be no point—but resort to force or other means of influence. As McCarthy puts it, "As suppositions we cannot avoid making while engaged in processes of mutual understanding, they are actually effective in structuring communication, and at the same time they are typically counterfactual."[44] The organizing capacity of these ideal presuppositions is apparently what Habermas means when he says that these "counterfactuals" may nevertheless create "social facts."[45]

Beyond this, Habermas asserts that participants in discussion presume that their arguments have *unconditional* validity, that is, that these claims transcend place and time, that what is being proposed is not merely "socially accepted" but "truth." Although all arguments are indeed socially and historically situated, participants' validity claims are presumed by them to be good for all times and places, that they will be in principle defensible against all future challenges.[46] Here Habermas draws on Charles Sanders Peirce's attempt to make sense out of what scientists do in face of the fact that all scientific reasoning is also historically situated.[47] Newton did not say "my theories are true for seventeenth-century England and its colonies." They are presumed to be true for all time, until a theory that better accommodates all the established facts and is fruitful for opening up new lines of research (like Einstein's) emerges. It is hard to see what other presupposition could organize scientific activity and discourse through time.

Habermas contends that validity claims transcend the situatedness of reason from inside the discussion itself. Arguments that would *only* appeal to a local consensus are not binding because we would have to ask if the consensus was rationally arrived at. This would then raise anew the question of reasons for accepting the arguments. The appeal therefore transcends the situation, pointing beyond to an ideal consensus. That is, the arguments imply that any rational person at any time would accept them.

We of course cannot establish the latter *a priori* because reasoning is indeed always context-bound. Therefore this is a "fallibilistic" consciousness, open to better reasons and/or refutation in the future. Again citing Peirce, Habermas argues that, given the fact that all reasoning is situated, "truth" must be conceived as "warranted assertability." What is the truth is only projected into the future, that the reasons for assertions will be sustained against all future criticisms. The court for the adjudication of reasons is the ideal community extended into the future, the court of "final opinion," counterfactual because the last day never comes. This is a "projection," as Habermas states, but a necessary one if we are to make sense of the social practice of discourses on various matters.[48]

Habermas's theory is an attempt to reconstruct existing social practices, to explain why they take the form they do. The concept of idealizations furthers this end. However the ultimate importance of these idealizations depends on how crucial it is in social life to reach understanding with others, that is, the importance of the concept depends on Habermas's social theory as a whole. The fruit of Habermas's expansion of the concept of rationality, the articulation of the contrast between communicative action and strategic action, and the notion of idealizations is that he can restate what cultural rationalization entails and how this leads to social rationalization.

CULTURAL RATIONALIZATION AND SOCIAL RATIONALIZATION

Like Weber, Habermas argues that prior cultural developments are necessary for increasing the rationality of social life. Cultural rationalization refers to the path of worldviews from mythology to argument from first principles based on "God, Being, or Nature" to the ultimate disintegration of unified worldviews into discrete, autonomous value spheres.[49] This rationalization expands the range of possibility for new directions in social life, thereby forming a kind of "logic" of social development. Specifically, cultural rationalization establishes opportunities for "learning processes" that can be drawn on for innovatively addressing problems facing society. An obvious example is scientific research.

The rationalization of worldviews frees the inner logic of development of central values in, respectively, science, art, and morals. In this way each sphere grows more distant from the others. "Value-enhancement" in natural science means refining an instrumental approach to nature through methodical experimentation that generates technological possibilities.[50] In regard to art, Habermas argues that there is no "progress" in the sense of science, in which later developments decisively displace earlier work. Instead, developing the logic of aesthetic value means exploring "authentic" expressions of subjectivity without regard to instrumental purposes or moral concerns.[51] Habermas does not say so, but art also becomes more and more self-referential. For example, many art works of the last century only make sense as a reaction to the perceived constraints of earlier art, leading to attempts to eliminate artistic illusion by revealing the history of the process itself (leaving drips and stray marks on the canvas—abstract expressionists), reducing art to its allegedly basic elements of shape and color (abstraction in general), experimentation with new materials of almost any origin, and even demystifying the role of the artist herself or himself in the production of art (Duchamps's "readymades"). The only thing that makes sense of a blank canvas hanging on a museum wall is the history of art to which the artist was referring and responding.

For both science and art, cultural rationalization means the expansion of intellectual and practical arenas in which a specific attitude toward the world can be explored without considering the other cultural values. In our day the logic of science leads to cloning, nuclear power, and genetic manipulation of life forms, all of which develop by ignoring perspectives formed in other value spheres. Equally so, the logic of art yields various forms increasingly distant from contemporary mass audiences such as minimalist art, fusion jazz, experimental theater and film, disjointed narrative in novels and film, and, in other realms of subjective expression, romanticism and eroticism that single-mindedly seek their own kind of "authenticity." It is clear that developments within these spheres can become separated from everyday conceptions of what these values should entail.

The moral–practical sphere develops its own logic in two ways. First, Habermas argues that moral perspectives are increasingly formulated as rationally defensible universal principles that are less and less grounded in specific forms of social life. The test of such principles is not whether they conform to a particular society's self-conception but whether such principles would be rationally accepted by participants in an unconstrained discussion, that is, in freedom and on the basis of mutual recognition. Habermas sometimes calls this "value generalization."

The second way in which the moral–practical sphere develops is through the separation of morals and law. Law is less and less tied to specific moral conceptions and thereby progressively freed for decision making distant from moral concerns. This is the development of positive law, law based on enactment by authorized decision makers through legitimate procedures.[52] We will have much more to say about this later.

However, cultural rationalization does not immediately lead to a broader rationalization of social life. For the latter to occur, for these cultural potentials to become "empirically effective," cultural developments must promote the transformation of social practices and displace traditional ways of doing things. This can be furthered in several

ways. One way is through the work of intellectuals in sharpening doctrines and through social movements inspired by these perspectives.
As Weber argues, interests must be legitimized. For this purpose
they require arguments establishing their validity. Although doctrinal
content depends partly on "external factors" such as the specific
potential carrier strata, the trajectory of historical development can
be influenced by intellectuals who rigorously address the question of
legitimacy of social practices. As Habermas notes, legitimation of
social action must be "supported with reasons and can thus also
be influenced by the intellectual treatment of internal relations of
meaning, by what Weber calls 'intellectualization.' "[53]

Habermas and Weber both also argue that social movements that
are forged from these various currents are important for bringing new
cultural possibilities to bear on social life.[54] According to Weber,
Calvinism encouraged new social practices by shaping individual
"action orientations." The concepts of the calling and predestination
freed individuals from traditional constraints on pursuing the accumulation of wealth through exchange. In this case, cultural rationalization
entered social life by being institutionalized in Calvinist religious con-
gregations and by the socialization of individuals in Calvinist families.[55]
Habermas adds that scientific communities and art markets can also
institutionalize cultural potentials, thereby aiding social rationalization.

For both Weber and Habermas, however, the crucial area through
which cultural rationalization can become fruitful for social rationalization is "moral–legal representations." This sets Habermas and
Weber apart from those who would stress the autonomous developments in science, technology, or economy. Habermas has long argued
the importance of normative development for social evolution, in
Communication and the Evolution of Society referring to normative
development as "the pacemaker of social evolution."[56] Habermas
argues this partly for the reason that moral–legal changes allow the
emergence of new forms of social relations that can lead to "height-
ened social complexity."

Social rationalization is firmly established with the legal organization of capitalist enterprises and a modern state based on taxation, a
monopoly on the legitimate use of force in a territory, and a bureaucratized administration. Especially important for these is the elaboration of formal law, based on enactment rather than tradition, to create
both the capitalist economy and the modern state and to regulate
their interactions with each other.

Once established, capitalist enterprises and the administrative state
prove more rational than alternatives in that they are organized
around calculability. One way in which both business organizations

and public bureaucracies increase their internal predictability is by separating the office from the individual. As Weber puts it, in both business organizations and in bureaucracies the individuals who work there are separated from the "means of production." As has often been stated, clear hierarchies of authority, formalized work rules, and performance measures increase the instrumental rationality, or efficiency, of these organizations when compared to their competitors. Finally, modern formal law develops by becoming more systematic through abstract principles, which means it is less tied to individual circumstances and more coherent overall, thereby increasing the predictability of the law.[57] This in turn helps establish a calculable environment for enterprises and bureaucracies.

Through these developments instrumental rationality is institutionalized in society. However, as argued in chapter one, Weber believes that this institutionalization of instrumental rationality and the emergence of compensatory "life orders" ultimately erodes the moral conceptions that prepared the soil for them. The resulting conflicts of "action orientations" of individuals create a crisis of meaning. A meaningful life cannot be constructed from the modern precipitates of mere economic instrumentalism and hedonism.[58] This kind of life has no point.

Unlike Weber, Habermas rejects the idea that social conflict is grounded merely in the dilemmas that modern social life poses for individuals. These dilemmas are at most symptoms of a more profound *structural* dynamic of modern society. In contemporary capitalism, one specific type of rationality, cognitive–instrumental rationality, is privileged by the expansion of the market economy and by the necessary interventions of the welfare state. The market economy and a bureaucratized public administration establish realms of action that ultimately impinge upon other areas of social life that cannot be sustained through instrumental or strategic action.

In brief, Habermas insists that there are actually two ways in which contemporary society is held together: "social integration" (reproduction of society as a meaningful whole for its participants) and "system integration" (reproduction of society as a self-maintaining system). These two modes of the integration of modern social life are distinct aspects of how contemporary society reproduces itself over time. The problem is that the particular manner by which these two dimensions of social life contribute to reproducing society as a whole tend to interfere with each other, creating social and political conflict in a number of areas. To explicate this, the central thesis of Habermas's social theory, we need to now explore his dualistic conception of society as a "lifeworld" and as a "system."

CHAPTER 4

SOCIETY AS LIFEWORLD AND SYSTEM

Drawing on various developments in twentieth-century philosophy and social theory since Weber—the painstaking analysis of language, the culturalist turn of Western Marxism, systems theory—and reflecting on the course of postwar capitalist society, Habermas approaches the issue of social rationalization anew. His social theory culminates in a "dualistic" reconceptualization of contemporary society. As mentioned, in order to comprehend the dynamic of social life, society must be conceived as both a meaningful whole (from the standpoint of the participants) and as a self-maintaining system constituted of subsystems fulfilling various functions (an observer perspective). From the first viewpoint, society is a "lifeworld" in which participants are immersed and which they reproduce in a characteristic way. The coherence of the lifeworld depends on maintaining cultural continuities, sustaining social relations the legitimacy of which is grounded in background assumptions and tested by experience, and the socialization of succeeding generations in such a way that they can construct coherent life histories by participating in social life. Reproduction of the lifeworld therefore revolves around the three structural components of "culture," "society" (a word Habermas uses in a specific as well as the more familiar general sense), and "personality."

On the other hand, in order to grasp the functional imperatives necessary for survival, society must be conceived as a self-maintaining system that is integrated through processes that occur "behind the backs" of society's members. We need both approaches if we are to comprehend the multiple ways in which modern society is reproduced and, thereby, be in a position to trace the contemporary sources of social conflict. Simply, there are two distinct integrative processes of society, "social" and "systemic," and these two modes of integration are irreducible to each other.

SOCIETY AS LIFEWORLD

In order to formulate his own theory of cultural and social rationalization Habermas employs a conception of society as a lifeworld. The "lifeworld" is another key concept of twentieth-century philosophy. It is a philosophical concept for organizing investigations into how the world immediately presents itself to us, that is, a "phenomenology" of the world. Fred Dallmayr gives a good overview of the importance and use of this investigatory strategy in contemporary philosophy.[1] However Habermas alters the traditional concept of the world as lifeworld in two ways. First, he stresses the importance of *language* in structuring and reproducing the lifeworld rather than conceiving the lifeworld as more ambiguous fundamental structures of *consciousness*. Second, he expands the concept beyond a mere reference to culture so as to make it more useful for sociological analysis.

For several reasons the conception of society as a lifeworld enjoys a certain priority over the systems conception. First of all, the systemic aspects of social life only emerge historically because of cultural changes in the lifeworld. Second, key systemic processes must always be in some way "anchored" in the lifeworld if they are to be regarded as legitimate processes of social life. Finally, the ultimate identification of *one* "society" depends on the understandings of society's participants, which take place in the lifeworld. Therefore we need to examine this conception of society first.

In articulating the idea of society as a lifeworld, Habermas is engaged once again in what he calls a "reconstruction." That is, Habermas begins with the "astonishing lifeworld fact of social integration" without violence and asks how this is possible, how so much social coordination of the "action plans" of individuals can unfold without threats of coercion.[2] He consistently rejects the view, associated with rational choice theory, that a society of merely self-interested individuals could be sustained. Habermas argues that a society of strategic actors cannot be stabilized because, *qua* strategic actors, they have no commitment to rules. Strategic or instrumental actors regard rules as obstacles to doing what one wants, to be evaded if possible. But without a generalized commitment to rules, institutions that bring people together cannot be sustained over time. Strategic actors therefore cannot reproduce the very institutions that give them an arena of action. Referring specifically to democratic theory, "if rational citizens were to describe their practices in empiricist categories, they would not have sufficient reason to observe the democratic rules of the game."[3] Simply put, pure strategic actors would treat everyone else as mere "suckers" and their relations would collapse, an argument that dates at least back to Plato's discussion in *The Republic* of why there must be "justice among thieves." Indeed, Habermas contends that rational choice theorists of democracy cannot explain the grounds of their own normative commitment to democracy.

To the contrary, Habermas argues that social coordination relies on the background consensus of members of society of what are the relevant facts in a situation and what are legitimate courses of action.[4] In problematic situations actors attempt to reach understanding with each other based on their explicit reasoning as to what would be an appropriate course of action. Understanding cannot be compelled; it can only be intersubjectively achieved. Individuals trying to understand each other can only restore their common convictions on the basis of reasons; for the attempt to be successful, participants must surrender to the "force of the better argument." That is, understanding can only be achieved if the participants are sincere in their engagement of reasons, rather than merely manipulating the opinions of others for their own strategic ends. As stated earlier, Habermas readily admits that in actual discussions of facts and legitimacy the presumption of sincere and fair participation may be false— counterfactual—but insists that participants *must* presume this or no one would ever even attempt to reach understanding with each other. They would simply resort to other inducements. Therefore, those trying to strategically manipulate the discussion must at least pretend to be arguing in good faith, the compliment that vice pays to virtue.

The general idea expressed in the concept of the lifeworld is that all thought relies on background assumptions or "preunderstandings." We can never, in principle, be aware of all the background contexts within which argument and action take place. For this reason Edmund Husserl referred to the lifeworld as the "always already," a phrase that recurs in Habermas's works.[5] The lifeworld is the inescapable context of knowing and acting; as an encompassing whole it cannot be seen and therefore is beyond doubt. We are always standing somewhere. As Habermas states the point, "Everyday communicative practice is not compatible with the hypothesis that everything could be entirely different."[6] More simply, following Peirce, he doubts the possibility of absolute doubt.

Although these background presuppositions can never be revealed as a whole to participants in social life, we do become aware of some of our silent presumptions when they become relevant to "goals and plans of action." Which assumptions come into view—are "thematized"—depends on the actions being pursued. Themes create "situations" in which the "horizon" (Husserl's term) formed by the lifeworld on our beliefs can be seen.[7] As we encounter problematic situations we become aware of some of the presuppositions of our reasoning and acting.

This analysis now connects with the previous discussion of communicative action as the mutual negotiation of situation definitions. Habermas calls the lifeworld "a culturally transmitted and linguistically organized stock of interpretive patterns" that sustains collective identity. "Collectivities maintain their identities only to the extent that the ideas members have of their lifeworld overlap sufficiently and condense into unproblematic background convictions."[8] In problematic situations the traditional and largely implicit interpretations that would ordinarily coordinate actions lose their certainty. The presuppositions of belief and action, this "segment" of the lifeworld, now appear "contingent," as open to other interpretations.[9] When situation definitions do not "overlap sufficiently" among actors for mutual understanding to coordinate actions, the problematic elements of the situation can then be consciously raised and "repair work" engaged in for restoring agreement on the grounds of action.

However, Habermas's conception of the lifeworld goes far beyond merely reaching agreement on the facts of the situation, relevant and defensible norms, and what is appropriately valued or felt in the situation. He contends that the emergence of the lifeworld is part of human *speciation* itself. Habermas follows George Herbert Mead's social anthropology in arguing that humans distinguish themselves from the animal world with the development of "linguistically mediated, normatively guided interaction." The genesis of the human species is occasioned by the development of language that creates sociation based on mutual understanding. The lifeworld is this system of symbols that emerges in the evolution of the human species as the framework for social existence.

There is a confusion that we must avoid if we are to appreciate how important the role of language is in Habermas's social theory. It is quite common to speak of "using language" (as I have done earlier), but this implies that language is a mere means to an end, a tool that is employed for the logically separate goal of reaching understanding. This is much too close to an "intentionalist semantics" that Habermas explicitly rejects.[10] Language and understanding are more tightly interwoven than the word "use" suggests. Habermas's (and Mead's) position is that understanding *emerges* through linguistic practices; it is not brought about by them, as if first language existed *then* understanding is reached. If one rejects the paradigm of "consciousness," as

Habermas does, there is no prior consciousness to wield language as a tool for reaching understanding. Our language, however frail, is all there is. The development of language and the coordination of social action through mutual understanding—the human mode of association—is therefore one and the same process. We are linguistic beings through and through.

Habermas argues that social life is reproduced through this network of communicative actions and background presuppositions called the lifeworld. To put it another way, the lifeworld fulfills certain functions in reproducing society as a coherent whole. First, the lifeworld sustains the conditions of mutual understanding through the "transmission and renewal of cultural knowledge." Second, it enables social action by maintaining the "solidarity" of individuals with each other; it integrates individuals into social groups that maintain the coherence of the collective, the sense of being one of a "we." Third, the lifeworld forms personal identities in that one's sense of self arises from one's interactions with others. The individual's identity is constituted by seeing oneself through the eyes of another, as the "other" of this other standing across from me. That is, following Mead, Habermas argues that personal identity is fundamentally constructed and stabilized through communicative action with others.[11]

The reproduction of the lifeworld is therefore also the reproduction of what Habermas calls "the structural components of the lifeworld: culture, society, and person."[12] These lifeworld structures are sustained by the "continuation of valid knowledge," "stabilization of group solidarity," and "socialization of responsible actors." With this it becomes clear that, in Habermas's usage, the lifeworld is much more than mere cultural presuppositions. To a considerable extent, Habermas thinks of culture, society, and person as precipitates or nodes of the reproductive processes of the lifeworld. Habermas seriously conceives society from a "structuralist" perspective, to employ the term he repeatedly uses.[13] Society is not an aggregation of individuals but fundamentally a network of communicative actions that engage the functional tasks of maintaining cultural continuity, sustaining legitimate social orders, and creating competent actors.[14] He even goes so far as to say that, "Individuals and groups are 'members' of a lifeworld only in a metaphorical sense."[15] The lifeworld is constituted by communicative actions, the success of which allows society to be reproduced over time. "Individuals" are not the atom of society but rather the consequence of a network of communicative actions that is functioning properly.

Culture, society, and person are symbolic constructions. They form as a way of reproducing the lifeworld over time, that is, reproducing this form of sociation, the heart of our very speciation as humans. This is, of course, not the way culture, social relations, and individuality are *experienced* by participants in society. This role of the lifeworld can only be appreciated from the perspective of an *observer* attempting to see the lifeworld as a whole and therefore revealing the manner and considerations of its reproduction.

It follows from the above that culture, society, and personal identity have no existence independent of or prior to the lifeworld. However, the reproduction of these structural components of the lifeworld is not a merely passive process. The lifeworld is reproduced when social actors are capable of plausibly connecting "new situations" with preexisting situations, that is with existing cultural interpretations, legitimate social relationships, and individual life histories. Actors must engage in communicative practices in order to sustain the lifeworld itself as a coherent set of presuppositions of social action. In doing so they maintain the coherence of their culture and the legitimacy of their social relations, and thereby help reproduce themselves as competent actors.

To the extent that these communicative practices fail, the structural components of the lifeworld—culture, society, and person—are threatened in ways specific to the component. In regard to culture, if the "cultural stock of knowledge" proves insufficient for sustaining mutual understanding in the face of new situations, that is, if the existing "interpretive schemes" are incapable of comprehending new situations by meaningfully connecting them with the existing cultural situation, loss of meaning occurs. As he puts it, "the resource 'meaning' becomes scarce." As the cultural tradition loses its coherence, the uncontested presuppositions for considering social relations legitimate and the cultural resources for making sense of individual life—collective identity (society) and personal identities (person)—are eroded. Disruption of the continuity of culture therefore results in "corresponding legitimation and orientation crises."

Second, social integration is maintained when new situations can be reconciled with the existing normative regulation of social groups. Successful social integration "stabilizes the identity of groups" by sustaining the legitimacy of social relations. If new situations cannot be accommodated within the existing "inventory of legitimate orders," the "resource 'social solidarity' becomes scarce." The consequence is a widespread sense that existing social relations are incoherent and unreliable, that is, "anomie."

Finally, socialization needs to connect the new situations with the existing situation over "historical time," that is, to forge continuity through succeeding generations. Habermas refers to this reproductive process as creating "generalized competences for action" and "responsibility of persons." This requires communicative action that allows individuals to establish personal identity by building "individual life histories" that make sense. If socialization processes weaken, the "resource 'ego strength' becomes scarce." Individuals are driven to psychological "defensive strategies" that obstruct social interaction, resulting in "psychopathologies" and "alienation."[16]

If the communicative reproduction of any of the three lifeworld structures is altered or disrupted, all of them are threatened because each provides resources for the others. Successful *cultural* reproduction provides reasons for legitimating "existing institutions" and resources for "the acquisition of generalized competences," that is to say, socialization. Successful *social integration* strengthens the cultural values that are manifested in "legitimate orders" and maintains the sense of personal "obligations." Successful *socialization* ("strong identities") creates individuals who can "deal on a realistic basis with the situations that come up in their lifeworld," increasing the capacity for innovatively interpreting and integrating new knowledge (culture) and increasing the likelihood of "motivations for actions that conform to norms" (society).[17] It is this network of communicative actions that sustains the sociation of humans through linguistic or symbolic interaction. Only when the network is maintained can individuals make sense of their social life.

THE RATIONALIZATION OF THE LIFEWORLD

Habermas goes beyond Weber by conceiving cultural rationalization as the rationalization of the lifeworld. This rationalization is manifested as a disempowering of tradition in stabilizing a coherent social life. Various modernization processes destroy the "naturalness" of key aspects of the lifeworld. Traditional certainties are eroded by the inner logic of scientific discovery, as it frees itself from religious and metaphysical commitments, by the pluralization of cultures and religions, and therefore, the emergence of rival conceptions of what are legitimate social relations, and by the modern construction of a realm of subjectivity that can only develop if it is unconstrained by ethical or practical concerns. It is also eroded by social differentiation of roles, occupations, and interests.[18]

Habermas argues that the rationalization of the lifeworld affects all three structural components of the lifeworld. Increasingly, cultural knowledge must be based on reasoned reflection rather than relying on what is traditionally given. Due to the pluralization of social roles and beliefs, the existing norms that regulate and legitimate group relations are more and more subject to testing by universalistic principles, intensifying the demands for a rational defense of the terms under which we live together. Finally, the rationality of identity formation increases to the extent that individuals are motivated to criticize received wisdom and also capable of taking responsibility for life choices, reconciling conflicting demands of diverse social roles, and forging a life history that makes sense.[19]

An additional aspect of the rationalization of the lifeworld is that the reproduction processes of cultural renewal and socialization of new generations tend to become the provinces of professionals. We have discussed this in regard to culture, but it also true of socialization. In fact, the role of professionals in virtually every aspect of the socialization and education of youth is one of the most prominent features of contemporary social life. Professionalization means an increase in the level of "reflection" in analysis and recommendations in this area. Consequently, traditional ways of raising youth are derided, delegitimated, and displaced.

Although increasing professionalization strikes many as elitist and exclusionary, rationalization in regard to the third structural component of the lifeworld, society, or group relations, unfolds in a different way. Habermas argues that the reproduction of legitimate social relations becomes more reflective due to the establishment of democracy. Although law as a field of *cultural* knowledge relies on professional jurisprudence, in regard to the lifeworld structure of *society* (in the specific sense) democratic procedures actually institute a kind of "discursive will-formation" that erodes traditional authority in justifying the organization of social relations. From this perspective the development of democracy itself is part and parcel of increasing rationalization of the lifeworld, an argument to which we will return.[20]

As the examples of socialization and democracy indicate, the rationalization of the lifeworld should not be construed as something that only concerns cultural knowledge. Habermas's *sociological* conception of the lifeworld, rather than a merely *philosophical* conception, refers not only to common knowledge but also to traditional and customary ways of doing things. Actors in society not only rely on "cultural certainties" but also on "individual skills as well—the intuitive knowledge of *how* one deals with situations—and socially customary practices too—the intuitive knowledge of *what* one can count on in situations...well-established solidarities and proven competences."[21] These "loyalties" and "skills" have been "tested" in social life in that what reactions one can anticipate from others in one's group or community, and traditional approaches in handling new situations, have been trustworthy in the past in coordinating one's actions with others.

This means that rationalization of the lifeworld not only challenges received wisdom but also disrupts customary *practices* that utilize typical skills and presume ordinary relations within one's group. These practices cannot be reduced to the cultural knowledge they embody and the increasing unreliability of these practices generally takes place behind the backs—"*a tergo*"—of society's members. Of course culture, social relations, and socialization all depend on each other for resources, so the specific causal relations of change are difficult to sort out. The main point here is to not reduce rationalization of the lifeworld to mere conscious cultural struggles. Background suppositions of how one's associates will relate to one and what skilled approaches will work in handling new experiences are also part of the lifeworld in a sociological sense, and the experience of rationalization includes the proliferation of situations where these traditional expectations prove wanting.

The rationalization of the lifeworld means that a general awareness of the contingency of the cultural tradition, social relations, and individual life paths emerges. This increases the demands on communicative action. "[T]he further the structural components of the lifeworld and the processes that contribute to maintaining them get differentiated, the more interaction contexts come under conditions of rationally motivated mutual understanding, that is, of consensus formation that rests *in the end* on the authority of the better argument."[22] The lifeworld is no longer reproduced more or less unproblematically through implicit communicative action but rather becomes dependent on "the interpretive accomplishments of the actors themselves." Ascribed consensus is replaced by "*achieved*" consensus.[23]

In this way various background assumptions on which social unity, meaningfulness, and coordinated social action are based become fragile. Situation definitions—what are the facts of the case, what is morally defensible in a certain situation, or what is appropriately felt or valued in a situation—lose their obviousness. Increasingly, agreement on factual matters, on moral and ethical positions regarding social relations, and need interpretations and evaluations must be consciously achieved. Communicative action organized around a presumption of seeking understanding becomes necessary for restoring social integration. In contemporary society this effort to reach understanding about the situation can only be accomplished by weighing the plausibility of various "validity claims": truth of statements, appropriateness, sincerity of the participants.

Modern development therefore displaces the traditional agreements and background assumptions that orient action through our understanding of each other, on which depends our sense of participating in a common world. To the extent that traditional preunderstandings are undermined, the unity of the lifeworld is threatened. Problematization breaks out in society as traditional reasons are disempowered, group cohesion and expectations weaken, and personal identities and the "know-how" of navigating social life are thrown into doubt. We should not, however, fall into the illusion that *all* things have lost certainty and are now subject to debate. The very idea of the lifeworld entails that it is not possible to question all things at once, to stand in the air. Therefore the lifeworld always forms an "unshakeable rock of background assumptions, loyalties, and skills."[24] It is a "conservative counterweight" to the possibility of disagreement that always accompanies communicative action. But things do change with modernity. The emergence of independent cultural value spheres, expert elaborations, and the general diversity of social relations, roles, and identities dramatically challenge what may be considered *plausible* reasons and expectations.[25]

The increasing burdens on communicative action as the mode of social integration, coupled with the dislocations engendered by the fragmentation of reason, provoke political and social reactions. There are attempts to overcome the decentering of reason by restoring the metaphysical or religious unity of worldviews, restoring a principle for ordering the claims of the different cultural spheres. There are also political projects in many parts of the world for restoring the ethical unity of society by force. All these reactionary policies will ultimately fail because previous reasons are indeed disempowered and a restoration of mutual understanding cannot be achieved with bayonets. As Roger Williams, the seventeenth-century religious dissenter, pointed out, all that these strategies can create is a nation of hypocrites, at most pretending to the authorities to believe.

In detraditionalized societies the pressures on coordinating social life through communicative action are enormous, but there is an alternative to reaction. Habermas states that contemporary society has alleviated some of these burdens by the establishment of delimited social contexts in which individuals are freed to make decisions based on self-interest rather than on reaching understanding with each other. A market economy and a bureaucratic public administration are areas of social life that are not "steered" by traditional consensus nor by reasoned agreement. Instead these social interactions are coordinated by conditioning the decisions of individuals through automatic rewards and punishments. In this way the burgeoning need for achieved mutual understanding in society as a whole is provided with a relief valve, reducing the pressure. In order to analyze these aspects of contemporary society, the systems-theoretic approach is necessary.

SOCIETY AS A SYSTEM

With modernization Habermas argues that the lifeworld perspective proves insufficient to capture the complexity and dynamic of social life. Society does not persist solely by sustaining the common understandings of its participants. Actions within society must also fulfill certain objective *functional* requirements if society is to reproduce itself: material reproduction, cultural elaboration and transmission, normative integration, and the development of certain competences in society's participants through socialization. Informed by the work of Talcott Parsons, Habermas argues that in order to analyze these functional imperatives, beyond the notion of society as a meaningful whole, we must also conceive modern society as a self-regulating system made up of subsystems differentiated according to specific functional processes. Although in premodern societies the lifeworld aspects of society (processes which maintain society as comprehensible to its participants) and the systemic aspects (the often unintended fulfillment of functional demands necessary for social life to be sustained) are bound together, with the development of a market economy and a bureaucratic state these dimensions of social life are "uncoupled" from each other. Therefore the need for a systems theory of society actually arises historically, at a certain point in "social evolution."[26] If we are to grasp all the ways in which integration of contemporary societies occurs, the analysis of society as a lifeworld must be complemented by a reconceptualization of society as a self-maintaining system.

The systems conception of society is developed from biological models, by regarding society as much like an organism attempting to maintain itself in a certain environment. Organisms respond to complex environmental challenges by increasing their own internal complexity over generations. For a social system this means developing subsystems that specialize in specific functional tasks that contribute to sustaining the whole. The proper functioning of each of these subsystems depends on obtaining "resources" (useful inputs) from the other subsystems. Overall system integration of society is achieved with the successful interchange of resources of these subsystems with one another, allowing society as a whole to be maintained over time.

From this analytical viewpoint, there are three subsystems in contemporary capitalist societies that engage the functional requirements mentioned above: the economic, the public administrative, and the "lifeworld." The economic and administrative subsystems are responsible for the material reproduction of society. Correspondingly, from the systems perspective, the lifeworld is theoretically reinterpreted as the subsystem that engages "processes of cultural reproduction, social integration, and socialization."[27] Unlike the lifeworld "subsystem," the subsystems of the economy and administration are not internally coordinated by reaching understanding through communicative action. Rather, these subsystems are steered by, respectively, the "media" of money and power. In contrast to the linguistically attained coordination of action in lifeworld processes, here media substitute for discourse.

It is important to note that *all* subsystems—not just the economy and administration—are engaged in satisfying the functional requirements for the integration and reproduction of society. Furthermore, both the "monetary–bureaucratic complex" *and* lifeworld processes are "distant from the immediate experience of the participants in interaction," but in different ways. In regard to lifeworld functions, participants are "intuitively aware of orders established by social integration," even if they could not necessarily identify how this order is generated. On the other hand, system integration through media simply cannot be captured from a participant's perspective. Access requires "counterintuitive" systems concepts.[28]

Habermas's dualistic theory might be called dialectical in the specific sense that the more one tries to grasp society from the participant's perspective, the more a functional analysis that transcends this perspective appears necessary. No matter how unchallenged the common understandings of society, no matter how smoothly the culture, group identity, and socialization of individuals support each other, if the society cannot provide for the material needs of its members, over time it will crumble. From the other direction, systems theory can be utilized only to a point because of the issue of the "identity" of the system being maintained. A society can only be identified as the *same* society, that is, for example, we can only distinguish a society's "destruction" from its mere "transformation," by appealing to the sense of identity of its *members*. One can try to comprehend the integration of social life from either a participant's perspective or from an observer's perspective, but either would soon be inadequate. A large part of *The Theory of Communicative Action* is devoted to demonstrating why this is the case.

REAL ABSTRACTION

In order to analyze the economy and the administration as self-regulating, media-steered subsystems, Habermas invokes the concept of "real abstraction" in Marx. We have already briefly encountered the idea in discussing Lukács; now we have to see how Habermas uses it to elaborate his systems perspective. The specific context in which Marx employs this concept is in formulating his labor theory of value. The laws of motion of capitalism—its autonomous and specific dynamic—come into existence with the increasing importance of exchange relations for mediating the social division of labor. As argued before, under capitalism the interchange of products of individual, private labors in the division of labor takes the form of the exchange of commodities. According to Marx, for commodities to be exchanged they must have some quality in common. Marx concludes that the commensurability of different products of the division of labor lies in the fact that they embody "socially necessary labor-time," the average time in a particular society it takes to produce something. Furthermore, the ratio at which commodities exchange is their relative incorporation of socially necessary labor-time, which determines their respective values. If it takes more time, on average, to find, mine, and refine gold than to find, fell, and cut up trees, then gold will be more expensive than lumber.

Unlike earlier societies, which sometimes utilized markets, capitalism is a society not only in which products are exchanged but in which they are produced *for* exchange. The coherence of the capitalist economy stems from the regulation of this exchange by the law of value. In this way the discrete, specific labors in capitalist society are brought together in a self-regulating whole. The productive activities of a professor and an autoworker can only be exchanged for each other if the products are regarded—from the standpoint of the economic *system*—as both embodying socially necessary labor-time. As Marx puts it, "concrete labor" is transformed into "abstract labor." This transformation rests on an "abstraction" from the varied and specific kinds of labor performed in social life. But it is a "real" abstraction in that the capitalist economy can only function—can only organize a society-wide division of labor as a series of exchanges of commodities, rather than, say, individual contributions to a community, or mutual gift-giving—by surreptitiously making this abstraction.

In appropriating Marx's concept of real abstraction Habermas typically cites secondary sources so it is not immediately apparent which specific passages in Marx's work have stimulated his theory. However, one of Marx's clearest statements on the topic is in *A Contribution to the Critique of Political Economy*: "To measure the exchange-value of commodities by the labor-time they contain, the different kinds of labor have to be reduced to uniform, homogeneous, simple labor, in short to labor of uniform quality, whose only difference therefore is quantity. This reduction appears to be an abstraction, but it is an abstraction which is made every day in the social process of production."[29] Later, in *Capital*, Marx states that the reduction of discrete, concrete labors to "simple average labor" is a "social process that goes on behind the backs of the producers."[30]

Habermas is not the only social theorist to focus on Marx's concept of real abstraction. Besides Lukács, I. I. Rubin discusses this aspect of Marx's argument in order to clarify the theory of value and emphasize the historically limited nature of the theory's application. More recently, Moishe Postone discusses the process of real abstraction as part of his innovative reinterpretation of the role of "value" in capitalism and the historical specificity of this mode of organizing social life.[31]

Unlike Lukács, Rubin, and Postone, Habermas's own adoption of the concept of real abstraction is hardly an endorsement of Marx's theory of value, a theory which he has repeatedly rejected.[32] Instead, Habermas uses the concept as a framework for analyzing how meaningful, purposive *actions* in the lifeworld of social groups are utilized—"behind the backs" or "over the heads" of individuals— as *performances* that maintain the *functioning* of the social system as a whole.[33] Habermas contends that the capitalist economy must be analyzed as more than an arena for the subordination and exploitation of labor, that is, a realm of social classes. The capitalist economy must also be conceived as a self-regulating subsystem of society that fulfills the task of the material reproduction of social groups by successfully extracting resources from society's members, and, along with the administrative subsystem, historically has done so exceedingly *well*.

The Economy as Subsystem

According to Habermas, Marx erred in not seeing the development of the market economy as an evolutionary advance of society through functional differentiation that allows it to expand its capacity to provide for material reproduction. Marx did not distinguish between "the *level of system differentiation* attained in the modern period and the *class-specific forms* in which it has been institutionalized."

> Marx is convinced a priori that in capital he has before him *nothing more* than the mystified form of a class relation. This interpretation excludes from the start the question of whether the systemic interconnection of the capitalist economy and the modern state administration do not *also* represent a higher and evolutionarily advantageous level of integration by comparison to traditional societies.[34]

In contrast, Habermas considers the above an evolutionary advance for two reasons. Not only does this self-regulating process increase material production, but also the emergence of media-steered subsystems reduces the burden of communication processes of a detraditionalized lifeworld. The increasing need for achieved consensus in regard to cultural reproduction, legitimate social order, and socialization threatens to overwhelm the lifeworld. Turning coordination of some reproductive functions of social life over to autonomic subsystems increases the possible density of social interaction without overburdening the lifeworld processes of social integration.

Media can perform this task because they produce a kind of "delinguistified" coordination of social action. "Media such as money and power attach to empirical ties; they encode a purposive-rational attitude toward calculable amounts of value and make it possible to exert generalized, strategic influence on the decisions of other participants while *bypassing* processes of consensus-oriented communication."[35] Although the phrase "empirical ties" is somewhat obscure, Habermas's argument is actually quite common. The institutionalization of media such as money and power simplifies social interaction in large spheres of social life by reducing the conditions necessary for coordinating action. For example, prices can on their own steer the interactions of individuals who do not even live in the same country, thereby increasing the density and velocity of market exchanges and, arguably, the material efficiency of the whole. As defenders of the market from the conservative Friedrich Hayek to the socialist Alec Nove have urged, among other things, the market should be seen as a large, efficient information network.[36] Prices (the medium of money) succinctly convey information that can automatically coordinate the interactions of strategically acting individuals or firms.

Habermas argues that the market economy increases the "complexity" of society, allowing it room to perform efficiently in reproducing the material conditions of the lifeworld without regard for lifeworld restrictions. The economic subsystem is created by law ("formally organized") and thereby circumscribed in its functioning by law. It is for this reason that media-steering can occur. It unfolds in a specialized context where individuals are faced with delimited choices that do not require communication beyond a binary "code" of acceptance or rejection of monetary offers.[37] Within the subsystem, individuals are free to act in a strategic instrumental fashion, oriented only to the consequences of action, because the situation is already legally defined, eliminating other normative considerations.[38] In this way law carves out areas of social interaction in which one can behave in a purely strategic manner. The legitimacy of these arenas of social life stems from the fact that the laws which create them have been passed by legally constituted authorities. Importantly, it is the legitimacy of the legal system that ultimately assures actors of the legitimacy of their activities in these realms. The legitimacy of the legal system must therefore be sustained if subsystems are to retain their position in contemporary society.

Media-steered subsystems regard other areas of social life as "environments" from which subsystems extract resources. The economy procures the performances necessary for its functioning through the legal institution of the labor contract. (Habermas even says that the role of employee is created by "legal fiat."[39]) Labor must be monetarized because a subsystem "can relate to its environment only via its own medium."[40] This allows the functioning of the subsystem which then puts out "goods and services" exchanged for monetary demand. The interchange therefore has its input exchange, wages for labor, and an output exchange, goods and services for consumer demand.

PUBLIC ADMINISTRATION AS SUBSYSTEM

Habermas acknowledges that this economy is not harmonious; he says that it is "crisis-ridden" or subject to "disequilibria." According to Habermas, disequilibria are normal to a subsystem as it adapts to changing environments.[41] These disturbances in the capitalist economy are handled by a bureaucratized administration that also functions as a subsystem, steered by the medium "power." In regard to administration, the hierarchy of offices invested with power and decision simplifies the situation in which individuals interact, although not to the same extent as in the economic subsystem. Here processes of reaching understanding with each other are also bypassed. Individuals are faced with the choice of either obeying or suffering sanctions. The legally constituted authority of the administration can always compel obedience, therefore reasoning with the recalcitrant is unnecessary.

Habermas argues that public administration has interchanges similar to the economy: "organizational performances" (i.e. managing the economy) for taxes (input) and "political decisions" (e.g. social programs) for "mass loyalty" (output). Corresponding to the lifeworld division between public and private, there are, then, four interchange relations between the lifeworld and the economic and administrative subsystems: employee and consumer (private), and welfare state client and citizen (public). Around the interchange relations these four social roles "crystallize."

Under democratic conditions, mass loyalty depends on "social welfare programs," "offers that can be checked as to fulfillment."[42] Habermas argues that this mode of extracting mass loyalty, along with the exclusion of certain political topics, impoverishes the public arena in contemporary welfare states, downplaying the role of "citizen" and enhancing the role of "client."[43] The client role is characterized by the bureaucratic formulation—power in the form of laws that define who is entitled to what services under what conditions—and delivery of social services ("use-values"). As we will discuss later, the symmetry of this analysis is hardly perfect. The point here is that administrative "production" must *also* take the form of its medium, thereby requiring another, noneconomic, form of real abstraction. Just as the economic subsystem must transform individuals into "labor," the administrative subsystem transforms individuals into clients of welfare state bureaucracies.

System Integration

There are many ambiguities connected with Habermas's attempt to conceive society as a self-regulating system, further discussion of which is best deferred to my criticisms of his social and political theory. However, one immediate question must be raised here. Society coheres as a system when the actions of individuals within social life can be utilized in fulfilling subsystem tasks. But since the appropriation of actions as socially relevant performances takes place behind the backs of society's members, how can we *know* that the actions are such that they quietly contribute to system processes? That is, how we can know that this social order actually fulfills the functions necessary for maintaining society, since it is notoriously difficult to even state *specifically* which functions are "imperatives" for maintaining social life? In response, Habermas relies on the system concept of "feedback."

> To be sure, the material reproduction of the lifeworld does not, even in limiting cases, shrink down to surveyable dimensions such that it might be represented as the intended outcome of collective cooperation. Normally it takes place as the fulfillment of latent functions *going beyond the action orientations* of those involved. Insofar as the aggregate effects of cooperative actions fulfill imperatives of maintaining the material substratum, these complexes of action can be stabilized functionally, that is, through feedback from functional side effects. This is what Parsons means by "functional," in contrast to "social," integration.[44]

For example, a market economy is characterized by the fact of unintended consequences of actions that are then coordinated behind the backs of participants. This creates a dense network of exchange that cannot be captured from within the lifeworld, so the functional significance of their actions typically escapes individuals. The effectiveness of this realm of "norm-free sociality" is established by the fact of the material successes of societies that have freed action in this way.[45]

Although at first glance this functional stabilization of social life may appear unlikely, the idea of order emerging of its own, through the interlocking of consequences, has been powerfully advanced by the relatively new field of "complexity" studies. For example, the biologist Stuart Kauffman argues that life itself may have emerged when a dense chemical soup made it possible for molecules to serve as catalysts for each other and therefore for a collection of molecules to reproduce itself. With sufficient density and diversity of molecules, "the chances that an autocatalytic system—a self-maintaining and self-reproducing metabolism—will spring forth becomes a near certainty."[46] He calls this "order for free." There are many other examples of self-sustaining patterns emerging in which one would anticipate randomness. A recent demonstration in regard to certain economic topics is presented in Paul Krugman's *The Self-Organizing Economy*.[47] Therefore, Habermas's arguments for the autonomic stabilization of interacting subsystems must not be rejected out of hand, even if the notion is counterintuitive.

Habermas argues that the development of media-steered subsystems has been very successful in providing for the material reproduction of contemporary societies, ultimately displacing the traditional conflicts endemic to capitalism. He does acknowledge that contemporary capitalism is still a class society in the sense of "private disposition over the means of producing social wealth."[48] However, as alluded to before, welfare policies effectively "dam up" conflict based on social class by (1) stimulating a "continuous rise in the standard of living" and other "compensations," and (2) creating a new set of social cleavages that cut across the old. The consequence is that "conflicts over distribution . . . lose their explosive power."[49] As Habermas repeatedly states, ownership of property dissipates as an issue in this situation: "[S]truggle over property forms has (long since) lost its dogmatic meaning."[50] Class relations simply lose their relevance for the lifeworld as struggles over distribution are reduced in importance.

This hardly means that social conflict disappears. The autonomous dynamic of economic and administrative subsystems, necessary for the material reproduction of society, causes serious tensions to arise between the lifeworld and system dimensions of social life, tensions that may explain the rise of various social movements in the past four decades. These social conflicts, and the new progressive political project that Habermas believes that they require, must now be examined.

CHAPTER 5

SOCIAL CONFLICT AND
PROGRESSIVE POLITICS

Habermas contends that contemporary society is held together in two ways: social integration and system integration. However, these distinct ways of reproducing social life tend to clash with each other, resulting in a variety of fierce social and political struggles. A major theoretical advantage of Habermas's dualistic social theory is that it allows him to reconsider the origins of conflict in advanced capitalist societies and to try to account for the new social movements that have surfaced in the wake of subsystem dynamics.

THE COLONIZATION THESIS

The fragmentation of reason that is part of cultural rationalization already leads to a widely perceived loss of meaning and weakening of social solidarity, a firm belief in what kind of social relations are legitimate. Habermas argues that the unsettling of social life caused by the partial rationalization of the lifeworld is deepened by attempts of the administrative state to handle various disequilibria of the economic system. Administrative action must utilize the media of power and money in its interventions, using law to, among other things, manage the various dislocations of the market economy. The consequence is that difficulties of social life that previously were more or less informally addressed—aid to the poor or disabled, support for the elderly, education and training of youth, relations between parents and children—are now recast as *legal* relations, with all the formally specified rights, responsibilities, forms, caseworkers, and bureaucratic monitoring and enforcement that this entails. According to Habermas, this "juridification" of social relations displaces communicative action aimed at reaching understanding and agreement with others. When law regulates social relations, people do not have to labor to understand each other. When communicative action is disrupted in this way, actors take a strategic attitude toward each other, but this is not the important theoretical point for Habermas. This strategic attitude is a symptom of the clash of the two modes of societal integration, as media displace reaching understanding in areas that, Habermas contends, can only be reproduced through communicative action.

Although Habermas gives few details, the general idea of the potential conflict between these modes of societal integration is easily demonstrated. When traditionalism has loosened its grip on cultural interpretations, cultural renewal and coherence can only be sustained by the offering of new interpretations and perspectives evaluated solely on the strength of the reasons that can be marshalled in their favor. Equally, when the norms that render reliable and defensible the social interactions among society's members are confronted with new situations, such as the immigration of groups from places with a very different idea of what is proper, an effort must be made to determine principles that can accommodate the new diversity and restore social solidarity. For example, he offers the principle that all affected should participate in deciding what is in the general interest.

The extent to which the media of money or power influence cultural reproduction or normative regulation, the latter processes are disrupted. If certain cultural perspectives are privileged and others proscribed by threats, bribes, or simply administrative narrowness, the culture becomes inauthentic. If the only books published or art works presented are a consequence of what will generate the most money for the presenters, or if certain ideas and forms of art are excluded by law, the "official" culture loses its ability to help people make sense of a changing world. When public policy can be purchased, if alternative political parties are legally excluded, or when the needs of various groups in a community are marginalized by the manipulations of money or power, the credibility of the rules that govern social life is eroded. Social solidarity can only be generated by the mutual accommodation of the interests and perspectives of all those subject to these rules. If this is lacking, individuals will find it difficult to identify with the social order, and alienation and cynicism gain ground.

Perhaps this illustration can further clarify the conflict here. On a small canvas, a college classroom involves both the necessary functioning of cultural renewal and normative regulation. If the topics discussed and perspectives allowed are limited by administrative threats or promises of early promotion for the instructor, the transmission of knowledge based on reasoned consideration of alternative relevant perspectives is obstructed and the teaching becomes suspect. If the grades in a course are not assigned by effort, a principle that students in the class recognize as defensible, but rather on the basis of whose parents donate the most money to the college or what the president of the college "suggests," the enterprise collapses. Finally, if a professor were to respond to any critical questioning by students with a sheer assertion of her or his administratively authorized control of classroom discussion, learning, which requires the comprehension and weighing of *reasons*, cannot take place. Only reasoning can generate common *convictions*, which reproduces the solidarity of the participants. For a college classroom to "work," the knowledge produced must be based on reasoning open to counterarguments and the rules governing the setting must be based on equal respect. The influence of power and money rend this delicate fabric.

Returning to the larger canvas, juridification is, specifically, the sign of subsystem encroachment on lifeworld processes because subsystems are organized through formal law. Habermas employs the examples of the increasing juridification of schools and family relations to illustrate the tensions that result when an alien frame is placed on relations that can only be reproduced communicatively. This is why education and family policy are intense areas of conflict today. However, he only indicates this as a line of future research. Although the concept "real abstraction" is taken from Marx's economic theory, Habermas says the "model case" of "colonization" is the transformation of citizens into clients of welfare state bureaucracies.[1] That is, for political reasons, the real force of his theory concerns welfare compensations.

Welfare state compensations result in "paternalism," "custodial supervision," and a "civil privatism" in which citizens are transformed into private consumers and clients of social programs.[2] Sounding very much like conservatives back to Herbert Hoover, Habermas argues that in this way welfare policies contribute to the erosion of traditional sources of social solidarity.

[T]raditional duties of caring have been replaced by bureaucratically administered provisions of basic necessities. As this transformation occurred, the consciousness of belonging to a community that was held together, not simply through abstract legal relationships but also through solidarity, fell by the wayside. Deteriorating relationships of solidarity cannot be regenerated among isolated clients who lay claim to entitlements from welfare bureaucracies.[3]

From a systems perspective, in its actions the administrative subsystem is actually seeking to reduce the complexity of its "environment"—the other subsystems of the economy and the lifeworld—by "extracting mass loyalty," thereby becoming "self-programming."[4] From the lifeworld perspective, however, social relations become ever more rigid, constrained, isolating, and foreign.

Habermas famously refers to this as "the colonization of the lifeworld," comparing the process to the destruction of local meaning-giving cultures by an imperial power pursuing its own narrow designs. The dynamic by which subsystems reconfigure other social processes as environments, from which resources must be extracted, is disorienting from the perspective of society's participants.[5] Furthermore, as the media of money and power extend their domains, there emerge "more and more complex networks that no one has to comprehend or be responsible for."[6] Aspects of social life "burst the bounds of the lifeworld"; as Habermas puts it, these activities are "deworlded." People increasingly find themselves in a web of social relations that appear "objective," like something in the natural world, that sometimes confronts them like a force of nature. That is, they experience a "loss of freedom," Weber's famous "iron cage." This is Habermas's restatement of Lukács's thesis of reification, the way in which capitalist social relations, especially social production, take on the appearance of a relation between things because of the dominance of commodity exchange.

However, Habermas hastens to add that the "uncoupling" of system and lifeworld processes in contemporary society does not in itself lead to intractable social problems. Media work well in areas of material reproduction, which is why the "welfare state compromise" could be stabilized. Social crisis, properly so-called, only emerges when media overflow their domains in material production and attempt to reconfigure areas of social life that cannot be steered by media: cultural renewal and transmission, group identity and the legitimacy of social relations, and the socialization of new generations. These aspects of social life depend on communicative action for their reproduction and coherence. When media interactions extend into these areas, this amounts to a colonization of lifeworld domains and produces conflict around the objectification of social relations that cannot function if objectified.

Colonization becomes *necessary* with the growth of the monetary–bureaucratic complex in order to satisfy the need for use-values and the reconfiguration of social roles this requires. "[C]apitalist growth triggers conflicts within the lifeworld chiefly as a consequence of the expansion and the increasing density of the monetary–bureaucratic complex; this happens, first of all, where socially integrated contexts of life are redefined around the roles of consumer and client and assimilated to systemically-integrated domains of action."[7] Colonization is *possible* because the lifeworld has been detraditionalized but is only partly rationalized due to the fact that rationality potentials made available by cultural change are largely "encapsulated" in expert cultures and not diffused in everyday life experience. The possibilities for broad-based innovative responses to social problems—"learning processes"—and for renewing social solidarity are thereby stunted.

> [T]he differentiation of science, morality, and art, which is characteristic of occidental rationalism, results not only in a growing autonomy for sectors dealt with by specialists, but also in the splitting off of these sectors from a stream of tradition continuing on in everyday practice in a quasi-natural fashion ... Everyday consciousness sees itself thrown back on traditions whose claims to validity have already been suspended; where it does escape the spell of traditionalism, it is hopelessly splintered.[8]

Where the "traditionalist padding" has especially "worn through," cultural reproduction, social integration, and socialization processes are "drawn into the vortex of economic growth and therefore of juridification."[9] Resistance to colonization is difficult because the lifeworld is only *partly* rationalized, denying the plausibility of traditional understandings, but not having the cultural resources, especially, as we will see, mobilized by a healthy "public sphere," to block the extension of media-steering.

But there is resistance. Habermas argues that instead of the classic loci of conflicts predicted by traditional socialists—property, distribution, and workplace—social conflict today breaks out "along the seams between system and lifeworld."[10] In this regard Habermas mentions the more or less full panoply of so-called "new social movements" that have dominated protest politics for the last several decades: youth movements, antinuclear campaigns, the environmental movement, and a variety of participatory democracy projects and citizens initiatives on the local, national, and international levels. (This leaves aside movements based on more traditional demands for freedom and equality such as minority movements and feminism.) These movements distinguish themselves from previous conflicts in that they are not focused on production and distribution issues (not "productivist"), their organizational style emphasizes individual involvement ("politics in the first person"), and they are largely populated by youths, the middle classes, and the educated. Habermas states that, "The bond that unites these heterogeneous groups is the critique of growth."[11] The new social movements especially focus on quality of life issues that cannot be remedied through further welfare state compensations. As Claus Offe points out, they are also primarily defensive; it is no surprise that their slogans frequently contain the words "stop," "end," or "ban."[12]

This transformation of the sites and issues of social conflict in contemporary capitalism does not mean that the processes of material reproduction are displaced from social and historical importance. Habermas insists that the economy is still the crucial origin of these conflicts, but the problems are manifested in other areas of social life.

> I still explain these pathologies ["loss of meaning, anomic conditions, psychopathologies"] by referring to the mechanism driving capitalism forward, namely economic growth, but I *assess* them in terms of the systemically induced predominance of economic and bureaucratic, indeed of all cognitive-instrumental forms of rationality within a one-sided or "alienated" everyday communicative practice.[13]

The consequence of the extension of instrumental rationality is a generalized "unsettling of collective identity" (culture), alienation (person), and especially the danger of "anomie" (society).[14] Following our earlier remarks considering the priority of the lifeworld, Habermas defines "crisis" as "when relevant social groups *experience* systematically induced structural changes as critical to their continued existence and feel their identities threatened."[15] Colonization caused by the growth of the interventionist welfare state provokes a crisis when it interferes with the processes that maintain cultural integrity, solidary social relations, and personal identity. These cannot be reproduced by instrumental action, which regards persons and social relations as "things" to be manipulated, but rather only by attempting to reach understanding with each other through communicative action.

Although welfare state interventions have the above effects, unlike conservatives, Habermas still considers welfare provisions to be necessary given the dislocations and inequalities engendered by market economies. His arguments in *The Theory of Communicative Action* were formulated in the early 1980s, at the very beginning of the assault on the welfare state, when welfare state policies were still largely intact. Regarding the crisis tendencies articulated then, Habermas has more recently discussed the further strains on social solidarity that result from the ubiquitous *retreat* of interventionist welfare state programs: increasing inequality and "loss of collective goods" in advanced capitalist societies that "affect different social classes selectively," increasing inequalities between North and South, and immigration problems caused by this, poverty and urban blight, ecological problems, and "ethnic, national, and religious wars."[16] In general, peoples in many places are experiencing the "moral erosion of the society, which inevitably undermines the universalistic core of any republican polity."[17] Thus the quality of life issues stimulated by the growth of the welfare state are now overlaid, with its decline, with a set of issues quite familiar to traditional socialist theory. We will explore this more fully later.

When he turns to more organized political responses to these issues, Habermas especially focuses attention on the above mentioned "moral erosion" of society. Although cultural disarray and disruptions of identity formation—leading, respectively, to a loss of meaning and alienation—are important conflicts, Habermas has long argued that the crucial arena of conflict is that regarding social solidarity, the legitimacy of social relations. The "social" (in the narrow sense) component of the lifeworld is crucial because it is here, not in culture or personality, that the media of money and power are institutionally "anchored" and legitimated. In a highly compressed discussion, Habermas asserts that when "steering" difficulties of the subsystems engaged in material production threaten the legitimacy of the use of the media of money and power, these difficulties are in some way shunted off onto the areas of culture and person. Some weakening of cultural coherence and even alienation are allowed to emerge as a trade-off to avoid outright "anomie."[18]

This analysis would need much more discussion than either Habermas gives or we can try to reconstruct here. Suffice it to say that Habermas believes that the maintenance of legitimate social relations is the core of social coherence. The general problem is that by encouraging privatism and clientelism, and by supplanting more traditional sources of solidarity, the welfare state itself undermines the sense of "we" that is necessary to sustain social relations that can only be reproduced through intersubjective consensus. On the other hand, the retreat of the welfare state also weakens social solidarity. Therein lies the dilemma.

THE ROLE OF LAW

Social solidarity in contemporary societies is therefore under assault in two ways. The fragmentation of reason that allows the elaboration of distinct attitudes toward the world erodes, among others things, the consensus on the legitimacy of social relations. Solidarity is also threatened by the administrative management of market "imperatives" and welfare compensations. Solidarity, the agreement on "legitimate orders," is now the key endangered "resource" of society.

> In complex societies, the scarcest resources are neither the productivity of a market economy nor the regulatory capacity of the public administration. It is above all the resources of an exhausted economy of nature and of a disintegrating social solidarity that require a nurturing approach. The forces of social solidarity can be regenerated in complex societies only in the forms of communicative practices of self-determination.[19]

Contrary to various fundamentalisms around the world, in contemporary societies solidarity cannot be restored by appealing to "traditional values." The rationalization of the lifeworld has permanently foreclosed that option. As Max Horkheimer once noted, "The very fact that tradition has to be invoked today shows that it has lost its hold on the people."[20] According to Habermas, the only alternative now is the deliberative construction of rationally defensible principles for regulating social life. Somewhat paradoxically, given his earlier criticism of "juridification," Habermas contends that the vehicle of solidarity is law.

The central form of integration of complex societies must be law for two reasons. First, in a situation of cultural pluralism—a permanent situation of complex societies—"[l]aw is the only medium through which a 'solidarity with strangers' can be secured."[21] Second, the media-steered subsystems of economy and administration are formally organized through law. This allows law to influence the dynamics of these subsystems. "For translations *into* special codes, [ordinary language] remains dependent on the law that communicates with the steering media of money and administrative power. Normatively substantive messages can circulate *throughout society* only in the language of law."[22] With the rationalization and pluralization of social life, communicative action "can neither unload nor seriously bear the burden of social integration falling to it."[23] Law can sustain social integration because it connects "all three sources of integration": (1) "social solidarity" of a communicatively grounded enactment, (2) markets, and (3) administration.[24]

Law is therefore the only alternative for social solidarity in complex societies. However, the preeminence of law must not be misconstrued as the legislative body commanding the whole. Habermas has repeatedly described contemporary society as "decentered," a society that has no "summit." A functionally differentiated society cannot be conceived as a "macrosubject" that can act on itself.[25] Society is complex in that it is a set of autonomous subsystems that serve as environments for each other, exchanging necessary inputs. Even the lawmaking body—referred to variously as "parliament," the "political system," or "politics"—cannot be conceived as a center from which the whole society is ordered. This is true especially because the political system depends on its fiscal resources from the proper operation of the subsystems, the taxes that pay for universities, highways, national health insurance, parks, and other use-values citizens want.[26] "Politics indeed continues to be the addressee for all unmanaged integration problems. But political steering can often take only an indirect approach and must, as we have seen, leave intact the modes of operation internal to functional systems and other highly organized spheres of action."[27] The political subsystem cannot simply command the resources that it needs. As a consequence, we must "give up holistic aspirations to a self-organizing society, aspirations that also undergirded Marxist ideas of social revolution."

Given that the political is only one subsystem among many, Habermas argues that the idea of the self-organizing *society* must be reduced to a notion of a self-organizing *legal community* that can affect the other subsystems without taking them over.[28] To perform this function in a context of cultural pluralism, to create a "solidarity of strangers," it will have to be a legal community of a particular kind. Partly through fear of punishment, the legal system contributes to solidarity by "stabilizing behavioral expectations" among society's members. However, Habermas rejects the idea that a legal system could function merely on the basis of fear or coercion. The legal system has a dual character: It stabilizes behavior by both the threat of coercion but also by allowing the possibility of obedience through acknowledged legitimacy, that the law is "right." "In the legal mode of validity, the facticity of the *enforcement* of law is intertwined with the legitimacy of a *genesis* of law that claims to be rational because it guarantees liberty."[29] For legal regulation to be effective in sustaining social solidarity, people must obey the law not only from fear of punishment but because they can at least in principle recognize themselves in it. Habermas argues that in the absence of any divine sanctions or other traditionalist guarantees for the legitimacy of the law, its legitimacy can only be secured by agreement. This is the teaching of social contractarians and "modern natural law" doctrine, which Habermas is reformulating in intersubjective terms, not as a mere contract of self-interested individuals but as active, reasoned agreement.

In a way very similar to Rousseau, Habermas is arguing that members of the legal community must not only be able to see themselves as "addressees" of the law but also as its "authors."[30] As in his conception of communicative action, Habermas approaches the idea of a legal community in a "reconstructive" manner, bringing forth the idealizations that must be present to explain the fact of stable legal communities. "A reconstructive legal theory follows a methodology premised on the idea that the counterfactual self-understanding of constitutional democracy finds expression in unavoidable, yet factually efficacious idealizations that are presupposed by the relevant practices."[31] If he can articulate these unavoidable idealizations, Habermas can show that certain inescapable normative commitments organize legal relations, and it is these that allow law to shore up social solidarity. Moreover, since they are already present in existing practices, normative arguments can avoid the form of an "impotent ought" facing a stubborn social reality. Since they already organize the practices of a legal community—even if counterfactually—the progressive political project can be reoriented as strategies to reinforce these unavoidable normative premises.

Habermas applies the notion of idealizations to the constitution of a legal community by asking what must be presupposed for individuals to rationally agree to become members of a legal community. Specifically, "what rights must citizens mutually grant one another if they decide to constitute themselves as a voluntary association of legal consociates and legitimately to regulate their living together by means of positive law [i.e. enacted by legislatures]?"[32] The immediate problem is how these rights are grounded. First, in a situation of ethical pluralism, alleged "natural rights" have no uncontested existence and therefore cannot be the legitimate foundation of a political order to which all would agree. Although there may be general agreement that there is such a thing as natural rights, there is no agreement on just what those rights are; lists of rights are often incompatible, for example, the right to choose abortion versus the "rights of the unborn." In brief, all assertions of natural rights land us back in a variety of the natural law/positive law dichotomy, in which a natural moral order is merely put into effect through enacted law, a position that cannot be sustained in a situation where the ethical unity underlying natural law has dissolved. Second, any formulation of natural rights necessarily places a limit on the extent of popular sovereignty—self-determination—thereby denying a recognition of "authorship" of the law.

Rousseau's solution was to argue that the only legitimate order is one in which individuals, after having entered the political community, remain as free as before. Only this would protect "autonomy," literally, living by laws one gives oneself. Further, rational individuals would only agree to form a political community if the laws under which they placed themselves ensured that they would be treated equally. In this view, the rights that citizens have are granted *by themselves to themselves* as necessary for the reciprocity that would have allowed rational individuals to enter in the first place. This allows obeying the laws but still recognizing oneself as obeying one's own will, that is, being "author" of the laws one is under.

Rousseau tried to institutionalize these principles by restricting the "law" properly so-called to only those broad subject matters that affect all equally. (Everything else is "decrees.") He also tried to ensure a strong consensus of the community, allowing it to be more easily governed by a "general will," by encouraging a simplicity of social life. Habermas, on the other hand, forges his own position by invoking his "discourse principle": "Just those action norms are valid to which all possibly affected persons could agree as participants in rational discourses."[33] Consensus is not obtained through a more tightly constrained ethical community but through public discourse.

> [T]he claim that a norm lies equally in the interest of everyone has the sense of rational acceptability: all those possibly affected should be able to accept the norm on the basis of good reasons. But this can become clear only under the *pragmatic* conditions of rational discourses in which the only thing that counts is the compelling force of the better argument based on the relevant information.[34]

Under these circumstances, individuals are free in two senses: They are self-determining as authors of the laws under which they live, but they also accord themselves specific rights that allow them to participate in political life and, furthermore, ensure that individuals can pursue their own life projects in a pluralistic society in which conceptions of the good life differ. Not only is some form of popular sovereignty necessary, but so also are certain rights guaranteeing "negative freedom," the freedom to do as one wishes. In this way Habermas clearly avoids the charge of totalitarian democracy, a democracy that swallows up the individual, frequently leveled (rightly or wrongly) against Rousseau.

It needs mentioning that when talking about law in a democracy, "good reasons" are not only moral perspectives. In an important emendation of earlier arguments, Habermas now emphasizes that there are three different "employments" of "practical reason": consideration of the "moral" dimension (what is universally defensible, what is good for *all* anywhere), consideration of the "ethical" dimension (the irreducibly particularistic issue of the identity of a specific community and conception of the good life, what is good for *us* in *this* society), and consideration of the "practical" dimension (what is actually feasible in this particular situation). All these dimensions must be considered in the legitimate legal regulation of society.[35]

The discourse principle requires that the interests of all affected be taken into account for laws to be legitimate. This strikes many as much too demanding, even utopian, a requirement. Habermas has often been criticized for ignoring that many interests may not be compatible and therefore bargaining and compromise would be the only possible option. To the contrary, Habermas has always recognized this, recently even stating that "Compromises make up the bulk of political decision-making processes."[36] However, unlike others, he believes that even seeking compromises brings forth a normative dimension. First, we can only find out which topics require compromise, what are and are not generalizable interests, through open discourse. Second, if the results are to be rationally acceptable to the participants, bargaining and compromise must be fair. Although bargaining/compromises can be accepted for different reasons, fair compromises require that all exert equal pressure in affecting the outcome.[37] Here as elsewhere, the normative basis for social solidarity cannot be evaded.

RETHINKING THE PROGRESSIVE PROJECT

Although a strong antistate animus was one of the distinctive aspects of various protest movements of the 1960s, socialist politics of the last century largely revolved around expanding the role of the state in social life. However, an increasing number of progressive thinkers now join conservatives in disparaging the utility of state action.[38] The collapse of the planned economies of "existing socialism" destroyed any lingering hope for a democratization of those societies that could have left the state-centric version of the socialist project intact. Furthermore, the *mode* of revolutionary upsurge that engendered the collapse suggested a new model for progressive politics. Specifically, this collapse stimulated a new appreciation for the power of "civil society" to resist the state in ways that could lead to its democratic transformation.

Habermas builds on all these currents in formulating an alternative progressive political project that he nonetheless continues to regard as a *socialist* approach, although chastened by the complexity of contemporary society. Historically, the socialist project has been to regard the above-described network of "objectified" social relations as alienation, as the estranged powers of society that must be reabsorbed by abolishing the market economy. Habermas repudiates this position first of all because of the evolutionary importance of media-steered subsystems. The planned economies of the traditional socialist project must be rejected because they destroy the independent economic subsystem, depriving society of the productivity that stems from the dense interactions made possible by the operation of autonomous subsystems. Second, from Habermas's perspective, traditional socialism means simply replacing the medium of money with another, the medium of power. However, since power, like money, also conditions decisions without discussion, its further extension expands the areas of social life that are no longer reproduced through communicative action, intensifying the colonization of the lifeworld. Power is not the "innocent medium" that earlier socialists presumed. "Producing new forms of life is beyond the capacities of political power."[39]

Finally, a more rationalized lifeworld—one in which culture, social order, and the formation of personal identity are increasingly based on a consensus achieved through reasoned discourse rather than on traditional preunderstandings—requires an unburdening of social coordination that can only be accomplished by maintaining areas of social interaction that are steered not by communicative action but by media.[40] It is only through such further rationalization that the encroachments of media-steered subsystems can be successfully resisted and the reproduction of the lifeworld secured. Eliminating media-steered subsystems could actually disrupt progressive rationalization of the lifeworld in that the overwhelming range of subjects on which mutual understanding must be achieved in pluralistic societies might provoke authoritarian attempts to reestablish society as a culturally and ethically unified whole.

Habermas breaks in another way with traditional socialist responses to social conflict. For a long time Habermas has argued that the complexity of contemporary societies displaces revolution as a serious option.[41] The possibility of total collapse and consequent new barbarisms is simply too great. Although the revolutionary desire to "rebuild the existing order" continues, "we have lost our confidence that conditions can be changed by revolution."[42] The task for those who still regard themselves as socialists, then, becomes articulating "the set of necessary conditions for emancipated forms of life about which the participants *themselves* must first reach an understanding."

Socialist theory must try to rescue the emancipatory impulse without reducing socialism to a preordained specific set of social arrangements.[43]

From these considerations the following project emerges. We must restrain the actions of subsystems so that they do not disrupt the reproduction of the lifeworld, but without destroying the social evolutionary gains that come from a differentiated society of media-steered subsystems. Furthermore, we must try to envision a way in which administrative and economic power can be guided without presuming a unified subject standing above them. Rather than "de-differentiating" society we must articulate a new "balance of powers" that can constrain media to their proper spheres of operation. It is here that Habermas's theoretical reconstruction of the "public sphere" reveals its importance.

In his earliest book, *The Structural Transformation of the Public Sphere*, Habermas analyzed the eighteenth-century emergence of a public sphere in European societies that affected political decision making without actually usurping the decision-making role.[44] In light of his social theoretical work since, he has now deepened that analysis to address contemporary issues. Habermas proposes that although contemporary society is decentered in the way indicated above, a public sphere emerges from the activities of nonstate, noneconomic organizations, that is from "civil society."

Proceeding from the work of Hannah Arendt, Habermas argues that the public sphere is a "*social space* generated in communicative action." In Habermas's version, this social space is constituted when people relate through speech acts, as opposed to merely reacting to each other in a strategic manner.[45] The public sphere comes into existence because of the need for reasoned arguments regarding contested terrain in social life and is institutionally grounded in civil society organizations such as citizens groups, religious institutions, single-issue groups, environmental organizations, and community organizations. The political, social, and cultural discussions that form the public sphere create a "higher-level intersubjectivity" that can generate solidarity regarding legitimate social forms and processes.[46] This is the emergence of a qualitatively new kind of power that Habermas calls "communicative power" or "communicatively generated power."

Habermas believes that the need for legitimacy of law, the idealization that necessarily organizes a legal community, is the wedge that keeps the door open for communicative power to resist encroachments by media. "[O]ne cannot adequately describe the operation of a constitutionally organized political system, even at an empirical level, without referring to the validity dimension of law and the legitimating force of the democratic genesis of law."[47] A robust civil society can anchor this public sphere, strengthening the traces of "existing reason" in social life.[48] However, unlike in classical republican theory, the public sphere does not require that *individual* citizens be well-informed. It is the quality of public discussion *as a whole* that is important. The concept of the public sphere therefore shifts the discussion of "deliberative democracy" from an individual-level analysis of how to stimulate public spiritedness and civic virtue in citizens to how to encourage open and balanced *processes* of deliberation via anonymous communication among the public, "replac[ing] the expectation of virtue with a supposition of rationality."[49]

The public sphere serves basically two functions in a differentiated society. First, it constitutes a series of "sensors" for "the perception, identification, and treatment of problems affecting the whole society."[50] One might say that in a way the public sphere creates a channel for a different kind of "feedback" for the social system. Second, the public sphere creates the normative context within which law making occurs and thereby affects the operation of the subsystems without displacing them. The legal system must be legitimized, and this only occurs if the participants in society recognize themselves as the "authors" of the law. The legal system is therefore subject to the normative constraints generated by the public sphere. In a pluralistic society a public sphere must be supported by the establishment of constitutional liberties that enable discussion. Persuasive (and therefore motivating) normative grounds can only emerge if procedures for an open deliberation are established and convictions result from consideration of the "interests of all affected."

With the generation of the public sphere communicative power emerges as a power that can counterbalance the corrosive effects of money and administration on social solidarity. However, Habermas says quite rightly that "the key question is how communicative power ought to be related to administrative and social power."[51] The transmission belt for social problems is the key issue, how these problems are persuasively conveyed to decision makers. His answer is the development of a multidimensional deliberative democracy on the basis of constitutional civil liberties and elected parliaments that institutionalize communicative procedures and allow an interplay of these institutions with "informally developed public opinions." "The flow of communication between public opinion-formation, institutionalized elections, and legislative decisions is meant to guarantee that influence and communicative power are transformed through legislation into administrative power."[52] "Influence" affects the decisions of others without actually commanding them or eliminating their decision-making capacity and exists to the extent that its source is considered in one way or another "authentic." Habermas's discussion brings to mind Theodor Mommsen's characterization of the "authority" of the Roman Senate as "more than advice and less than a command, an advice which one may not safely ignore."[53]

In this context Habermas is using the word "influence" in an entirely different way than he used it before in contrasting strategic action with reaching understanding (chapter 3). Starting from Parsons's examination of influence as a third kind of medium or "quasi-medium," Habermas explains that influence (or "trust") based on scientific authority, moral authority, or professional reputation affects other people's motivations without having to be backed up by specific reasons here and now. Unlike the true media of money and power, however, influence is always embedded in the sphere of communicative action, in the lifeworld, in that it is ultimately dependent on "consensus formation in language." He further explains that influence requires "technologies of communication by means of which a public sphere can develop," such as the printing press and electronic media.[54]

Still, these comments are not particularly helpful. In fact, exactly what the content of "influence" is supposed to be is perhaps the most ambiguous aspect of Habermas's political argument. The ambiguity is deepened in that Habermas insists that the public sphere must be more than a mere *sensor* of societal strains: "Besides the 'signal' function, there must be an effective problematization."[55] He does mention that since the administration is dependent on others for knowledge, often biased by interest groups, the public sphere's influence can be felt by "mobilizing counterknowledge."[56] However, there are few other examples regarding this central issue and considerably differing possibilities, some of which pose problems for Habermas's overall political framework, as I will explore later.

An obvious objection to this reorientation of progressive politics is that inequalities of power pervade the public sphere, a problem that Habermas fully recognizes. He acknowledges the importance of resources and threats to get one's perspective heard and the danger of manipulation of public opinion by unequal social power.[57] He also notes the attempts of interest groups to influence the administration through other channels, displacing communicative power. In an arresting passage, he even brings up the persisting importance of class structures. "Only in an egalitarian public of citizens that has emerged from the confines of class and thrown off the millennia-old shackles of social stratification and exploitation can the potential of an unleashed cultural pluralism fully develop."[58] In sum, besides various inequalities, "communicatively generated power" must struggle against "the social power of actors with credible threats" (i.e. interest groups) and the "administrative power of officeholders."[59] It is crucial that this be addressed for his political perspective to be plausible.

Habermas's response to these dangers is fourfold. Unless the public sphere is constituted of the interplay of reasoned arguments, it cannot sustain legitimacy nor have the motivating power ascribed to it. In this way the public sphere is to some extent inherently resistant to corruption. The very need to provide reasons constrains participants to at least pretend to be arguing in good faith and requires an at least rhetorical commitment to "shared value orientations."[60] Attempts to manipulate the public sphere, once exposed, destroy the very legitimating power that those attempting to manipulate it want.

Second, Habermas repeatedly states that it must be possible for private individuals to have the material resources to function as citizens and acknowledges the role of welfare interventions in furthering this.[61] He therefore includes among the tasks of social integration, "income redistribution and social welfare."[62] However, although he acknowledges deep inequalities, Habermas gives a very Arendtian reminder that autonomy, not distribution, must be the focus.[63] Mindful of the debilitating effects of welfare policies in general, Habermas would apparently support redistribution only to the extent necessary to maintaining an autonomous citizenry.

Third, he suggests institutional changes that would intensify public legitimation pressures and thereby strengthen the role of communicative power by opening up more channels for it, more opportunities for challenges, for example, requiring that courts give more justifications for decisions. Habermas even argues for some sort of "democratization" of the administration.[64] Since we would never be able to tell the extent to which the public sphere is actually corrupted by unequal power, Habermas's strategy appears to be to establish an institutional framework that would most *likely* promote authenticity.[65]

Finally, there are certain cultural prerequisites. A robust public sphere cannot emerge under just any circumstances. Habermas always insists that a rationalized lifeworld must meet these proposals "halfway," even speaking of a "populace accustomed to freedom."[66] "The communicative power of shared convictions issues only from structures of undamaged intersubjectivity."[67] This power can only be fully mobilized where cultural developments, normative principles, and socialization practices have lost their traditionalist supports—have become "reflexive"—and an orientation to validity claims has become unavoidable.[68] Progressives must therefore be sure that their political agenda not inadvertently derail these processes of rationalization, for example by overtaxing communicative action by abolishing media-steered subsystems.

The task is to strengthen democracy so that the public (not socialist intellectuals) determines the future. Similarly to Marx of the *Manifesto*, socialists must confine themselves to clarifying the conditions that would help nurture an autonomous public. In this progressives must be guided by what Habermas calls the "dogmatic core" of his own position: "the idea of autonomy according to which human beings act as free subjects only insofar as they obey just those laws they give themselves in accordance with insights they have acquired intersubjectively."[69] In contrast, Marx and other socialists have often been "too concrete": "It is not the common control of social cooperation that forms the core of intentionally established social relations. Rather, this core resides in a normative regulation of life in common."[70] If it is to be democratic and authentic, socialist theory must limit itself to pointing out the necessary features of a humane, emancipated, and morally defensible existence but leave the details to the specific actors in specific circumstances who will suffer the consequences of potentially disastrous decisions. This means focusing on *procedural* questions rather than engage in substantive recommendations.[71] Any authentic socialism must be a result of "authorship" by the people. Nothing less would be sustainable in the long run.

Chapter 6

Contested Terrain: Language, Art, and Gender

Habermas's work of four decades has resulted in an innovative and provocative analysis of contemporary society. Many parts of his social and political theory are contestable and in passing we have already noted some difficulties with specific positions. Moreover, key arguments in his work are in considerable need of further elaboration, a fact often acknowledged by Habermas himself. "I am aware that I have not put forward a mature theory.... It was my concern in writing *The Theory of Communicative Action* to provide the foundation for a project sufficiently fertile to be pursued, as it were, radially, in different directions."[1] The present work is concerned with Habermas's substantive portrayal of contemporary society and politics so I will focus more detailed attention on difficulties with these topics. However, before turning in that direction it is worth briefly examining a few of the more prominent areas of criticism of Habermas's general theory that have some bearing on our main concerns. This should also help clarify some puzzling issues that have accumulated along our way.

Lyotard: Language as Contest

Habermas's theoretical edifice is crucially founded on the idea that communicative action sustains the coherence of social life. Linguistic practices bind the whole together by maintaining a common sense of what is factually the case, what is normatively appropriate, and on shared subjective evaluations. When this sense of the common is shaken by new experiences, an attempt must be made to restore consensus through reasoned discussion.

Many recent social theorists, associated with the perspective of postmodernism, are deeply suspicious of the very idea of consensus. If consensus is to seek what is common it must necessarily exclude that which cannot be held in common, that which cannot be assimilated. To the extent that consensus is considered necessary to maintaining order, it must engage in a war on the different and thereby become oppressive. The linguistic practices that constitute social life are therefore an arena of contest, a struggle between the assimilated and the different.

Jean-François Lyotard is one of the most prominent to pursue this line of argument against Habermas's theory, especially in Lyotard's oft-cited work *The Postmodern Condition*.[2] In this work the immediate concern of Lyotard is to analyze the status of scientific knowledge in the wake of "postempiricist" criticisms of scientific practices. Contemporary philosophers of science dispute the common understanding of the history of science as more or less continuous attempts to refine ever-closer approximations of reality, that is, to create through scientific practice a "mirror of nature." Instead, these critics argue that the observations of science are always in important respects predetermined by the theories employed. All theories delimit the range of possible observation and therefore all facts are necessarily "theory-laden." There are no "plain facts."

Utilizing Wittgenstein's analysis of language, Lyotard conceives scientific discourse as a kind of "language game." As in games, scientific discussion is constituted by rules that govern what are legitimate or meaningful utterances, "moves" within the game. Lyotard argues that social life itself is properly characterized as a multiplicity of such language games. That which Weber and Habermas refer to as "cultural value spheres"—the separation of the good, the true, and the beautiful—are actually discrete language games, the utterances of which cannot be translated into each other. "[T]here is no possibility that language games can be unified or totalized in any metadiscourse." As a consequence, "The social subject itself seems to dissolve in this dissemination of language games."[3] In effect, Lyotard is restating Weber's portrayal of modern social life as a struggle among cultural "gods," now from the standpoint of linguistic analysis.

In this new city of Babel the scientific enterprise itself can no longer be justified by claiming that science contributes to the emancipation of humanity or by other legitimizing narratives. The evaluative or normative language of "emancipation" is inapplicable to the very different language of facts with which science is solely concerned. These discourses are incommensurable with each other.

There is no comprehensive narrative that can order and justify the varied practices that make up social life. As Lyotard puts it, all such "grand narratives" or "metanarratives" of society or history—such as progress—have collapsed.[4] Therefore no unity of discourses, such as that presumed by Habermas's theory of rationality, is possible.

In reflecting on the status of scientific knowledge Lyotard goes beyond the argument that a broad consensus, expressed in a grand narrative, is impossible. He contends that consensus is not even desirable. Referring to recent developments in scientific discussion, such as the uncertainty principle of quantum mechanics, mathematical arguments that cast doubt on the idea of "precise measurement" (fractals), and the impossibility of predicting the future of certain kinds of unstable systems ("catastrophe theory"), Lyotard turns these scientific discoveries on the practice of science itself. Science is an enterprise in which new discoveries are unpredictable, therefore science itself is characterized by abrupt breaks and shifts of perspective.

Science's goal is to pursue the unknown, to generate new knowledge. Lyotard argues that this is not possible by remaining within the prevailing scientific consensus but only by challenging the rules that constitute "normal science" (Thomas Kuhn's term). Rather than the reigning consensus that forces research down the path of exploiting existing lines of thought, the generation of new ideas comes from exploiting "instabilities" and uncovering "difference." Lyotard argues that in general good "moves" in a language game are those that say something new. He approvingly quotes a game theorist who says that the usefulness of game theory resides in the fact that it generates ideas, and *"having ideas* is the scientist's highest accomplishment."[5] A good performance in the language game of science means creating new, unexpected moves, moves that "displace" the other participants, that acknowledge the "agonistics" (contested nature) of all language games. In contrast, seeking consensus is at least a kind of violence and perhaps even a "terror" that threatens to silence (remove from the game) those who challenge the rules that constitute the existing practice.

Lyotard is therefore critical of Habermas's project in several ways. First, the legitimizing narrative of emancipation is no longer plausible because of the plethora of incommensurable language games that make up social life. Second, Habermas misconceives language when he argues that it is grounded on an attempt to reach understanding with each other. On the contrary, the use of utterances is actually conflictual, provocative, displacing, in a word, agonistic. Third, attempts at achieving consensus in this circumstance must necessarily be oppressive, a silencing or denial of practices that expose and pursue the different.

Lyotard's postmodern account of scientific practice is quite similar, and not accidentally, to descriptions of the path of modern art, the "tradition of the new" in the phrase of art critic Harold Rosenberg. There is a kind of aestheticizing of scientific practice here, that science must be understood such that it can generate new scientific values from within itself. Lyotard's argument is intriguing as a "move," displacing us, seeking out instabilities in current understandings so as to provoke new perspectives. However, it suffers from several limitations. For one, Lyotard's portrayal of society as fragmenting into a multiplicity of language games is itself a "grand narrative" that should be impossible given his own premises. As Habermas states the issue, "But if there is no such thing as a form of reason that can transcend its own context, then the philosopher who proposes this same picture may not lay claim to a perspective that allows him this overview."[6] That is, here and in other ways, Lyotard's argument results in a performative contradiction.

Lyotard believes that since knowledge is fragmented into mutually exclusive and internally contested language games, seeking consensus is necessarily authoritarian. In contrast, he valorizes the different, the marginalized, the excluded, the incommensurable, the pursuit of which is essential for the generation of new knowledge. In support, Lyotard favorably cites Heraclitus on conflict as the father of all things.[7] The difficulty is that although attention to difference may well advance scientific discovery, as Lyotard contends, it is unclear why we need support the advance of science. If linguistic practice is as fractured and hermetically sealed against other games as he says, neither this nor *any* preference can be grounded, including a preference for scientific advance or, for that matter, openness rather than conformity. That is, the basis for this *evaluation* of *scientific* practice remains unclear. (It is also jarring to have a postempiricist say, "the facts speak for themselves."[8]) The agonistic model suggests that this requirement for scientific advance is at most a fact about science, and an inherently contestable and unstable fact at that. This is an example, noted by Habermas, of the recurring odd conjunction of assertions of the incommensurability of language games, a diversity that should deny us a universal basis for evaluation, with the "hypercritical" attitude of postmodern arguments.[9]

Moreover, although language can indeed be seen as an arena of contest, the idea of language as an attempt to reach agreement cannot be so easily escaped. One must employ language to promote an alternative understanding of language and in so doing give reasons for why the reader should see it the same way. As Habermas never tires of stating, only reason itself can uncover its own limitations.[10] Exploring the limits of reason requires further reasoning, as Lyotard's work demonstrates. Implicit in the very pursuit of Lyotard's argument regarding science and society is the unspoken, "Don't you agree?"

Lyotard asks a revealing question regarding Habermas's intentions: "Is the aim of the project of modernity the constitution of sociocultural unity within which all the elements of daily life and of thought would take their places as in an organic whole?"[11] Peter Dews argues that this question shows that Lyotard confuses the concepts "sphere of value" and "validity." Lyotard believes that Habermas is seeking a "vertical" ordering of the different discourses that result from the fragmentation of modern culture into separate spheres of value. However Habermas actually tries to uncover a "horizontal" relation, pointing out what the modes of argumentation *within* the separate value spheres have in common. All language games share the raising of claims of validity within the discourse. The discourses, in their particular ways, are all constituted by the offering of *reasons* for the judgments in which the specific spheres specialize. The practice of raising "validity claims" arises within *all* language games and therefore provides a commonality of practice within the diversity, a commonality that can be used to articulate a *general* idea of what rationality entails. This is different from seeking, from above, to reduce all language games to a common tongue.[12]

For all these problems, it must be acknowledged that Lyotard's argument is related to others that have caused Habermas to alter his position in an important respect. As previously mentioned, many have argued that Habermas's analysis of the three claims of validity implicit in all speech acts—truth, moral appropriateness, sincerity—ignores the crucial function of language as disclosing the world as a whole. Since all contact with reality is through the linguistic structures that convey awareness, language determines the very way in which the world is opened to us. As the physical structure of the human eye only allows us to perceive a small part of the electromagnetic spectrum (not radio waves nor microwaves), so our language as a whole limits and guides our awareness of the world.

As noted earlier, Habermas has now accepted this criticism, although with caveats that we need to expand here. Responding to the arguments of Charles Taylor, Habermas says that "Taylor demonstrates how every language opens up a grammatically prestructured space, how it permits what is in-the-world to appear there in a certain manner and, at the same time, enables interpersonal relations to be regulated legitimately as well as making possible the spontaneous self-presentation of creative-expressive subjects."[13] However, Habermas argues against placing too much emphasis on this for three reasons. First, he fears that emphasizing the world-constituitive function can lead to an overly deterministic view of how language structures our possible thinking.

> If, on this view, linguistic analysis becomes entirely preoccupied with the question of how members of a linguistic community are guided in all that they do by an unavoidable, holistic pre-understanding of the world operating behind their backs, so to speak, then the very right to the communicative use of language falls by the wayside. The pragmatics of speech proceeds from the question of how communicative participants—in the context of a shared lifeworld (or sufficiently overlapping lifeworlds)—can *achieve* an understanding about something in the world.[14]

Emphasizing world-disclosure, as many postmodernists do, obscures the "problem-solving capacity of language" that Habermas details in his theory of communicative action. Second, this also ignores how the learning processes initiated *within* a linguistically disclosed world may potentially "have a retroactive effect on the previous understanding of the world."[15]

In many ways Habermas believes that postmodern analyses have had a "healthy influence," sensitizing us to the importance of the dissimilar and noncontinuous in social life. However, he warns us, third, that too much emphasis on the linguistic construction of society marginalizes the processes of the material reproduction of social life. "[Y]ounger sociologists now write the history of modern societies in the concepts of a history of modern social theory—as if the material structure of society were made up of the concepts and discourses of social scientists."[16] In taking into account the world-*disclosive* function of language we must not confuse it with the position that language *constitutes* the world as a whole. Such linguistic idealism is not helpful in analyzing contemporary capitalism. For that, Habermas argues, a dualistic social theory is necessary. We will appraise that particular contention in the next chapter.

THE ROLE OF THE AESTHETIC

Another area of dispute regarding Habermas's theory concerns the third domain of rationality analyzed by Habermas, the "aesthetic-expressive" or "aesthetic-practical." Although he favors the latter term, a difficulty is already indicated here.[17] Habermas admits to not having given a full account of aesthetics, referring to his "scattered remarks" on the subject occasioned by other topics.[18] This is an important topic nevertheless because a society that has a balanced rather than selective rationalization requires that all three cultural value spheres shape social life.

> A selective pattern of rationalization occurs when (at least) one of the three constituitive components of the cultural tradition is not systematically worked up, or when (at least) one cultural value sphere is insufficiently institutionalized, that is, is without any structure-forming effect on society as a whole, or when (at least) one sphere predominates to such an extent that it subjects life-orders to a form of rationality that is alien to them.[19]

The status of the aesthetic is also important because, as the previous arguments of Adorno and Marcuse attest, it is often raised by those attempting to develop a critical view of society. The most that can be accomplished here is to indicate the ambiguities of Habermas's own discussion of the aesthetic and how he has reconsidered his position to take account of criticisms.

The immediate problem in Habermas's theory is the conflation of the expressive and the aesthetic in one mode of rationality. The former is the presentation of subjectivity by articulating needs and desires, assessed by the criterion of sincerity or truthfulness, whereas the latter is an *evaluation* of an art "object" or performance, assessed by its capacity to alter our sensibilities or perception of our world. Habermas tries to connect the two through their manifestation of "authenticity." However, as David Ingram notes, "[I]t is unclear how the presumed truthfulness of speakers oriented toward reaching agreement for purposes of coordinating action has anything whatsoever to do with art."[20]

A second difficulty is that in some ways the realm of the aesthetic seems radically different from the other two cultural spheres. For example, art and music are nonlinguistic, creating an important asymmetry for a conception of reason that is constructed on discussion. There is also a huge gulf between the art world and everyday aesthetic intuitions and it is difficult to see how this is to be overcome. As Habermas points out, the real "arguments" in this field are the works themselves, in their impact on the audience. Public architecture, sculpture, and the influence of modern art on advertising may help, but unless people are motivated to experience paintings or musical performances firsthand, they rarely encounter the "arguments." More so than other spheres, developments in art are not only encapsulated in expert cultures, they seem to be hermetically sealed.

Ingram further argues that aesthetic judgments differ from the cognitive and moral in that they do not, even as a counterfactual, propose evaluations that could be universally accepted. Rather, evaluative standards are always localized in a particular community. However, as noted earlier, Habermas does argue that the rationality of evaluations includes an ability and propensity to reflect on the prevailing standards of one's community. Ingram is nonetheless justified in doubting that this distancing from one's own can be taken very far.[21]

Habermas has attempted to clarify his position in the following way. First, that art is a kind of "knowing" is demonstrated by the fact that it can be criticized. We try to distinguish bad art from good art. Habermas proposes that art can be judged by the criteria of "unity (harmony)," "authenticity," and in regard to "their expressions by which they can be measured and in terms of which they may fail."[22] On their own, these phrases more or less simply beg the question, but Habermas is more helpful when he articulates the experience of art. He says that art suspends our usual orientations in the world, that through art "the routines of daily action and conventions of ordinary life are destroyed," creating a decentered, unbound subjectivity that alters our sensibility. Speaking almost as a postmodernist, art opens us to the "unassimilated," "the expurgated elements of the unconscious, the fantastic, and the mad, the material and the bodily."[23] The "learning process" stimulated by art is the expansion of the possible realm of subjective experience. As a consequence, Habermas introduces what appears to be a *fourth* validity claim specific to art that separates the criterion of valid subjective expression from the criterion of valid aesthetic creation. He now speaks of "propositional truth, normative rightness, subjective truthfulness, and aesthetic harmony."[24]

The validity claim associated with art is essentially that good art advances new modes of perception, enabling us to see the familiar in new ways. As the art theorist Arthur Danto puts it, art effects a "transfiguration of the commonplace."[25] This "eye-opening," as Habermas says in regard to literature, is an appropriate expression.[26] To see the familiar in a new way or to bring to consciousness perceptions previously on the margins certainly accounts for the success of some of the most imaginative of recent works, such as Christo's curtaining off a valley in Colorado, John Cage's "musical" work "4′33″," in which no sound is produced from the stage for the stated amount of time, making us aware of the usually ignored "ambient" sound, or James Turrell's explorations of how we perceive light, one piece of which requires patrons to sit in a completely dark room for as long as they would like to stay.

However, Ingram points out an ambiguity in Habermas's expanded position. Much of the discussion revolves around an individual subject's encounter with an aesthetic object. But Habermas strongly suggests that the realm of the aesthetic not only has an impact on individuals but also on the *whole* world, that is, on all three rationality complexes, the cognitive, the moral–practical, and (now) the subjective expression of needs and desires, that are precipitated out from *within* the constitution of the world as a whole. Habermas states that the distinct validity claim of art "stands for a *potential* for 'truth' that can be released only in the whole complexity of life-experience" or in its altering "world-shaping modes of perception."[27]

This is possible because although each elaborates one particular validity claim, the three cultural value spheres are not unaffected by developments in each other. Differentiated, they still "communicate with each other," albeit in ways that do not interfere with each one's elaboration of one specific cultural value. Habermas argues that this permeability is necessary in order to avoid the blind purities of, respectively, "objectivism," "moralism," and "aestheticism."[28] Ingram, drawing on the work of Martin Seel, has elaborated this point in a striking way.

> One who lacks aesthetic imagination will be at a disadvantage as a scientist or moral agent; one who lacks cognitive understanding will be a poor art critic or moral agent; and one who lacks moral understanding will be deficient as a researcher or evaluator of art. However, what distinguishes aesthetic criticism and its peculiar type of experiential rationality from other forms of integrated reasoning is that it alone involves a "presentative" reflection on the basic attitudes and "ways of seeing" that globally encompass and define the possibilities and limits of our cognitions, moral evaluations, and aesthetic sensibilities.[29]

On this view, the aesthetic has a kind of double position, as one cultural value sphere but also with a global effect on perspectives of the whole, akin to the world-disclosive function of language.

It should be noted that ambiguities regarding the aesthetic sphere stem partly from the path taken by contemporary art itself. Even professional art critics have been challenged by the diversity of styles, materials, and animating intuitions of practicing artists today. Danto describes the development of art as a "history of erasures" of the boundaries of what could be considered art. "[A]nd it is reasonably clear what kind of product must be the terminus of conceptual erasures. It is pretty much the blank canvas—and that leaves the philosophical question, as all blank canvases look pretty much alike, which of them were works of art and which of them were not."[30] Danto concludes that the "master narrative" of art has come to an end. We have entered the "post-historical period," in which what should count as the "making of art" is difficult to determine. It is not for nothing that another well-known art critic, Harold Rosenberg, entitled collections of his essays with phrases such as *The Anxious Object* (because it does not know if it is art or not) and *The De-definition of Art*.[31] Andy Warhol once famously responded to a question about what made one of his productions "art" with the completely circular, "Well, first of all, it was made by an artist, and, second, that would come out as art."[32] This is the self-referentiality of art shrinking down into a black hole, even a singularity. Given this situation, one would be forgiven for wondering if the "inner logic" of the aesthetic is to eventually efface its own subject matter, a kind of nihilistic impulse of what could then only *rhetorically* continue to be considered an art "world." If this is the practice, theoretical confusion is not surprising.

Further attempts to clarify the role of the aesthetic in Habermas's theory would take us far beyond our present purpose. For his part Habermas frequently simply notes "countermovements" within each cultural sphere to overcome a sterile insularity. However, he also argues that these movements *within* expert cultures are not the real place to look for such mediation. "Everyday life . . . is a more promising medium for regaining the lost unity of reason than are today's expert cultures or yesteryear's classical philosophy of reason."[33] Nevertheless, an intriguing line of exploration would be to try to link the fourth validity claim of art with the fourth, world-disclosive function of language. To the extent that this is successful, one might then be able to elaborate Adorno's conception of art as an intimation of a reconciled world and also more effectively state Marcuse's idea of the political possibilities of a new aesthetic sensibility. Shelley may well have been right to say that "Poets are the unacknowledged legislators of the world."

GENDER

A third major area of criticism of Habermas's theory is on issues of gender. Feminist critics have assailed the theory on a number of grounds, some of which overlap with Lyotard's concern with how the different can be excluded and oppressed. It is necessary to consider some of the perceived problems of Habermas's theory that have caused as Habermasian a thinker as Jean Cohen to once refer to "Habermas's prejudices regarding feminism."[34]

The criticisms are wide-ranging. Marie Fleming, for example, attacks Habermas's theory of social evolution. Habermas argues that the key development in completed hominization occurred when the division of labor of collective male hunters and collective female raising of children was superceded by the establishment of the family. Until then, as in ape societies, the male could only occupy one role in a rank ordering of males, based on the ability to physically threaten. Habermas argues that eventually the "egalitarian relations within the hunting band" conflicted with this rank ordering for sexual access. Only with the establishment of the "father" role within the context of having children, that is with the emergence of discrete "families," do the reciprocal *expectations* that constitute social "roles" come to regulate social interaction, "moralizing" the "motives for action."[35]

Fleming argues that Habermas is here guilty of propagating "another version of the patriarchal story of origins." For Habermas, a " 'human' society requires a father-centered family structure." She traces this blindness to Habermas's focus on hunting as the productive activity, like Marx, excluding the socialization of the young from his concept of social labor.[36] Even though Habermas acknowledges that "care for the young" is equally important for the reproduction of the species, he nevertheless in the same sentence distinguishes it from social labor.[37] Fleming contends that Habermas's argument for the importance of the father role in social evolution relies on a definition of social labor that, distorted by gender biases of what constitutes "productive" work, diminishes the role of women in the evolution of human society. We will return to the issue of social labor with our discussion of Nancy Fraser.

Another focus of feminist critique has been on the abstract, disembodied nature of the "moral" perspective, an abstraction that Habermas elaborates partly by appropriating Lawrence Kohlberg's theory of the developmental stages of moral reasoning. Habermas agrees with Kohlberg that at the highest stage of moral development individuals have learned to make principled judgments based on distinguishing the moral perspective—what is good for all—from evaluations of the good life for a particular community. The moral perspective requires an abstract conception of self if moral judgments are to be applicable to all people in all times and places. The reason that feminist theorists in particular focus on this argument is that it seems biased against different possible qualities of moral action that are more associated with women's customary role in society.

Drawing on the work of Carol Gilligan, Seyla Benhabib argues that the use of this "generalized other" only foregrounds certain aspects of the moral perspective. If instead one acknowledges that individuals are always found within a specific set of social relations, that is, that all selves are "situated," encountering a "concrete other," then a different set of morally relevant concerns are highlighted. Ricardo Blaug summarizes the difference of perspective well.

> In abstracting individuals from their particular life histories and emotional constitutions, [the generalized other] stresses what speaking and acting subjects have in common, and ushers in moral categories such as right, obligation, respect, and duty. Against this, the concrete other is the manner in which we encounter the other in contextualist moral theory. Here, the other appears as an individual with particular experiences and emotional constitutions, and ushers in moral categories such as love, sympathy, care, and responsibility.[38]

Benhabib contrasts the two resulting positions as "an ethics of justice and rights" and "an ethics of care and responsibility."[39]

Habermas responds that the latter conception confuses the ethical idea of the good life for *us* with the universalistic moral perspective. He further argues that these issues especially concern not moral judgment but the separate problem of "anchoring of moral insights" in individual motivations.[40] In turn, Benhabib insists that these concrete concerns are actually amenable to, and must be evaluated by, a universalistic moral perspective. Using the example of whether we can say that it is better for *all* that families show internal solidarity, Benhabib argues that issues of "care" can be regarded from a universal perspective.[41] Through arguments such as these Benhabib intends not to abolish the distinction between "moral" and "ethical" judgments but to rethink how the distinction is conceived.

In further arguing for a moral theory based on situated selves, Benhabib reminds us that the nurturing of children is necessary for the development of moral competence, but this very process forges an identity that carries with it attachments that cannot be set aside. She also points out that in stating that "solidarity" is the "obverse" of justice, Habermas, like Gilligan, recognizes the relevance of protecting "fragile human relations," thereby providing a theoretical opportunity for integrating an ethic of care into universalist moral philosophy.[42] In this way Benhabib hopes to promote an "interactive" conception of universality, a universality that emerges from the concrete relationships within which we are always found, instead of an abstract universality superimposed on real relations from above.[43]

Benhabib concludes that the question of "justice" does not exhaust the content of the "moral," that "issues of care" and responsibility rooted in real relations with others can also be subjected to universalistic judgments.[44]

It is clear that the qualities occluded by Kohlberg and Habermas are those often associated with women, suggesting a gender bias in Habermas's abstract moral philosophy. However, the status of this ethic of care is sharply contended within feminist theory itself. The argument that women typically express these other morally relevant qualities veers toward "essentialism," that women as a group have a certain ineluctable essence. Other feminist thinkers argue that this portrayal of "feminine" values reinforces oppressive stereotypes of women.[45] Although the dispute within feminism will no doubt continue, these criticisms of Habermas are nonetheless probing.

A third area of Habermas's theory criticized by feminist theorists parallels aspects of Lyotard's critique. Among other things, Iris Marion Young contends that Habermas's conception of "impartiality" artificially and unnecessarily excludes the affective dimension of human life. Young argues that the concept of impartiality central to modern moral reasoning has been construed to mean being above particular interests and desires. To "not be partial" is to see the whole by distancing oneself from the particular. "In modern moral discourse, being impartial means especially being dispassionate: being entirely unaffected by feelings in one's judgement."[46] The idea is that a unifying perspective can only be achieved by "expelling" the particularizing "desire, affectivity, and the body." This premise of moral reasoning again results in the abstract "desituated" self criticized by Benhabib and many others.

Young, in contrast, uses this as a springboard to connect with Adorno's criticism of "identity thinking." In Young's argument, the desituated self emerges from a conception of rationality, not as merely "giving an account" of one's reasons, but as formulating a "ratio," bringing all things under a "common measure." Identity thinking is the mode of thought that attempts "to think things as a unity" by finding what particulars have in common. Young admits that all conceptual thinking must do this but wishes to draw attention to implications that might otherwise be overlooked.

First, the *logic* of identity is ultimately totalizing, driven, as Horkheimer and Adorno indicated, by a project of control: "[T]hrough it thought seeks to have everything under control, to eliminate all uncertainty and unpredictability." Second, for this reason, identity thinking must necessarily strive to "eliminate otherness."

In trying to conceive the ratio, identity thinking must "expel" the qualities that are *not* in common, resulting in "leftovers," that which cannot be integrated, which are typically evaluated as "lesser" or even "bad." Young insists that identity thinking is especially at war with desire because desire particularizes subjects.[47]

Young argues that although the ancients, Aristotle for example, distinguished between good desires and bad desires and ordered their political life so as to cultivate the former, the tendency of modern moral reasoning is to reject desire because particularizing desires are in themselves inferior and inimical to reason. This brings her to the feminist issue at stake here. "Thus as a consequence of the opposition of reason and desire, moral decisions grounded in considerations of sympathy, caring and an assessment of differentiated need are defined as not rational, not 'objective,' merely sentimental. To the degree that women exemplify or are identified with such styles of moral decision-making, then, women are excluded from moral rationality."[48] The political consequence is a division between a "universal public realm" based on reasoned common interests and the "particular private realm of needs and desires," associated historically with women caring for a household. The persisting exclusion of women, and *others* associated with untamed desire, from public life is no accident.[49] Further, Young warns that the official exclusion of desire is actually dangerous in that desire and affectivity will ultimately find expression. "They sprout again, menacing because they have been expelled from reason."[50]

Young does believe that Habermas's theory of communicative action holds out the best possibility for integrating desires because of his focus on reason not as "monological authoritarianism" but as intersubjective "giving reasons." However, Young asserts that the possibilities contained in this approach are hindered, first, by Habermas's conception of impartial judgment that reproduces the dichotomy between reason and desire and, second, because of an overly narrow conception of communication. On the first, although intersubjectively anchored, Habermas still conceives impartiality as reaching agreement by setting aside every motive except seeking the truth. In the public realm he focuses on common interests, not expressions of need.[51] This reproduces the distinction between reason and desire.

It should be pointed out that this is a rather selective reading of Habermas. Habermas frequently speaks of expressing needs, presents the public good as percolating up from unrestrained discussions in the public sphere about needs and interests, and his phrase "the force of the better argument" can be interpreted in more than one way, depending on what counts as an "argument." Agreeing with Benhabib, Young argues that "In his scheme discussion about individual need and feeling is separate from discussion about norms."[52] However, in several places Habermas notes the importance of compassion or indignation for arousing our moral concern.[53] It is nevertheless true that for Habermas, norms exist at a higher level of abstraction, so this topic will no doubt remain contentious.

In regard to the second point, Young also criticizes Habermas for a conception of communicative action that reduces the "meaning" of an act to the reasons that can be given for it. Young argues that Habermas's conception of communication devalues its "expressive and bodily aspects," the playful, dramatic, metaphorical, emotional, etc. As Fredric Jameson puts it, Habermas seems to conceive communicative action as a "passing of tokens from hand to hand."[54] Anticipating Habermas's probable defense, Young insists that the above elements of communication are not merely "derivative" from straightforward speech but basic to our everyday experience of communication. Further, these varied elements allow "multiple meanings" of the same utterance, resulting in "the irreducible multiplicity and ambiguity of meaning."[55]

The relevant point for us is Young's recommendation for a public sphere in which the expression of difference sometimes takes precedence over producing "consensus," a public sphere in which the aesthetic, passion, and play are not considered off-limits, a public that is truly "open." "In such a public, consensus and sharing may not always be the goal, but the recognition and appreciation of differences, in the context of confrontation with power."[56]

Finally, many feminist thinkers have criticized Habermas for not fully appreciating more specific ways in which gender refracts the dynamic of contemporary society that he analyzes. Benhabib, for example, argues that the "gender–sex system," "the social–historical, symbolic constitution, and interpretations of the anatomical differences of the sexes," is a central way in which social life is constructed. "[F]or feminist theory the gender–sex system is not a contingent but an essential way in which social reality is organized, symbolically divided and lived through experientially."[57] Feminists sympathetic to Habermas's project therefore argue that examining how gender socially situates individuals is crucial for overcoming the abstractions of his social and political theory.

Nancy Fraser has registered several criticisms of Habermas's theory on these grounds, for example the way in which Habermas's theory separates lifeworld processes from the media-steered sub-systems responsible for maintaining material production. Among other things, this conceptual distinction tends to understate how money and power pervade the household. The power exercised in the household is a different kind of power, one based on gender constructions, and therefore cannot be captured by the idea of colonization, an invasion of power from outside. Habermas's definition of power as a medium of bureaucracy prevents the adequate theorizing of other types of power, especially the power relations of the household, and therefore fails to integrate gender relations into his social theory.[58]

Equally important, Fraser argues that the separation of the household and "work" that emerged with capitalism informs and genders the four central social roles analyzed by Habermas. Historically, this separation relegated women to caretaker of the household and elevated the role of "male breadwinner." From its origins, the employee role is therefore a gendered role. It is no accident that women's participation in the workforce has been, historically, as an extension of the service role (nurse, teacher, waitress), nor that these occupations are largely low paying. They have been perceived as contingent positions intended to supplement the income of the male breadwinner.

Fraser demonstrates how the consumer and the citizen roles also reflect differences in gender. The consumer has historically been regarded as female, as an extension of supplying and maintaining the household. The citizen role, on the other hand, has been identified with men in a number of ways, especially in regard to participation, in which empirical studies show that men tend to steer and dominate discussions, reinforcing this domination by physical gestures.[59] Young expands this point by arguing that the historical contrast between public sphere and private life designated the home as the place for sentiment, as opposed to reason, a place of nurturing and refuge.[60] Fraser, like Jean Cohen, also points to the importance of the soldier as a dimension of citizenship that is ignored by Habermas and therefore obscures the historical maleness of the role of citizen. As Fraser puts it, the citizen-soldier is the traditional "defender of the polity and protector of those—women, children, the elderly—who allegedly cannot protect themselves."[61]

Finally, feminist theorists have given special attention to the ways in which the client role of contemporary welfare states is gendered. The relegation of women to low-paid "helper" occupations, the general marginalization of these occupations as a "second income," and the emphasis on women as the primary nurturers of children have all contributed to the feminization of poverty. Fraser states that Habermas "fails to see that the new client role has a gender, that it is a paradigmatically feminine role. He overlooks that it is overwhelmingly women who are the clients of the welfare state, especially older women, poor women, and single women with children." She argues forcefully that welfare, in the narrow American sense of aid to needy families, is especially "oriented to what are understood as domestic 'failures,' that is, to families without a male breadwinner." In sum, gender identity runs through all four social roles "like pink and blue threads."[62] To understand the actual dynamic of contemporary capitalism and the political struggles that ensue, we must acknowledge the way gender structures the dynamic in specific ways.

Extending the previously discussed objections of Fleming, Fraser argues that Habermas's theory also misses the importance of gender by excluding household labor, especially the socialization of children—the nurturer role—from his notion of social labor. Habermas confines social labor to the systemic role of employee and relegates household activities to the lifeworld. From Fraser's perspective, this simply ignores the fact that household labor is essentially unpaid, and therefore exploited, labor. This is a crucial point because "the separation of the official economic sphere from the domestic sphere and the enclaving of childrearing from the rest of social labor" is "one—if not the—linchpin of modern women's subordination."[63] Fraser further argues that, contrary to what the lifeworld/system dichotomy suggests, the rearing and socialization of the young is not merely a symbolic activity. It also involves the *biological* survival of children and therefore the physical survival of society itself.[64] Reconsideration of these dimensions of the household tends to explode any rigid separation of lifeworld and system processes.

Needless to say, there are serious disagreements among feminists on the issues targeted by Fraser. For example, Fraser and Cohen disagree over whether household labor should be waged or not, with Cohen resisting the straightforward assimilation of families to production. They also disagree over whether gender should be considered a new "medium" guiding social interaction, with power actually an "expression of masculinity" (Fraser), or, as Cohen contends, that gender is a communication "code" that simply steers the medium of power, "so constructed as to stop questioning at a supposedly unchallengeable meaning-complex that is defined as 'natural.' "[65] Regardless of variations, feminist theorists are in complete agreement that gender is crucial for structuring social life and therefore must have a central, rather than subsidiary role, in social theory.

Feminists have been equally critical of some of Habermas's political perspectives. Habermas describes the women's movement as in some ways a classical "bourgeois-socialist liberation movement," struggling for equality, although he also mentions some more particularizing tendencies which present the danger of "withdrawal." Fraser and others argue that this portrayal misunderstands the importance of this "particularism" for, among other things, constructing a space in which women can interpret themselves rather than merely acceding to prevailing interpretations that disadvantage women.[66] Cohen further defends the necessarily "dualistic" politics of the feminist movement by arguing that "identity politics" was crucial for thematizing certain issues in the public sphere.

> [A]ttaining group consciousness involved an explicit challenge to traditional norms that identified women primarily in terms of the roles of mother and wife and justified inequalities, exclusion, and discrimination. In short, the traditional understanding of women's place and identity had to be changed and new identities constructed, before challenges to sex discrimination could appear as a legitimate issue and women could be mobilized around them.[67]

Before a frontal political assault was possible, a new sense of identity had to be articulated and propagated. What was traditionally considered personal had to be politicized.

This aspect of the women's movement should therefore not be interpreted as a retreat from a universalistic perspective. On the contrary, it was necessary to break down the already *existing* "particularist sexist norms and practices" in order to *open* communication in the public sphere by increasing sensitivity to previously hidden forms of exclusion caused by gender stereotyping. Cohen argues that "Such projects are universalist insofar as they challenge restrictions and inequalities in the communicative processes (in public and in private) that generate norms, interpret traditions, and construct identities."[68] That is, this aspect of feminist thought and practice bears on all three of what Habermas calls the structural components of the lifeworld: culture, norm-governed social orders, and socialization.

In regard to specifically political matters, feminist theorists tend to agree with Habermas's analysis of the ambivalence of welfare legislation. Habermas recognizes that welfare state provisions are necessary to give substance to the purely formal equality of the Lockean liberal state. On the other hand, he also notes that welfare state interventions are necessarily bureaucratic, mediatizing family life (to name one area), and therefore reducing the range of free action of individuals caught in this net.

Since welfare policy especially affects women, feminists have sharpened our understanding of this dilemma. Due to Habermas's restricted notion of power, he does not see how power already pervades family life and therefore he cannot completely appreciate the extent to which some juridification of family relations protects women and children from domestic violence and oppression. Cohen argues particularly well how law can be used to "dismantle the position of the paterfamilias in favor of a more equal distribution of competences and entitlements among family members."[69] Fraser even compares these legal protections of members of the household to the rights achieved by the workers movement in the workplace.[70]

However, like Habermas but in greater detail, feminists also note the oppressive "normalizing" effects of welfare policy rights, especially in regard to women. Cohen's explanation is not only pointed, it further clarifies the meaning of colonization.

> Experts (judges or therapists) become the adjudicators of the new rights and the conflicts around them. They intervene with their juridical or administrative means into social relations that become formalized, dissociated, and reconstructed as individualized cases to be handled administratively or juridically like any other set of adversary relations....Formal, individualizing, and hence universalizing judgments that cannot deal with contextual complexities disempower clients by preempting their capacities to participate actively in finding solutions to their problems. It is thus the medium of law itself that violates the communicative structures of the sphere that has been juridified in this way.[71]

As Fraser indicates, quoting Carol Brown, the outcome can be "private patriarchy replaced by public patriarchy," reinforcing stereotypes of gender. The political lesson, Cohen argues, is that when juridical forms go beyond merely "supplement[ing]" socially integrated contexts with legal institutions," "vertical" structures replace the horizontal relations that are necessary for communication and solidarity.

Habermas has included many of these arguments and perspectives in his later works. In response to feminist arguments regarding the positive protections of family law, but especially because of the increased importance of legal regulation in his political argument, Habermas now has a more measured view regarding the effects of law. For example, in one place he refers to his "perhaps over-presumptuous" arguments in *The Theory of Communicative Action* on juridification, and in a discussion of "Asian values" he argues that legal protections, contrary to traditionalists, will not destroy the integrity of family life.[72] On the other hand, he further specifies the gender effects of juridification by arguing that legal attempts to acknowledge the specific needs of women—"special regulations regarding pregnancy, motherhood, and the social burdens of divorce"—can create a new "paternalism" that reinforces stereotypes of gender.[73] In doing so, these laws "become part of the problem they are meant to solve."

In regard to the latter, in *Between Facts and Norms* Habermas states that the feminist critique of welfare law clarifies the reasons why we must reject the two dominant paradigms of law, both the liberal (in the Lockean sense) conception and the social welfare conception. The former argues that equality is served if certain basic individual rights are protected. Negative liberties on their own are sufficient for assuring equal political participation. In contrast, the welfarist conception recognizes that real social inequalities can make these rights purely formal, so social rights are necessary to provide the resources for effective participation in public life. Habermas, however, contends that these two paradigms of law share a misleading "productivist" understanding of law and a privatistic conception of social life. "This society is supposed to function in such a way that the expectation of social justice can be satisfied by securing each individual's private pursuit of his or her conception of the good life." Both agree that private lives, suitably equipped, will produce social justice. The only real point of contention is exactly what kind of resources must be provided to assure this.

To the contrary, Habermas argues that the expectation that private autonomy will automatically *produce* public autonomy is flawed in a number of ways. The welfarist conception suggests that the factual inequality of women can be solved by more or less paternalistically bringing women up to the status of men. However, first of all, this ignores the fact that there are *two* gender identities that need to be put in question, not just one.[74] Second, this privatistic conception fails to see that what are the *relevant* dimensions of equality can only be established through public discussion. "[I]n the final analysis, private legal subjects cannot enjoy even equal individual liberties if they themselves do not jointly exercise their civic autonomy in order to specify clearly which interests and standards are justified, and to agree on the relevant respects that determine when like cases should be treated alike and different cases differently."[75] Private autonomy (rights and resources) is necessary for public autonomy (participation), but the determination of what *kinds* of inequality must be remedied in private life so people *can* act publicly is itself a public question, only decideable through deliberation. Based on this understanding, Habermas now fully recognizes, with Cohen and Fraser, that the "struggle for recognition" of women and other excluded groups requires a moment of "consciousness-raising" so that certain themes can first be articulated within a group and then become thematic for public discussion as a whole.[76]

The result is a dialectical understanding of private and public autonomy: Equality is necessary for public participation but what the relevant dimensions of equality *are* can only by discovered through public discussion. On the other hand, effective participation in the public sphere cannot occur unless private autonomy has been secured. The concepts of private autonomy and public autonomy therefore mutually presuppose each other, they are "co-original." However, although Habermas now recognizes the need for feminist consciousness-raising, in this public discussion, "[e]ven the feminist avant-garde does not have a monopoly on definition."[77] As Habermas always says, in processes of enlightenment, there can only be participants.

CHAPTER 7

THE LIMITATIONS OF HABERMAS'S SOCIAL AND POLITICAL ARGUMENT

Many of the criticisms of Habermas's theory presented in the preceding chapter are based on considerations brought from "outside" his own social theoretical framework. However, there are also important difficulties internal to his theory, especially stemming from his dualistic conception of society, which require a more "immanent" critique. First, there are many perplexities in regard to the relation between the lifeworld and system aspects of society, especially revealed in Habermas's analysis of the contemporary capitalist economy. It is particularly important to examine Habermas's portrayal of the economy because his unrealistic conception of an autonomous economic sphere, shorn of his theoretical terminology, is a very common assumption of social and political discussion today. Second, Habermas's theory of the dual ways in which contemporary society reproduces itself leads to a much too chaste project of progressive political action. Even on his own terms, the integrity of the public sphere, the key to a healthy and just democracy, can only be preserved through more direct political confrontations with the fundamental processes of contemporary capitalism. I conclude that the concerns of traditional socialist thought are not as easily displaced as Habermas and many other progressives today seem to think.

THE DUALISTIC THEORY OF SOCIETY

In regard to Habermas's broad social theory, Postone states that Habermas tries to express the duality of social life by "combin[ing] two one-sided approaches."[1] The theoretical merits of that witticism aside, the most pervasive difficulty of Habermas's social theory is precisely how the two aspects of society as lifeworld and as system intersect once distinguished. Unfortunately, this topic involves some of the thorniest and most abstract arguments of Habermas's social theory. We must nevertheless try to engage those arguments here if we are to have a clearer picture of Habermas's theory of contemporary society and the limitations of that theory. I contend that a sharp separation of system and lifeworld processes cannot be sustained in regard to the capitalist economy and so leads to a false conception of the autonomy of capitalist processes. It consequently causes Habermas to underestimate the full range of likely sites of conflict in contemporary society.

Much confusion ensued from *The Theory of Communicative Action* on whether this social dualism was merely an analytical distinction, pursued for methodological reasons, or was intended in some more emphatic sense as "real." In response to criticisms by Thomas McCarthy and others, Habermas has now clearly stated that although all societies have social and systemic processes that can be analytically distinguished, in modern societies "both aspects of society, which are initially introduced merely as different perspectives adopted in observing the same phenomena, also acquire essentialist connotations for modern societies and open up a view of differently structured domains of social reality itself."[2]

This relatively forthright statement actually intensifies the problem of the empirical referent of the concept "subsystem," those aspects of social life that are the "domain" of subsystem dynamics. That is, exactly to which aspects of social life does the idea of "subsystems" refer and how can their dynamic be conceived as autonomous from the rest of social life as we consciously experience it, as a lifeworld? Specifically in regard to the economic subsystem, there are two intertwined relations that need clarification: the relation between the economic subsystem and organizational forms (e.g. business firms), and the relation between the economic subsystem and action orientations (conscious purposes) of individuals. We have to try to reconstruct Habermas's argument from a number of conflicting comments if we are to judge its usefulness.

First, in regard to organizational forms, Habermas states that subsystems are not institutions: "[T]he functional contexts of media-steered subsystems cannot simply be marked off topologically from one another and made to match certain institutional complexes."[3] Subsystems are not institutions but *processes* responding to functional needs for maintaining society. The functions that actions satisfy are typically "latent," that is, the functional significance of actions is not consciously or collectively intended and often not apparent from within a participant's perspective of society. The systems theoretic approach to social analysis is therefore pitched at a different level than the institutional one.

Functional processes do need an *"institutional complex* that anchors a newly emerging mechanism of system differentiation in the lifeworld."[4] The specific anchoring of the medium money is through "civil law" regarding "property and contract."[5] However, although media need anchoring and legitimation through legal institutionalization, this does not mean that subsystems *are* institutions. The anchoring of media merely legitimizes this form of social coordination and thereby unleashes the processes that build societal networks steered by media, like a chain reaction in the production of nuclear energy.

Although subsystems themselves are not actually institutionalized (only the medium is), in several places Habermas acknowledges that they do need appropriate organizations for their functioning. "A societal subsystem like the economy can be differentiated out via the money medium only if markets and forms of organization emerge that bring under monetary control the transactions within the system and, more important, its transactions with the relevant environments."[6] Habermas then mentions the development of "wage labor and the state based on taxation." In another place he refers to "new, objectified, organizationally-structured realities."[7]

However, again, even if organizations are necessary *conditions* for the functioning of subsystems, the subsystem cannot be identified with the organizations that facilitate media-steering. Instead, the subsystem's imperatives work through these organizations in such a way that the latter become increasingly autonomous. "[M]odern societies attain a level of system differentiation at which increasingly autonomous organizations are connected with one another via delinguistified media of communication: these systemic mechanisms—for example, money—steer a social intercourse that has been largely disconnected from norms and values...."[8] In some way the economic subsystem calls forth appropriate organizations, thereby having a "structure-forming effect."[9] This might be an example of the lifeworld being forced to "adapt" to the needs of steering media.[10] However, apparently these organizations can no more be equated with the subsystem than business firms can be equated with the market. Rather, the systemic quality comes from the way in which their *interaction* is steered by delimited motives—in this case, profitability, the money medium—in a context that has been legally specified. Because the considerations of actions are narrowed in this way, one small set of interactions among business firms automatically alters the calculations and actions of another set of business firms, which automatically alters the calculations and actions of a more distant set of firms. In this way social relations take on a life of their own, beyond anyone's calculation, comprehension, or control.

In sum, Habermas's position seems to be that subsystem domains develop by encouraging the creation of organizations (business enterprises and a bureaucratized state administration organized on the basis of taxation) that produce actions that have functionally beneficial effects. The flexibility to do this results from the fact that these organizations are legally constituted, allowing individuals and organizations to place at a distance any other orientations than strategic ones. Once the medium is legitimated through law, and the appropriate organizational forms are in place, media-steered networks of interaction expand of their own accord, far beyond the ken of society's members.

The Inescapable Embodiment of Subsystems

We can now see the source of various confusions regarding Habermas's economic analysis. Although in other parts of his social theory Habermas has been sensitive to the dangers of functionalist arguments,[11] here he falls prey to their classical weakness: functionalism begs the question of what makes itself possible. To say that something is functional does not explain how it came into existence. Just because something would be beneficial if it existed does not determine whether it can or will emerge. In order to underscore the necessity of systems analysis, Habermas downplays the fact that although the economic subsystem cannot be *identified* with institutionalization nor specific organizations, it can only be *actualized* through them. But if this is the case, then it is misleading for Habermas to say that subsystems cannot be "topologically" located. Particular organizational forms are necessary for media dynamics to unfold. These organizations must be of a particular kind or they will not be actually "steered" by media nor will actions within these organizations be such that they can be utilized as subsystem performances.

The point is that nothing ensures that these necessary organizational forms, necessary for subsystem dynamics to unfold, will actually emerge. There is nothing about subsystems in themselves that calls forth the required contract law, laws establishing wage labor, a property form that is freed from community restrictions, or laws that create the limited liability corporation. Simply, subsystems do not create their own conditions of existence. Rather, these conditions are the consequence of conscious decisions from within the lifeworld. To this extent, subsystems are less autonomous than Habermas suggests.

Habermas's theoretical project causes him to relatively neglect the ways in which the capitalist economy must be embodied. Acknowledgment of the prior conditions for the actualization of the economic subsystem means that (1) the economy is rooted more deeply in lifeworld forms than Habermas allows, (2) that processes of the subsystem are amenable to organizational control from within the lifeworld and therefore historically contingent, and (3) that there are therefore more potential channels of social conflict than Habermas suggests. Given the necessity for organizational embodiment, it is not surprising that in the more recent work *Between Facts and Norms* Habermas, in contrast to some of his statements in regard to the economy, identifies certain functional reproductive processes *of* the lifeworld with specific institutions *in* the lifeworld.[12]

Habermas also tries to separate the systemic and lifeworld dimensions of society in his discussion of the relation between the economic subsystem and "action orientations." According to Habermas, social integration occurs when action orientations (pursuit of goals) of society's members are coordinated through processes of reaching understanding. In contrast, system integration "bypasses" action orientations; it refers to the functional coordination of action *consequences*. Habermas reinforces the distinction in several ways in discussing system integration. "The adaptive capacity of an action system is measured only by what the aggregate effects of actions contribute to maintaining a system in a given environment; it matters not whether the objective purposiveness of the action consequences can be traced back to purposes of the subjects involved or not."[13] Again, in viewing society as a system trying to maintain itself over time, what is important is whether the intentional actions of society's members can be utilized by the system, even though the actors would be unaware of how the actions aided the functioning of society as a system. In bolstering this point Habermas denies that even "organizational rationality" rests on the rational purposes of those acting within organizations and speaks of "a level of organization at which organizational aims are detached from motivations of membership."[14]

The issue of the relation between individual motivations and system processes surfaces again in regard to the "place" of strategic action. In response to those who have interpreted him to say that strategic action is confined to subsystem domains and communicative action is confined to lifeworld processes, Habermas denies any such compartmentalization. Strategic action does occur in the lifeworld and would only cease if "non-repressive forms of life prevail." Communicative action also takes place in subsystem domains: "It is obvious that commercial enterprises and government offices, indeed economic and political contexts as a whole make use of communicative action that is embedded in a normative framework." In the same place, however, he reiterates the separation of action orientations and subsystems by retracting the phrase—ubiquitous in *The Theory of Communicative Action*—of "purposive-rationality" in conjunction with system processes. He states that in this regard, it is more appropriate to speak of a "functional form of reason."[15]

If subsystems merely "stabilize nonintended interconnections of actions by way of functionally intermeshing *action consequences*," then what actually motivates actors would be irrelevant.[16] The functional significance of actions is not identical to action orientations and is typically unseen by the actors. If this is true, then it would not really matter what an actor's motivations are which result in an action that helps the organization function. For example, this would be true of the Calvinist conception of the calling and the belief that material success is a sign of the elect that (arguably) helped functionally establish capitalism. From the standpoint of organizations operating in the economic subsystem, it does not matter if workers in fishing companies work for wages or for the greater glory of Reverend Moon. The functionality of the action, the successful transfiguration of actions into performances, is what counts.

However, the interpretations of Habermas's critics have a textual basis. There are many passages in which Habermas does directly relate action orientations to subsystem processes. For example, when Habermas discusses the requirements for a "media code" to function, he states that "actors are oriented only to the consequences of actions, that is, they have the freedom to make their decisions depend only on calculating the success of their actions."[17] Habermas also notes that juridification leads to strategic behavior on the part of individuals and throughout *Between Facts and Norms* identifies legal organization of subsystems with strategic action.[18] Finally, the very phrase "empirically motivated ties" of money and power suggests that *certain* actor orientations are indeed connected to the functioning of subsystems.[19]

Second, Habermas actually seems to argue that the uncoupling of organizational performance from members's orientations is an *achievement* by organizations necessary for subsystem functioning.

Subsystems regard other subsystems as environments on which they depend for inputs but from which they must protect themselves from disruption. From the systems theoretic perspective, even the lifeworld is regarded as part of the subsystem's environment. Therefore, Habermas argues that organizations that operate in formally organized domains ("modern enterprises and institutions") must "immunize" themselves against the contingencies of personality, ideology (cultural traditions), and norms in order to extract the performances they need to function. (These are again the three structural areas of the lifeworld: culture, society, and personality).[20]

The interactions of these organizations are media-steered, establishing subsystem dynamics, insofar as (1) these organizations can encourage individuals to engage in functionally significant practices, and (2) the organizations gain autonomy from lifeworld restrictions. The first is accomplished through "membership requirements" that individuals accept, creating the roles of "employee" and "client." By accepting these membership requirements, individuals become "bearers of certain performances."[21] This allows an "organizational rationality" to emerge that is not identical to the organizational participant's rational activity.[22] The second is accomplished by organizations immunizing themselves against restrictions from culture and society (personality is taken care of through the first).

However, this argument by Habermas is not only strained, it demonstrates that action orientations cannot actually be theoretically excluded from subsystem domains, a fact that he tries to sidestep by the phrase "membership requirements." Specifically, in regard to the economy, Habermas states that membership requirements of employment require a generalized willingness to work.

> The wage–labor relation neutralizes the performances of producers vis-à-vis the lifeworld contexts of their actions. It sets the conditions of organizational membership under which wage laborers declare their general willingness to expend their labor power as a suitably programmed contribution to maintaining the capitalist enterprise. It is this monetarized labor power, which is appropriated as a commodity and alienated from the life context of producers, that Marx calls "abstract labor."[23]

First of all, the "general willingness to expend their labor power" ignores fundamental facts of capitalist production. Habermas cites Claus Offe on the "fictitious" nature of the commodity "labor-power" but importantly neglects a crucial aspect of Offe's discussion: the subjectivity of labor-power, which distinguishes it from all other commodities, requires that labor must be extracted from the laborer.[24]

Unlike with other commodities, when labor-power is sold, the buyer and seller cannot go their separate ways. The seller of labor-power, the worker, is now subordinated to the buyer, the employer, for a certain amount of time, for which the worker receives wages. However, how much effective work will actually be performed in this time period is subject to great variation depending on inducements (a friendly working environment, threats, etc.) by the employer and the strategies and attitude of the worker (including what is considered an "honest day's work"). The extraction of useful "labor" from the commodity "labor-power"—to employ the distinction of Marx—is, of course, subject to much shopfloor bargaining and struggle on both sides.

In several places, Offe has explored how successful production under modern working conditions increasingly requires the anticipation of problems by workers, responsibilities that are very difficult to evaluate and supervise.[25] Given this situation, Offe contends that only a generalized *normative* commitment to the organization's success makes effective performances possible. Talcott Parsons argues this as well: Due to the increased employment of professionals, "line authority" cannot be implemented in the usual way. "The difference has modified both public and private 'bureaucratic' organizations, reducing the importance of line authority, so that the organizations have become more associational, for it is essential to secure the cooperation of specialists without asserting sheer authority. Much of modern 'bureaucracy' thus verges on the 'collegial' pattern."[26] Habermas's analysis evades this crucial topic of worker orientations by a proposed blanket acceptance of membership conditions.

Habermas is compelled to employ some such notion as a "general willingness" to labor or "follow orders"[27] in order to make plausible his argument about an independent organizational rationality based on media-steering. But, second, what are membership requirements if not an admission that actor orientations *cannot* be excluded from organizations operating in system domains? It may be true that a variety of motivations may animate actions that have favorable functional significance—obedience in hopes of a promotion, from religious belief, or from patriotic fervor—but motivations cannot be excluded as altogether irrelevant.

Furthermore, in places Habermas admits that the process of immunization might endanger identity by making actions in this type of organization meaningless from the participant perspective and he even recognizes that if mutual understanding coordination were completely banished, organizations would fail.[28] Although Habermas may be correct in that, ultimately, bureaucratic authority can simply appeal to its legal establishment and compel performances, thereby trumping or "disempowering" communication in this situation, organizations apparently must rely to some extent on communication to function. Therefore, in more ways than one, it is not true that system processes can bypass action orientations: They must work *through* them. Again, it is false to say that subsystem processes cannot be topologically located.

From the above, it is clear that subsystems can only be actualized through appropriate organization and appropriate motivations. Subsystems are therefore not only organized through law but require additional anchors in the lifeworld. If this is the case then at least two things follow. First, Habermas's portrayal of the likely focus of conflict in contemporary capitalism is too narrowly drawn. Second, the actualization of media-steered subsystems, and the existence of systemic integration itself, is more fragile and contingent than Habermas implies.

CONFLICT POTENTIALS AND THE ROLE OF THE STATE

Habermas states that conflict in advanced capitalist welfare states centers on the roles which form around the interchange relations between subsystems and lifeworld: employee and consumer, client and citizen. He argues that due to the weakness of the public sphere (citizen) and to the normalization of nonetheless "alienated" labor (employee), conflict is especially likely to emerge from the client and consumer roles. "[H]opes for self-actualization and self-determination" become "privatized," intensifying the social importance of these particular roles.[29]

Although at first glance this appears plausible given some of the themes of new social movements, it is actually built on curious asymmetries. Of the four roles, two are juridically determined (employee, client) and the other two (consumer, citizen) are legally *bolstered* but actually emerge from "prior self-formative processes in which preferences, value orientations, attitudes, and so forth have taken shape," orientations that "cannot be 'bought' or 'collected' by private or public organizations."[30] One would think that protest would either focus on the two roles that are directly subject to real abstraction (employee, client), or the roles of citizen and consumer, which

Habermas connects with classical "bourgeois ideals" that retain their importance.

What apparently ties the two roles of consumer and client together is the orientation to use-values. As he repeatedly states, even in an exchange society people are oriented toward use-values.[31] However, in contemporary welfare state capitalism these use-values can only be provided in a media-shaped form which is alienating. The money medium turns people into consumers as a condition for obtaining use-values from the economic system. Habermas indicates that in certain quarters there is resistance to this "consumerist redefinition of private spheres of life and personal life-styles."[32] Correspondingly, as Habermas's discussion of juridification suggests, the legally constituted power medium turns people into clients as a condition for obtaining use-values in the form of welfare policies (e.g. health care). Habermas even refers to clients as "customers who enjoy the rewards of the welfare state."

It is reasonable to trace the origins of certain new social movements to resistance to clientelization and consumerism. Much social protest today does indeed seem to be provoked by the imposition of inappropriate principles of evaluation and interaction in different social domains. These can be well-described as resistance to commodity culture and juridification, and both of these can be plausibly explained as necessitated by capitalist growth and the increased responsibilities of the interventionist state. The experience is quite common, for example, when creative expression is equated with the art market, or education is evaluated by vocational imperatives. Similarly, the redefinition of relations between children and parents as court-monitored legal relations or the required search by teachers for litigation-proof grades certainly strikes us as alien frames imposed on social relations constituted on other grounds.

However, Habermas's analysis of conflict in contemporary capitalism is limited in two important respects. First, as our discussion of membership conditions suggests, there is no real reason to believe that employees will not also challenge, through quiet foot-dragging or even sabotage, their transformation into commodities. There is enormous evidence from labor history and in the present that this role cannot be "normalized" in the way that Habermas's systems theory requires. It is not surprising that when Habermas turns to themes of new social movements, he does not confine himself to activities of clients and consumers. Even the normalized labor role is under attack, and "citizens initiatives" are obviously one of the key political forms of new social movements.[33]

The second and more important limitation is that Habermas's theory was actually intended to explain the discontents with a *successful* welfare state compromise. The welfare state is now not just disequilibrated but in crisis: Steering problems have resulted in a lack of good jobs, insufficient revenues for the compensations organized and distributed through the welfare state, and it appears that Keynesian policies have become obstructive. Already in the early 1980s Habermas reasonably argued that if welfare state compensations did not continue, older conflicts would resurface.

> [O]n the one hand, the conditions necessary to the welfare state compromise may be fulfilled—continuous, albeit restrained, economic growth. Then problems would arise that I would place under the heading of colonization of the life-world, an erosion or undermining of realms of communicatively-structured action. On other hand, the dynamics of growth may not be maintained; then we would see some variant of traditional conflicts.[34]

Although the problems internal to the welfare state have not disappeared, in the last two decades the development of a truly global economy has, in Habermas's own words, brought the welfare state to a point of "collapse." The political and social consequences of this are the focus of much of Habermas's political commentary in recent years. The capacity of his theory to integrate these enormous changes will be the subject of the concluding chapter. Before turning in that direction, however, a critical view of his more political theoretical arguments is necessary.

WEAKNESSES OF HABERMAS'S POLITICAL PROPOSALS

The ambiguities of the relation between lifeworld and system are deepened when we turn to Habermas's political proposals. Habermas's dualistic social theory results in a rethinking of socialist politics as a form of deliberative democracy, the crucial moment of which is an influential and authentic public sphere. It is especially mindful of the debilitating effects of administrative power on the coherence of social life. It therefore offers additional ammunition for the progressive critique of state-centrism that underlies the rejection of the traditional planned economies of socialism. However, Habermas's attempted reconstruction of socialist politics, at least as thus far developed, suffers serious limitations.

Besides the untenable separation of politics and economics,[35] Habermas's political project is unclear on the central issues: What is the public sphere supposed to *do* and what makes that possible? To begin, in Habermas's theory the public sphere is not intended to replace one set of decision makers (legislators, administrators, judges) with another set (e.g. public councils), nor to trump existing decision makers in some fashion. This would simply relocate instrumental political power to another level and reinforce a state-centric notion of political community that cannot be sustained in a complex society. Instead, the goal is to alter the *quality* of decisions by making them responsive to the felt needs and problems of "society as a whole." An authentic public sphere strengthens social solidarity by bringing attention to the disruptions of social life by the dynamic of subsystems and by maintaining a situation in which people can reasonably consider themselves authors of the laws to which they are subject. It thereby simultaneously serves justice by providing a place for articulating and bringing to bear the interests of all affected and shores up solidarity at a higher level, the level of legitimate law. If the public sphere is to be authentic, problem definitions must percolate up from below, not be formulated from above. The object of political theory must therefore be limited to indicating the broad conditions that would allow an authentic public sphere to emerge and reinforce the idealizations that partly organize the legal community.

Even if one respects these limitations on political theory, Habermas's project presents several difficulties. First, as indicated earlier, the content of the "influence" flowing from the public sphere is unclear. Many comments by Habermas stress the normative, that the public sphere is an "impulse-generating periphery that *surrounds* the political center: in cultivating normative reasons, it affects all parts of the political system without intending to conquer it."[36] In another place he states that "normative reasons remain the sole currency in which communicative power becomes operative. It can affect the administrative system by cultivating the pool of reasons on which administrative decisions, which are subject to the rule of law, must draw."[37] Instead of the common Newtonian conception of politics, of bodies exerting direct force on other bodies, an analogy with Einstein's theory is appropriate, that space has contours that determine the direction of energy without obstructing its flow. By generating normative limitations on potential legislation, the public sphere can shape the dynamic of subsystems without actually obstructing the flow of media.

One could defensibly argue that communicative power is "power" in that by mobilizing counter-knowledge, framing issues a certain way, and by generating normative constraints, it shapes the terrain over which battles will be fought. This would then be influence that does not seek command, "authority," rather than power, in the usual sense in which the latter term is used. However, the truth is that it must necessarily go far beyond that. Communicative power appears to have two moments that are frequently blurred. The public sphere does convey normative impulses that shape subsystem dynamics without obstructing them. An authentic public sphere thereby engenders the common conviction that reason *is* being followed in the legal regulation of public affairs. This is why the bourgeois citizenry of the eighteenth century could believe that rule of law under the influence of public opinion actually meant the end of "domination."[38]

However, second, the public sphere must also "convincingly and *influentially* thematize" problems.[39] In one place Habermas even goes so far as to say that the communicative power of public opinion "programs" or "directs" the administration, although "only the political system can 'act.'"[40] Once one tries to clarify what "effective problematization" would entail, the above distinction becomes unclear. Effective problematization would have to include all three "employments of practical reason." The discussions that constitute the public sphere would therefore take into account practical concerns, not merely normative ones. But if this is the case, the distinction between the impulses of the public sphere and the concrete deliberations and decisions of the legislature begins to evaporate. In focusing on the practical as well as normative aspects of social problems, the discussions of the public sphere must become much more pointed than Habermas states. The public sphere would then instruct the parliamentary and administrative bodies in a more immediate and detailed way than Habermas wants to admit.

Habermas would like to confine the specifics of public policy to the legislative body but this cannot be sustained for another reason. As both Joshua Cohen and William Forbath point out, unless specific substantive proposals are raised the public sphere will not be animated nor people engaged.[41] Cohen in particular emphasizes the need for local decision making, partly to engage citizens by focusing their attention on *problems* to be *solved*.[42] He thereby rejects Habermas's sharp distinction between opinion and decisions, noting that, "Otherwise radical democracy dissolves into a scheme in which open-ended debate among citizens proceeds in splendid isolation from the exercise of political power."[43]

Reflecting on the meaning of this "pool of reasons" raises a related ambiguity regarding the object of public policy. It would appear that the normative constraint results from the public sphere screening arguments so that only those that would respect the interests of all affected would be conveyed as authoritative limits on public policy. The problems to be addressed are those that affect society as a whole. The difficulty here is epistemological, resulting from Habermas's conception of society as "decentered." He argues that society must be conceived as an array of subsystems which provide no vantage point from which the whole can be seen, an impossibility given the "deworlded" nature of subsystem dynamics. However, he nonetheless repeatedly refers to "society as a whole" as the practical referent of political decision making and "the interests of all affected" as the principle of a morally defensible public policy.[44]

Again, the problem stems from the systems-theoretic aspects of Habermas's theory. From his theory imbalances in the operations of the subsystems will have effects that appear in the lifeworld—he refers to "the public" that "perceives" the "social intolerability of deficient or disturbed functional systems"[45]—but given the epistemological limitations he argues exist regarding our ability to comprehend system processes, it is hard to see what direction public policy should or could take.

Some comments by Habermas suggest a stronger conception of society, that the communication in the public sphere would allow a view of the whole on which a general will could be based. In one place he even diminishes the fragmentation of a society of subsystems: "Even the decentered society...[needs] the projected unity of an intersubjectively formed common will."[46] However, "society as a whole" allows a weaker interpretation as well. Legislative bodies may be influenced by rivulets from various sources. One may not be able to see the entire river system, every spring or creek that feeds into it, but each affects the whole by its flow. In this case, "society as a whole" would simply indicate that the reformist project is to improve opportunities for neglected social needs to gain a hearing.

If the latter is intended, the deterioration of politics into mere interest group activity is likely. If society as a whole only manifests itself as discrete rivulets, the screen of universalizability is lost. Although the universe of interests that gain influence would be expanded, democracy would still be limited to mere preference aggregation with all the well-known public choice difficulties that accompany this.[47] To use Rousseau's terminology, the general will would disintegrate into the mere "will of all."

The public sphere must be organized such that it can provide an arena in which citizens' preferences can become more universalist, rather than merely aggregated as they are. The public sphere must also be able to effectively influence decision makers, especially administration. These topics are more fully explored by various other theorists of deliberative democracy such as James Bohman, John Dryzek, Joshua Cohen, and numerous contributors to the journal *The Good Society*.[48] A problem with these alternative accounts is that they must reject or ignore Habermas's argument that the integrity of subsystem dynamics requires the limitations Habermas recommends. (Dryzek and Jean Cohen and Andrew Arato are exceptions.) Bohman even says, "As with arguments based on the efficiency of subsystems, it is necessary to ask: complexity for what?"[49] Habermas's response would be, to allow further rationalization of the lifeworld so that a rationalized culture can meet political prescriptions "halfway." This theoretical stalemate broaches the crucial limitation that Habermas places on democratic action. It also involves his theory in an important inconsistency, a topic to which we can now turn.

DEMOCRACY AND SUBSYSTEMS

Habermas's version of deliberative democracy is distinguished from a host of similar proposals precisely by his insistence on protecting subsystem dynamics from overweening lifeworld impulses. This is also what separates Habermas's political project, and that of Habermasians such as Jean Cohen and Andrew Arato, from traditional socialist strategies of democratization. Habermas has repeatedly rejected self-management schemes on the grounds that they presume a capacity of society to act on itself and because "complex societies are unable to reproduce themselves if they do not leave the logic of an economy that regulates itself through the market intact."[50] A "self-limiting" democracy is exemplified in Jean Cohen and Andrew Arato's discussion of workplace democracy and in Habermas's careful recommendations for more public participation in administration: both reject any interference with subsystem dynamics. Cohen and Arato argue that, although desirable, such democratic spaces within subsystem organizations must preserve the "self-regulation of steering systems."[51] Similarly, Habermas suggests that any democratization of the administration must be sensitive to eroding administrative "efficiency" and argues for at best "cautious experimentation."[52] This is quite similar to Samuel P. Huntington's formulation that democracy and efficiency are values that must be traded off against each other, that democracy should be "optimized" rather than "maximized."[53]

Progressives have long had good reason to be suspicious of this argument. The allegedly necessary trade-off between economic prosperity versus democracy is the stock in trade of virtually all authoritarian governments. In Habermas's case, the suggested balancing of democratic institutions and subsystem efficiency actually exposes a profound tension in his political project. In *Between Facts and Norms* Habermas specifically rejects attempts to interpret *norms* as just one "value" among others, allowing trade-offs or compromises.[54] Habermas's argument for this crucial distinction occurs in his discussion of an (alleged) tendency in German constitutional analysis called "value jurisprudence." In this judicial approach, court decisions are based on weighing values against each other according to the specific case. The approach necessarily creates considerable discretion on the part of judges and can lead to arbitrary rulings. This in turn hampers the coherence and predictability of the legal system as a whole.[55]

In opposition, Habermas explicitly argues that "rights must not be assimilated to values."[56] Norms and values differ in a number of respects, especially in that norms are deontological, *morally obligatory*, whereas values are teleological, they are *goods* to be pursued as best they can be. Other differences are that norms are either valid or not, whereas values can be realized in varying degrees; norms are universally binding but values are relative to a specific culture; and norms cannot conflict whereas values can be weighed against each other.[57] Attempts to escape this distinction by elevating values to *universal* goods make values so abstract that they become in effect deontological principles, for example, the "value" of human dignity.[58]

Habermas acknowledges that different norms may at first glance apply to a specific case, causing some to argue that different principles are being balanced against each other. However he says that this is mistaken. "Different norms must not contradict one another" because then we would be under conflicting obligations.[59] This would threaten the coherence of morality in general and, specifically, the coherence of the legal system as a whole. Given the extraordinary importance of the rule of law in pluralistic societies the coherence of the legal system must be protected, but in a way that is normatively defensible. To satisfy both, judges must not conceive their role as weighing *values* but weighing *reasons* for why a particular norm should apply, without thereby impugning the general validity of alternative norms that are rejected as inapplicable in this particular situation. Which norm applies to a case requires arguments of "appropriateness" but only one will ultimately be the right fit for a particular case.[60]

Based on this distinction between norms and values, Habermas specifically repudiates any "cost–benefit analysis" in regard to norms, any talk of "optimizing," and even denies that norms must be weighed against reasons for "functional efficiency" of organizations such as "security of the state" or "labor peace."[61] "The legal validity of the judgement has the deontological character of a command, and not the teleological character of a desirable good that we can achieve to a certain degree under the given circumstances and within the horizon of our preferences." This analytical distinction between norms and values must be respected, although Habermas acknowledges that the distinction is necessarily blurred in legal practice because positive law applies to a specific territory and therefore simultaneously advances moral (universally obligatory) and ethical (the good life for us) concerns.[62]

However, if one applies this reasoning to *democratic* norms it is clear that as norms they are obligations, not choices.[63] But if this is the case, then the suggested trade-off between democratization of the economy and administration against the efficiency of subsystems is forbidden. The self-limiting politics endorsed by Habermas and by Cohen and Arato thereby loses a major support. The question must not be how much democratization is compatible with efficiency, but, if public autonomy is to retain its privileged position, how much efficiency is compatible with autonomy.

In fact, in a discussion of the "Asian values" debate of the early 1990s, Habermas makes precisely this point regarding the priority of democracy over "functional arguments."

> These dictatorships consider themselves authorized by the "right of social development"—apparently understood as a collective right—to postpone the realization of liberal rights and rights of political participation until their countries have attained a level of economic development that allows them to satisfy the basic material needs of the population equally. For a population in misery, they claim, legal equality and freedom of opinion are not so relevant as the prospect of better living conditions. One cannot convert functional arguments into normative ones this easily.[64]

Indeed, one cannot. Of course Habermas et al. are arguing for a *self*-limiting democracy. That is, due to the consideration that the political cannot create administratively the economic (revenues from private investment) and cultural (a rationalized lifeworld yielding a liberal culture) preconditions for its own action, Habermas may be merely making a *practical* recommendation for a democratic decision to limit itself. Nevertheless, the discussion veers close to regarding democracy as one value among others. To this extent, the priority of democratic norms tends to get lost in the prescriptions for what contemporary socialists should do. The tension is exacerbated when one considers the tactics that are necessary to sustain the integrity of a public sphere.

THE PROGRESSIVE ROLE OF CONFLICT

Walling off subsystems from democratic interference in advance must also be rejected when one considers the actual politics necessary to establish an *authentic* public sphere in the contemporary context. A major question to ask of any theory of deliberative democracy is why legislators would listen to the problems and issues emerging from the public sensors. Habermas responds with the argument regarding unavoidable idealizations and the need for a legitimate legal system that can maintain social integration. However, in capitalist countries, those who control investment funds exercise tremendous veto power over public policy, the well-known "privileged position of business."[65] This social situation establishes what it is reasonable for the public to do or want and, indeed, in some respects may affect who "the public" is considered to be.

The privileged position of business is what class society means. It cannot be ameliorated by campaign finance reforms or other reforms that target resource inequality because it is not about distributional inequality in the retail sense. The threat of a capital strike inheres in a social structure in which investment funds are in the hands of a minority. Furthermore, as Dryzek points out, a capital strike need not be consciously organized or abetted. The capital strike can, and probably most often does, take the form of an anonymous withdrawal of investment, an "automatic recoil" of capital markets.[66] To be sure, the threat of a capital strike is not in itself absolute. As I have indicated elsewhere, in a capitalist system investors cannot for long simply refuse to invest. They must eventually invest somewhere.[67] Nevertheless, as long as there are reasonable investment opportunities in other places, the threat of a capital strike is a serious constraint on democracy.

This "structural dependence on capital," to use Adam Przeworski's phrase, *also* creates "social facts." In a market society the crucial role of capital in determining the availability of employment and the size of the tax base on which social spending depends allows a plausible identification of the class interests of capital with the general interest of society as a whole. If practical concerns are to be included in the public sphere's deliberation on what it is reasonable to do, then maintaining a "good business climate" is following reason under contemporary circumstances.

Obviously, in this situation many interests are excluded from serious consideration, reinforced by strategies, analyzed by Offe, for dividing society into the morally worthy and unworthy.[68] The referent of the term "we" is thereby narrowed in an attempt to maintain legitimacy. The only way to ensure the inclusion of all interests is for the marginalized to engage in tactics that alter the calculus of which policies are "reasonable" in a practical sense. This means effective resistance to marginalization.

Habermas himself mentions the need for "*veto* rights" of various groups to ensure that their voices are included.[69] He does not give this phrase content but in practice this has meant sit-ins, demonstrations, strikes, work to rule, even sabotage and threats of violence. Although Habermas typically emphasizes the educative aspects of civil disobedience,[70] it has also importantly always been an attempt to "stop the machine," as Thoreau put it, to force political agencies to confront demands. That is, creating a "veto" has often meant to purposefully disrupt economic and administrative efficiency. In contrast, Habermas's discussion of deliberative democracy appears, as James Scott put it, "to treat civil and political society as if it ought to be the perfect graduate student seminar."[71]

Furthermore, many have long argued—for example, Nicos Poulantzas throughout his works, and more recently Leo Panitch and Bohman—that if the public sphere is not to be shunted aside, the state apparatus itself must be subject to a thorough democratization, much more thorough than Habermas's gestures indicate.[72] Although this is true, even this does not reveal the full importance of the state's specific structure for the public sphere. The structure of the state is not important only to provide avenues for excluded perspectives. The existence and organization of the various departments, agencies, and branches concentrate or scatter particular interests and thereby to an important extent determine which perspectives are actually organized. The specific institutional structure of the state is in this way partly *constitutive* of the public sphere itself. Therefore, the very existence of an authentic public sphere, and *not* just the depth of influence of an already existing public sphere, requires a determined struggle over the basic constitutional order, the structure of state agencies, the place of local autonomy, and so on. Again, this may well disrupt the efficiency of public administration, but, if public autonomy must trump all else, then this must occur. Habermas simply does not appreciate how much the authenticity of public influence may seriously clash with the operations of the economic and administrative subsystems.

Finally, in response to Habermas's concern that such interventions may obstruct further rationalization of the lifeworld, the dynamic of this rationalization has been much too narrowly portrayed. As Habermas himself argues, the rationalization of the lifeworld is not merely a *cultural* phenomenon. We noted earlier that Habermas conceives the development of democracy itself as an aspect of the rationalization of the lifeworld. Whatever else it may require, a rationalized lifeworld entails that all perspectives in society are considered. As the above comments show, this can only be promoted by structural changes and public policies that raise the voices of the marginalized. Democracy increases the rationalization of the lifeworld by forcing those of differing beliefs to engage one another and, in doing so, necessarily reflect on why each holds the beliefs they do. Equally so, failure to struggle for democracy may itself diminish the opportunities for unleashing innovative thinking about social and political conflicts. Rather than a justice that is inclusive and therefore enduring, people will try to find comfort in rationalizations in the Freudian sense. As Ernesto Cortes, Jr., a community organizer in San Antonio, Texas once reminded us, "Powerlessness also corrupts."[73] *Democratization* must therefore meet a partly rationalized *lifeworld* "halfway."

Over the last several years international developments have pushed to the breaking point the domestic project of trying to balance an effective deliberative democracy against subsystem autonomy. Welfare state policies that, however ambivalently, have contributed to mass loyalty are under vigorous assault everywhere, due to liberalized trade regulations and the overwhelming threat of a capital strike. The moral universalism that maintains social solidarity has been seriously wounded, and the marginalization of groups increased as political communities redefine who is and who is not to be counted as part of the community. Habermas's general response, articulated in diverse commentaries on contemporary political developments, is to try to restore a balance by increasing binding decision making on the level of regional and international organizations, influenced, of course, by a global public sphere. The final chapter discusses Habermas's portrayal of the changing world situation and the limits of his theory for helping us think through an effective political strategy for the twenty-first century.

CHAPTER 8

HABERMAS AND THE POLITICS OF
THE TWENTY-FIRST CENTURY

Habermas's analysis of the problems resulting from the welfare state "taming" of capitalism were formulated in the 1970s and early 1980s. The world has, of course, dramatically altered its trajectory since then. The collapse of communist regimes in Europe, the deepening of the ties of the European Union, and the global unleashing of neoliberal policies by the International Monetary Fund and other agencies present new issues that displace the previously analyzed ones from attention, albeit without eliminating them. Habermas explores these developments in his contemporary political writings, articulating a political project, now on an international scale, that would protect the advances of the welfare state without corrupting the dynamic of a global market economy. Although he retains his ambivalence regarding the welfare state, with the collapse of state socialism he considers this option "the only one remaining."[1]

After examining Habermas's portrayal of the contemporary world, in conclusion there are two issues to be addressed. First, as in the previous discussion, we must ask whether the global economy is as autonomous as Habermas makes it out to be. Second, given that the welfare policies that contained class conflict have been partly dismantled, is it still reasonable to theoretically exclude the classical socialist topics of property, exploitation, and social class? These questions will help us assess the adequacy of Habermas's theory for understanding the challenges of the twenty-first century.

GLOBAL CAPITALISM

According to Habermas, the emergence of a truly global economy gravely weakens progressive domestic policies in a number of ways. He comprehends this economy as not merely an increase in world trade caused by an interlinking of financial markets, but further as the creation of "global networks of production." The diffusion of technologies associated with global production means a tremendous increase in international economic competition. Combined with the fluidity of financial markets, this intensifies the threat of "capital flight," discussed before in regard to domestic policy, for national economies as a whole.[2] An immediate consequence has not only been increasing inequality between North and South but also a general drop in the standard of living in the North itself as all become involved in a potential "race to the bottom."[3]

Occasionally Habermas acknowledges that the new global economic order is to some extent a political project, mentioning the role of the General Agreement on Tariffs and Trade (GATT) and the policies of the World Bank. He also discusses the European Union, noting that to the present its planners have emphasized "sheer economic criteria" and "economic rationality."[4] However, Habermas largely considers these political developments to be forced on the participants, referring frequently to the "domination of systemic imperatives."[5] As stated before, governments cannot simply command the resources they need to function. Since individual nations get their tax revenue from economic activity, they must tack with the winds of international competition. He also contends that in seeking solutions to their domestic economic problems, neoliberalism is easier because "dismantling trade barriers" has the "lowest implementation costs," since it is removing something rather than constructing anew.[6]

The resulting autonomy of the global economy is such that Habermas even speculates on whether "systemic processes" have "severed their ties with all contexts produced by political communication." For example, he argues that the administrative planners of the European Union, as systems theory predicts, tend to become "self-programming."[7] In one place Habermas now even states, in a very Marxian fashion, that the economic subsystem is the "pacemaker of evolution," "a self-referentially sealed economic system whose self-stabilization requires the absorption and the processing of all relevant information solely in the business management language of cost effectiveness."[8] Although he doubts that this situation is sustainable, it is nonetheless a danger to social cohesion that must be countered.

The consequences of these economic developments are many and fierce. First, the nation-state is increasingly hamstrung. Transnational corporations and banks have "undermined" the capacity of states to control their own economies to the extent that, combined with global communication networks, the nation-state is actually becoming an anachronism.[9] This is true of all states, not just developing countries. "Capitalism's new, apparently irrevocable globalizing dynamic drastically reduces the G7 states's freedom of action, which had enabled them, unlike the economically dependent states of the Third World, to hang on to a relative degree of independence."[10] Since " 'Keynesianism in one country' is no longer a possibility," full employment policies, already weakened by jobless growth, have become much more difficult.[11] Unsurprisingly, governments that can no longer produce the goods face declining legitimacy, that is, mass loyalty.

Second, these pressures lead to the marginalization of increasing numbers of the population, both within and without, domestically resulting in the creation of an "underclass." Habermas argues that since these "pauperized groups" are no longer necessary for production, they have no effective "veto" in regard to policies. This does not mean, however, that their situation can simply be ignored. Although to some extent confined to ghettoes and prisons, there are nonetheless debilitating effects on cities and entire regions, a phenomenon with which Americans are all too familiar.[12] Like other observers, Habermas sees the situation of the domestic poor as simply the local manifestation of the conditions of the poor in the world at large.

> The pattern of relations between the metropolises and the underdeveloped peripheral areas that has increasingly become established in the international arena seems to be repeating itself within the developed capitalist societies: the established powers are less and less dependent for their own reproduction on the labor and willingness to cooperate of those who are impoverished and disenfranchised.[13]

The most the excluded can do is engage in "self-destructive revolts," which of course leads to greater repression.

Global economic dislocations have also increased immigration to all advanced countries, often producing "chauvinism" on the part of the "relatively deprived classes" and sometimes even violence against immigrants.[14] Similarly, domestic disparities feed separatist movements in more affluent regions, for example in northern Italy. In general and in multiple ways, who are to be included in "our community" becomes ever-more constricted, requiring an almost willful blindness regarding the marginalized. "Since at least the Reagan presidency, it has been possible to observe in the largest U.S. cities the way the 'ins' can survive only by means of a neurotic defense system that protects them from seeing the 'outs.'" Social Darwinism, domestically and globally, results in a psychologically useful, naturalized conception of "winners" and "losers."[15]

Third, economic difficulties strengthen the neoconservative platform of supply-side economics, technocratic decision making removed from popular influence, and an intense focus on cultural politics. In regard to the latter, Habermas gives particular attention to the general demonization of intellectuals and to the reassertion of "traditional values." "[T]raditional culture and the stabilizing forces of conventional morality, patriotism, bourgeois religion, and folk culture are to be cultivated. Their function is to compensate the private lifeworld for personal burdens and to cushion it against the pressures of a competitive society and accelerated modernization."[16] This increased proximity of culture and politics powerfully supports a ubiquitous politics of symbols or, as President Clinton called it, the "politics of meaning."

Habermas well describes the cultural project of neoconservatism as a deliberate surrender of critical capacities. Although he is specifically analyzing cultural–political developments in Germany, he could as easily be talking about the recommendations of prominent American culture warriors such as Lynn Cheney or William Bennett. Neoconservatives hope to encourage "a process of reenchantment, by narrative without argument, inspirational literature, the creation of meaning, and empathic historicism."[17] This is not only true of the writing of national histories—in Germany, in the United States, in Japan—but also in regard to religious belief. Habermas thereby shows an affinity of the rise of fundamentalism to this broader, more consciously pursued neoconservative project.

Echoing Horkheimer on "tradition," Habermas understands fundamentalism as a desperate attempt to restore meaning in a fragmented world. "Fundamentalist movements can be understood as an ironic attempt to give one's own lifeworld ultrastability by restorative means. The irony lies in the way traditionalism misunderstands itself. In fact, it emerges from the vortex of social modernization and it apes a substance that has already disintegrated."[18] Religious fundamentalism, like nationalist movements, satisfies the longing for an "ascriptive" identity, one into which one is born and is therefore beyond doubt.[19] The desire for this is so strong, Habermas warns, that "religious socialization" such as that of Islamic fundamentalism can create "deeper fractures than differences in modes of production or class distinctions."[20]

Although global fundamentalisms may be a reaction to the destabilization of traditional lifeworlds, Habermas leaves no doubt that local elites must also share the blame for this development.[21] However, he also believes that the marginalized of the world generally have a dearth of alternatives. "[T]he masses from the impoverished regions of the world lack effective sanctions against the North: they cannot go on strike; at most, they can 'threaten' with waves of immigration."[22] Tying together the situation of the domestically and internationally marginalized once more, Habermas reiterates this position in a way that is very revealing. "Those who can no longer change their social situation on their own have fallen out of the solidarist context of state citizenship. They can no longer pose any kind of threat— any more than the former Third World can threaten the First."[23] The naiveté of that statement is no less breathtaking now for the fact that before September 11 it was universally shared.

Finally, and extremely important, the broad consequence for the advanced capitalist countries is that the welfare state, so crucial to the pacification of class conflict, is "in a state of disintegration."[24] Most remarkably, Habermas even entertains the possibility that welfare state protections were merely a historical episode, a time that is now past. "No matter how one looks at it, the globalization of the economy destroys a historical constellation that made the welfare state compromise temporarily possible. Even if this compromise was never the ideal solution for a problem inherent within capitalism itself, it nevertheless held capitalism's social costs within tolerable limits."[25] As related by Rudolf Meidner, even Sweden, the longtime hope for a "Third Way," has had to adjust to the pressures of a globalizing capitalism.[26]

Considering the social functions of welfare policy discussed earlier, this development presents nothing less than a political crisis. The domestic divisions and exclusions mentioned above, the social Darwinistically justified marginalization of certain groups, end up casting doubt on the legitimacy of *majority* decisions themselves since the shrinking of the relevant community causes the majority to act in an increasingly self-interested manner.

> In the long run, a loss of solidarity such as this will inevitably destroy a liberal political culture whose universalistic self-understanding democratic societies depend on. Procedurally correct majority decisions that merely reflect the fears and self-defensive reactions of social classes

threatened with downward mobility—decisions that reflect the senti-
ments of right-wing populism, in other words—will end up eroding
the legitimacy of democratic procedures and institutions themselves.[27]

Whatever social Darwinists might believe, the universalism of liberal
political culture cannot be tossed aside without consequences. This
development, coupled with the weakened capacity for action by
nation-states in the international arena, throws into doubt the very
relevance, for the twenty-first century, of the basic concepts of
democracy.[28]

POLITICAL PROPOSALS

Many today continue to insist that the state is based on a "prepolitical
entity" called the nation that then merely receives political expression.
As Habermas shows, already in the eighteenth century Rousseau and
other republican contractarians tried to replace this identification of
"ethnos" and "demos" with the notion of a people whose identity
resides in collective self-legislation, in common civic practices of
citizenship. The nationalism of the French Revolution furthered this
separation by creating a collective identity grounded not on ascribed
characteristics (real or alleged) but on the achieved identity of "citizens" of France.[29] Such state building in European history allowed for,
among other things, an overcoming of devastating religious differences.[30] Habermas contends that basing national identity on common
origins was in most circumstances "always a fiction" because, historically, states in Europe and elsewhere were often constructed from the
most disparate cultural elements. However, the cultural project of
neoconservatives described above, the longing for ascriptive and therefore intuitive identities, and the general movements of population
prompted by the global economy have all caused the question of the
relationship between ethnos and demos to resurface with enormous
force.

Habermas concludes that the nation-state is today challenged by
two great problems. The first, "from without," is finding room to
maneuver in face of the constraints of an unsentimental globalizing
economy. The second, "from within," is the "explosive potential of
multiculturalism."[31] He argues that it is becoming increasingly difficult to realistically conceive a "nation-state based on a culturally
homogeneous population," that is, the "nation" of the nation-state is
"disintegrating."[32] On the other hand, Habermas admits that some
kind of "cultural substrate" is still necessary to motivationally anchor

the solidarity on which democratic practices depend.[33] The question is what kind of cultural underpinning can be maintained in an age of an inescapable pluralism of worldviews.

Habermas proposes a political initiative on the national level to reduce this extreme fragmentation and "moral erosion," an initiative that then serves as a kind of template for his more international proposals. On the level of the individual nation Habermas repeatedly argues for a kind of "constitutional patriotism" (Dolf Sternberger's phrase). In the German context this means "a readiness to identify with the political order and the principles of the Basic Law."[34] Unlike the ethnos, this collective identity would neither require the suppression nor abstract leveling of cultural differences. It would recognize the plurality of cultures in which people's identities are formed while separating "ethical" integration from "abstract political integration."

The question, asked by Charles Taylor, among others, is what would ground this in individual motivations?[35] Habermas responds that only reinvigorated democracies can achieve the requisite anchoring. "My sense is that multicultural societies can be held together by a political culture, however much it has proven itself, only if democratic citizenship pays off not only in terms of liberal individual rights and rights of political participation, but also in the enjoyment of social and cultural rights."[36] Members must be able to recognize that the freedom to pursue their own conception of a good life can only be guaranteed by the reciprocal recognition of other subcultures in which identities of citizens are anchored, that therefore their distinctive identities are only protected if the distinctive identities of others are also protected. According to Habermas, this means that "fundamentalist immigrant cultures" that deny the right of alternative identities to exist can be properly excluded because they leave no room for "reasonable disagreement."[37] (This is something with which, for example, very open cultures such as that of The Netherlands have been struggling of late.) But we must also recognize, as our discussion of gender showed, that the mutual granting of "negative liberties" will not be enough. It is only political *participation* that can create a collectivity. "The strength of the democratic constitutional state lies precisely in its ability to close the holes of social integration through the political participation of its citizens."[38]

Habermas bolsters his argument for the adequacy of constitutional patriotism by insisting that the virtualization of democratic processes by a political public sphere has itself reduced the need for "cultural homogeneity." "A previous background consensus, constructed on the basis of cultural homogeneity and understood as a necessary catalyzing condition for democracy, becomes superfluous to the extent that public, discursively structured processes of opinion- and will-formation make a reasonable political understanding possible, even among strangers."[39] The collective identity of the people is not something simply given by history. It can emerge from "the fluid content of a circulatory process that is generated through the legal institutionalization of citizens' communication."[40] In this way, "collective identities are made, not found."[41] This public sphere must be supported by the full associational life of civil society and also by political parties that are not merely cogs in the political subsystem and can therefore still "mediate" between the public sphere and institutionalized decision making. It must also be supported by a rationalized lifeworld. "Rationalized lifeworlds, with their institutionalized discourses, have access to their own mechanism for generating new bonds and normative arrangements. In the sphere of the lifeworld, 'rationalization' does not plug the wellsprings of solidarity; rather, it discovers new ones as the old ones run dry."[42] Rationalized lifeworlds increase the possibility of "enter[ing] into new social ties and to creatively draft new rules for living together with others."[43] Habermas's argument, then, is that a rationalized lifeworld encourages a liberal political culture that, anchored in associational life, can produce new democratic collective identities. The argument rests rather heavily on the emergence of a rationalized lifeworld, and it should be recalled that this cannot be conjured up at will.[44]

These proposals are promising for handling some of the "centrifugal forces" afflicting the nation-state.[45] However, as argued above, the state also faces problems that clearly outrun any purely domestic capacities for action. Deteriorating welfare protections can only be shored up by "larger political entities which could manage to keep pace with the transnational economy."[46] This is also important from a moral perspective in that, with global capitalism, those "affected" and those making the decisions have been increasingly separated. Therefore, there appears to be a moral imperative that planning be shifted to a higher level.[47]

First, Habermas considers regional organizations such as the European Union for reducing the pressures on welfare policy. The emergence of regional organizations holds some promise for moderating the imperatives of global capitalism simply because it reduces the number of political actors in the world, making coordination easier. Larger political organizations therefore present possibilities for escaping the zero-sum game of "locational competition," that is, the unrelenting attempt to find advantage over competitors.[48] However,

Habermas contends that regional organizations like the European Union can only become truly effective if they, like nation-states, can encourage solidarity without eliminating national-cultural differences.[49] Again, like nation-states, this would require a thorough democratization of decision making, creating a sense of citizenship in a larger order. The prospects for this are uncertain due to the fact that the administrative planning bodies resist democratization and that "the role of citizen has hitherto only been institutionalized at the level of nation-states."[50] Given Habermas's arguments in other contexts, however, it is plausible that the rationalization of lifeworlds on a national level would increase the openness to innovative solutions on the regional level so that these levels could build on each other.

Habermas believes that attempts to create supranational political agencies are encouraged by other recent signs of principled international coordination. For example, he states that the role of the United Nations in the Persian Gulf war and its intervention into Somalia, whatever one might think of the concrete aims and interests involved, indicate at least a perceived need to justify actions in the international arena by an "appeal to norms."[51] In effect, Habermas sees the gradual establishment of a new idealization organizing interactions among nation-states, even if, as with the previously discussed idealizations, it is often counterfactual. "The institutions of the UN, and the basic principles of international law expressed in the UN Charter, embody what Hegel would have called a piece of 'existential reason.' ... It's no longer merely a vague ideal. There are certain demands that derive from this claim to legitimation."[52] The rise of the politics of human rights further shows that the claim of nonintervention in the name of the self-determination of nations is rapidly losing credence, increasing the tension that has always existed in international law between nonintervention in the domestic affairs of a nation and the commitment to advancing human rights.[53]

In accord with his understanding of the dynamic of contemporary democracies, Habermas argues that the primary source of continued growth of normative regulation in world politics will not be "mass action," whose day has passed, but the emergence of a global public sphere. World summits that "thematize" specific issues and prominent transnational groups such as Amnesty International, Greenpeace, and other associations, are helping to establish a trans-national civil society that stimulates public communication, forming a global political public sphere.[54] Ultimately, these developments indicate the potential for the emergence of a "cosmopolitan solidarity."[55]

These trends must be pushed further toward what Habermas calls a "world domestic policy," that is, in Kant's phrase, we must move in the direction of "cosmopolitan law." This differs from the familiar "international" law in the following respect. "Whereas international law, like all law in the state of nature, is only provisionally valid, cosmopolitan law would resemble state-sanctioned civil law in definitively bringing the state of nature to an end."[56] In order to do this, cosmopolitan law must be able to "bypass" state sovereignty and hold a country's citizens personally liable for actions.[57] Habermas has in mind the attempt to establish a permanent International Criminal Court that would regularize the proceedings of the ad hoc courts for crimes against humanity, such as the Nuremberg trials and the court presently trying the former leader of Yugoslavia.

Informed by his understanding of the necessity of communicative action for producing social solidarity, Habermas believes that greater international coordination will not come primarily from trying to accommodate the interest positions of the various actors. "The Hobbesian problem—how to create a stable social order—overtaxes the cooperative capacities of rational egoists, even on the global level."[58] Instead, global referenda on various issues, the influence of the global public sphere politically sharpened by transnational social movements, and the involvement of domestic political parties responding to the demands of constituents must shape the political terrain so as to encourage "transnational will-formation."[59]

Because world citizenship based on human rights is likely to remain largely "reactive," Habermas argues that it cannot substitute for the ethical identity forged within the individual nation-state. Therefore, he does not hope for nor even consider desirable a "world government."[60] However, his reading of the historical development of the nation-state strongly suggests that the creation of a more global sense of citizenship is not to be dismissed out of hand.

> [P]recisely the artificial conditions in which national consciousness arose argue against the defeatist assumption that a form of civic solidarity among strangers can only be generated within the confines of the nation. If this form of collective identity was due to a highly abstractive leap from the local and dynastic to national and then to democratic consciousness, why shouldn't this learning process be able to continue?[61]

It could be added that the progress of democracy and liberal political cultures on the domestic level further increase the chance of another historic leap in political integration in that, as Habermas often says, democracy itself opens up the possibility of learning and innovation. Nevertheless, Habermas argues, instead of world government the likeliest path would be a continuation of international negotiations, albeit within much more compelling normative constraints.

In a world of centrifugal forces, the prospects of a global solidarity of strangers may still seem fanciful. However, the question before us is not whether "we *can* learn from catastrophes," but increasingly whether "we *only* learn from catastrophes."[62]

HABERMAS'S SOCIAL THEORY AND TWENTY-FIRST-CENTURY CAPITALISM

Habermas's analysis of recent political and economic developments illuminates a number of pressing questions, such as the challenges of multiculturalism and the undermining of the welfare state by a globalizing capitalism. He is correct that a national strategy of attempting to improve competitiveness only presents an endless round of beggar thy neighbor, increasing the likelihood of a race to the bottom and all the suffering and conflict that that entails. However, the conceptual difficulties that dog his social theory return with renewed force when contemplating the possibilities of the future. For one, Habermas's distinction between lifeworld and system obstructs our ability to grasp the extent to which global capitalism is a political construction. In turn, this weakness is intimately bound up with the uncertainty of the role of class in Habermas's social theory.

In regard to the first, the effect of portraying economic processes as autonomous system processes, reinforced by Habermas's repeated references to the "anonymity" of economic imperatives, is to "naturalize" global capitalism. To the contrary, from the enclosure movement in sixteenth-century England to the land reforms of Asian countries in the latter half of the twentieth century to the present imposition by the International Monetary Fund of "structural adjustment" on developing countries that compels the opening of capital and consumer markets, capitalism is and has always been a political construction. The increased effectiveness of the capital strike to drive down wages results from politically conscious decisions to eliminate the controls on flows of investment capital into and out of a country, highly encouraged by the IMF. As Karl Polanyi, favorably quoted elsewhere by Habermas, put it in *The Great Transformation*, "There was nothing natural about *laissez-faire*; free markets could never have come into being merely by allowing things to take their course."[63]

On a different level, this is reinforced by William Roy's account of the rise of the industrial corporation in the United States. This crucial form of economic action was and continues to be an artificial legal construction, not the consequence of inherent economic development.[64] Earlier, Paul Hirst insisted on a similar point against the dominant Marxian view of the economy. He argued that Marxists, like neoconservatives, often regard the economy as something that comes into existence on its own and then merely assumes a legal *form*. This presupposes a realm of production that is constituted prior to its legal determination, "an economy which generates and determines its own conditions of existence."[65] Among other things, such a conception renders completely incomprehensible what legislatures *do* and derides the stakes involved.

By insisting that media must be anchored in law, Habermas's theory would appear to evade this criticism. However, his emphasis on how the free flow of media can construct ever-expanding networks on their own tends to reinstate the illusion of an autonomous, "naturally" emergent, economy. The meticulous elaboration of laws governing international trade today demonstrates that it is misleading to describe global capitalism as anonymous. As argued before, capitalism is only actualized through law and policy. That is, it is constructed by specific actors for specific purposes. For example, the placing of certain decisions beyond immediate democratic control—in the planning bodies of the European Union, with those who implement NAFTA, in the unelected World Trade Organization—is purposeful, to avoid democratic "interference" with economic decisions. It is also a kind of self-binding, to place the decisions beyond the weakness of will that those who are democratically accountable might experience in the future. They can then plausibly claim that their hands are tied because they arranged to have them tied beforehand, consciously limiting their options in the future. This is not evolution, this is "intelligent design."

Habermas also underestimates the political construction of global capitalism by ignoring the hegemony of the United States. The truth is that the sovereignty of all nations is not equally compromised, not all states are equally constrained. (Relevant to the above discussion, this also grounds the rejection by the United States of an International Criminal Court.) This may greatly complicate political analysis by disrupting symmetries, but no understanding of the global economy is possible without acknowledging this fact. Furthermore, decision makers in the United States are committed to a much more rapacious capitalism than other capitalist nations might be, as argued by John Gray, a former adviser to Margaret Thatcher, in his book *False Dawn*. The United States's control of the IMF, perhaps the key architect of an unrestrained global capitalism, promotes what even billionaire currency speculator George Soros refers to as "market fundamentalism."

We must not overstate the case. No doubt there is an objective dynamic of capitalism that pushes it in some directions rather than others. No doubt there are also unintended consequences that interlock in unanticipated ways. However, Habermas's commitment to the systems approach to the economy does not allow an analysis of the dynamic of capitalism in any detail. Habermas himself sometimes mentions "endogenously produced problems of economic accumulation," but his belief that material production is not "surveyable" suggests that we cannot specify what these problems are.[66] The conceptual array of systems theory of "inputs" and "feedback" simply seems barren for formulating the crucial questions, much less answering them. We need to know if global demand can be sustained with the increasing inequality of distribution, chronic unemployment in all but a few advanced capitalist countries, and declining standards of living everywhere, and to what extent globalized production and finance actually do constrain domestic responses and to what extent this is exaggerated as a political stratagem. In one place Habermas correctly notes the general absence of "economic analysis with a lasting political impact."[67] However on this issue, systems theory, at least at its present stage of development, obscures more than enlightens.

In sum, Habermas's social theory does not sufficiently integrate the fact that capitalism must be anchored in organizational forms and developed through specific policies, that these structures and policies cannot be taken for granted, and that this situation greatly expands the likelihood and avenues of social and political conflict. Like many who ponder globalization, Habermas greatly overplays the "weakness" of nation-states in the present situation. There are many today who glibly speak of the irresistible dynamic of capitalist globalization, as if the structural forms necessary for its expansion will be called into existence simply because they are functional. The promoters of NAFTA, the WTO, and coerced structural adjustment of vulnerable economies in large parts of the world—not to mention corporations that charter themselves in states with relaxed incorporation provisions—are under no such illusions. They are quite aware of the fact that capitalism, to borrow a phrase from Giovanni Arrighi, does not "operate over the heads" but "through the hands of state actors."[68]

Contrary to Habermas, this is also why property, the fundamental organizational form of the economic subsystem, is still a relevant question. As Hayek and many others have noted, "property right" is actually a bundle of rights.[69] This bundle of rights continues to go through various permutations, determined by multiple struggles: over environmental regulations (called in the United States the "takings" question), the intellectual property provisions of GATT, whether living organisms can be patented, and copyright in regard to various kinds of electronic media. Conflict over what is included or excluded from this bundle—and the consequences for the distribution of goods, services, and life chances—is inescapable. This is precisely why property right has been the political focus of traditional socialist theory, a focus that has hardly exhausted its capacity to inform.

This brings us to the second limitation of Habermas's social and political theory. Habermas's analysis of the dynamic of global capitalism heightens the theoretical uncertainty of the concept of social class in his work. Earlier he persistently argued that the welfare state compromise eliminates class conflict from the horizon of the lifeworld. He says in various places that struggles over distribution and the "doctrinal significance" of "forms of ownership" have lost their importance.[70] These alternative ways of understanding society had dissolved in the consumerism and clientelism of advanced capitalist democracy.

However, Habermas still insisted that although the *formation* of class-conscious actors was increasingly unlikely, class *structure* retained its significance for actually promoting the dynamic of contemporary capitalism. There are many passages in *Legitimation Crisis* that refer to "latent classes," "latently continuing class struggle," or "class contradictions yielding class-unspecific effects," and in *The Theory of Communicative Action* of "containment of class conflict," "pathological side effects of a class structure," "dynamics of class opposition," "pacifying the class conflict," and "social burdens resulting from class conflict."[71] At the time, Habermas's position appeared to be that overt class conflict could be indefinitely ameliorated by welfare state policies, thereby making colonization effects the major site of social conflict. However, this would only be true if "the social security system continues to hold good."[72] Now that the welfare state is in serious retreat and there is little hope, at least on the national level, that the trend can be reversed, one would expect that class would resurface as an important theoretical concern. Thus far it has not, and it is hard to see how it can unless the capitalist economy is conceived as much more than a media-steered subsystem.

On occasion Habermas criticizes other social theorists for neglecting the concept of class. For example, he specifically faults the systems theory of Niklas Luhmann in which "the class-specific distributive effects of the media's being anchored in property laws and constitutional norms do not come into view at all." He criticizes Talcott Parsons on the same grounds, that Parsons's focus on the "integrative subsystem" privileges moral and legal development, "whereas the dynamics of the material reproduction of the lifeworld recede into the background, and with them the conflicts that arise from class structures and the political order."[73] Unfortunately, at this point one could say the same about Habermas's own theory.

In the context of global politics this theoretical weakness manifests itself as an inability to specify the economic relationship between the developed and developing countries. Given Habermas's understanding that the generation of a surplus comes from developing science and technology, it is unsurprising that he typically denies that the growing inequality between North and South is a consequence of "exploitation." "These asymmetrical relationships can no longer (or at least not primarily) be characterized as relations of exploitation, since neither side can survive without the resources of the other."[74] Instead he argues that the inequalities grow because, first, "real markets" tend to reproduce preexisting "relative advantages," and second, citing Weber, that the lack of certain cultural prerequisites may have hampered the development of capitalism in other parts of the world, presumably reducing the competitive efficiency of their production.[75]

Several puzzles immediately present themselves here. The fact of mutual need hardly rules out an exploitative relationship. It is precisely because two sides need something from each other that exploitation, rather than mutual indifference, can emerge. Much depends on the options available to the two sides; those with more options can more effectively influence the terms of the exchange, exploiting the other's weakness. The puzzle is deepened by the fact that at least in one place Habermas suggests that the simultaneous growth of wealth and poverty is no accident. "I speak of a 'world society' because communication systems and markets have created a global network; at the same time, one must speak of a 'stratified' world society because the mechanism of the world market couples increasing productivity with growing impoverishment and, more generally, processes of economic development with processes of underdevelopment."[76] If the simultaneity of these processes is due to the fact that some areas develop technology and efficient markets more rapidly than others, one still need not interpret growing inequality as evidence of exploitation. Inequality could merely come from the differential returns of more and less productive capital. However, in that case the implied causal relation mentioned above, and how exactly this should be conceived as an *economically* unified world society, become entirely unclear.

To sort these questions out one would have to begin by acknowledging the way in which capitalism has been a *historical* construction in which certain regions of the world became economically subordinate, the effects of which continue today. His discussion of autonomous markets and disadvantaged developing countries, even the term "developing countries," suggests that capitalism is a kind of machine, originally invented domestically, that can at least in principle be adapted to a variety of conditions. But capitalism is no machine; it is a historic system that developed in a certain way with lasting effects, constraining the actions of some nations and privileging others. Once going, there no doubt was a "logic of development," to employ Habermas's phrase, strengths in specific departments of certain nations feeding strength in other departments in a positive feedback loop. All is not contingency, after all. However, a historical view of capitalism would, among other things, reveal how the uneven development of capitalism promoted and continues to promote specific class structures and political institutions in various countries. Whatever "imperatives" emerge from the global economy are then necessarily refracted through these local structures and institutions, another crucial way in which capitalism is an embodied rather than abstract dynamic. We cannot begin to understand this dynamic unless the concept of social class is restored to social and political theory.

Formulating the contemporary relevance of class is also crucial because any global public sphere will face tremendous forces of fragmentation, some of which at least can be traced to class conflict. This is not only true of the class interests behind present trade agreements but also possible conflicts within, broadly speaking, the global working classes. Workers in the dominant capitalist nations have an interest in maintaining the low cost of coffee and oil or obtaining inexpensive clothing from sweatshops far from sight. Workers in developing countries have an interest in the jobs fleeing the former nations, even if the jobs are low paying. These conflicts of interest must be negotiated but first they have to be identified.

Finally, we need class analysis to clarify the extent to which the ideological conflicts of the world are intensified by the economic dynamic. There were few means of support in Afghanistan except as soldiers for the Taliban or as students in the *madrassahs*. Any hope for the creation of a global public sphere must identify how economic forces, again refracted through local social structures, obstruct the rationalization of the lifeworld in *other* parts of the world. If Habermas's comment regarding the "shackles of class" is to become more than an aside or an idle wish, it must be placed at the center of social theory.

Habermas once noted that to many the argument for a vigorous public sphere probably has "the ring of an empty formula."[77] This would be even more likely on the global level. Even if binding international agreements are negotiated they will only include those who "count," those considered a part of the relevant community, and social Darwinism on a global scale writes off entire continents, for example Africa. A social and political theory that speaks to the contemporary world must reveal possibilities for resistance that will improve the chances that everyone will count. This is extraordinarily pressing because we now know well that for the "marginalized," for those left out, social pathology is not the only possible outcome. Fanatical obscurantism, piloting airplanes, can also be an outcome.

In brief, as several critics of Habermas have noted over the years, we need more Marx. James Marsh states that, "Habermasian critical theory, we could say, to too great an extent, is a critical theory without Marx and is thus a critical theory that is insufficiently critical."[78] In important respects Habermas's theory follows the same contours as that of Marx: Social conflict ultimately originates in material reproduction, media batter down all "Chinese Walls," and it is through cultural contexts that people become aware of dysfunctions of material reproduction. However, unlike Habermas's theory, Marx's emphasis on class relations expressed through property forms focuses our attention on the social structures that embody capitalism and, arguably, govern its historical trajectory. Any political project that seeks to influence that trajectory so as to actually bring the benefits of market arrangements to the global majority, as Habermas's evidently does, must analyze how these class relations steer the fruits of the vaunted efficiencies of capitalism into the pockets of the few.

Once formulated, such analyses will inform the politics of the twenty-first century only if a public sphere on the national and international level is constructed and sustained. But the authenticity and effectiveness of the public sphere requires that we recognize that reason without revolution is not possible. Today many progressives shrink from the socialist heritage, fearing disaster. But existing practices are already a disaster in large parts of the world. We are not in a position to either act or refrain from acting: We *always* act. The question is in which direction. Unfortunately, notwithstanding the powerful illumination of important topics, central premises of Habermas's theory constrain our ability to think through an answer.

NOTES

PREFACE

1. "Concluding Remarks," in *Habermas and the Public Sphere*, edited by Craig Calhoun (Cambridge, MA: MIT Press, 1992), p. 464.
2. Ibid., p. 469.
3. "Reason without Revolution? Habermas's *Theorie des kommunikativen Handelns*," in *Habermas and Modernity*, edited by Richard J. Bernstein (Cambridge, MA: MIT Press, 1985), pp. 95–121.

CHAPTER 1   WEBER AND MODERNITY

1. "The Social Psychology of the World Religions," in *From Max Weber: Essays in Interpretive Sociology*, edited by H. H. Gerth and C. Wright Mills (New York: Oxford University Press, 1958), pp. 293–294.
2. Ibid., p. 280.
3. "Religious Rejections of the World and Their Directions," in *From Max Weber*, p. 324. By "teleological consistency" Weber seems to be indicating the adequacy of ideas in furthering the stated end. The root of the word is the Greek word *telos*, meaning "end."
4. "The Social Psychology of the World Religions," p. 281, pp. 284–287.
5. Ibid., p. 284. See also Reinhard Bendix, *Max Weber: An Intellectual Portrait* (New York: Doubleday/Anchor Books, 1962), pp. 63–64.
6. Max Weber, *The Protestant Ethic and the Spirit of Capitalism* (New York: Charles Scribner's Sons, 1976), p. 98; *Economy and Society: An Outline of Interpretive Sociology*, volume I (Berkeley: University of California Press, 1978), pp. 6–7; "The Social Psychology of the World Religions," pp. 292, 300; "Religious Rejections of the World and Their Directions," p. 323; Bendix, op. cit., p. 274.
7. *The Protestant Ethic*, p. 26. On Roman religion see *Economy and Society*, volume I, pp. 408–409.
8. "Politics as a Vocation," in *From Max Weber*, p. 123; "The Social Psychology of the World Religions," p. 281.
9. "Politics as a Vocation," p. 122.
10. "The Social Psychology of the World Religions," pp. 271–272.

11. *Economy and Society*, volume I, p. 426, pp. 429–432; Bendix, pp. 88–89.
12. "The Social Psychology of the World Religions," pp. 279–280; "Religious Rejections of the World and Their Directions," p. 351.
13. "Religious Rejections of the World and Their Directions," p. 327. See also "The Social Psychology of the World Religions, p. 278.
14. "The Social Psychology of the World Religions," p. 275; *Economy and Society*, volume I, pp. 523–524.
15. "The Social Psychology of the World Religions," pp. 290–292; "Religious Rejections of the World and Their Directions," p. 325.
16. *The Protestant Ethic*, pp. 76–78. With one exception below, we will not challenge Weber's interpretation of Calvinism. Many others have done so and it is not necessary for the purpose of showing its contributions to Habermas's social theory.
17. *The Protestant Ethic*, pp. 103–104, p. 164; *Economy and Society*, volume I, pp. 522–523.
18. *The Protestant Ethic*, pp. 102–103, p. 109.
19. Ibid., pp. 102–104, p. 105.
20. Ibid., p. 155.
21. Ibid., p. 160, p. 159, p. 115. For comments on Martin Luther, ibid., pp. 80–83.
22. Ibid., p. 170. Carnegie's argument appears in his famous 1889 essay "Wealth."
23. *The Protestant Ethic*, p. 117; "The Social Psychology of the World Religions," p. 291.   .
24. "Science as a Vocation," in *From Max Weber*, p. 139; "Religious Rejections of the World and Their Directions," pp. 350–351; H. H. Gerth and C. Wright Mills, "Introduction: The Man and His Work," in *From Max Weber*, p. 51.
25. "The Social Psychology of the World Religions," p. 282, p. 281; "Religious Rejections of the World and Their Directions," p. 351.
26. *The Protestant Ethic*, p. 90. On his definition of capitalism, ibid., pp. 17–24 and p. 185 endnote 2.
27. "The Social Psychology of the World Religions," p. 281.
28. *The Protestant Ethic*, p. 175, pp. 174–177.
29. Ibid., p. 181, pp. 176–177, p. 182.
30. Ibid., p. 182.
31. Alasdair MacIntyre, *A Short History of Ethics* (New York: The Macmillan Company, 1966), p. 86. Weber discusses taboo differently in *Economy and Society*, volume I, pp. 432–437.
32. "Religious Rejections of the World and Their Directions," p. 330; "Politics as a Vocation," p. 123; "Science as a Vocation," p. 148.
33. "Religious Rejections of the World and Their Directions," p. 331, p. 339.
34. *The Protestant Ethic*, p. 104. This is a problematic position. Weber admits that some quasi-Calvinists like the Methodist John Wesley believed in the "universality of Grace" (ibid., p. 125) and that there were many internal

struggles within Protestantism on this issue. Weber's interpretation does not seem to accommodate the fact that early Puritans like John Winthrop and John Cotton stressed the importance of the role of the entire congregation in pursuing salvation. Cotton insisted that one should not be allowed to leave the congregation without permission and that neighbors should help neighbors from straying from the path. As Winthrop put it, "we must be knit in this work as one man." Given the import of this thesis for Habermas's own theory, it should be mentioned that the individualized character of salvation is perhaps stressed too much by Weber.

35. "The Protestant Sects and the Spirit of Capitalism," in *From Max Weber*, p. 322; "Religious Rejections of the World and Their Directions," pp. 332–333. Weber argues in the latter place that "mystics" also escape the inherent tension between brotherliness and economic activity by simply rejecting the latter altogether.

36. "Religious Rejections of the World and Their Directions," pp. 333–335. He points out that in war the state even usurps religion's role in defining the meaningfulness of death, as death in defense of one's country.

37. "Politics as a Vocation," pp. 119–122.

38. Ibid., p. 126. The same dilemma is explored in Jean-Paul Sartre's play "Dirty Hands" and in Albert Camus's play "The Just Assassins."

39. Plato, "The Crito," 48E–50A. For Thucydides, *The Peloponnesian War*, Book Five, "The Melian Dialogue."

40. "Religious Rejections of the World and Their Directions," pp. 339–340; "Politics as a Vocation," p. 121, p. 123, p. 127.

41. "Religious Rejections of the World and Their Directions," p. 342, pp. 341–343.

42. Ibid., pp. 344–347, p. 349.

43. *The Protestant Ethic*, p. 182.

44. "Science as a Vocation," pp. 143–154.

45. Ibid., p. 152.

46. Ibid., p. 151, p. 148.

47. Alasdair MacIntyre, *After Virtue: A Study in Moral Theory* (Second Edition) (Notre Dame, IN: University of Notre Dame Press, 1984), p. 26.

48. "Science as a Vocation," pp. 151–156.

49. *The Theory of Communicative Action, volume 2, Lifeworld and System: A Critique of Functionalist Reason* (Boston: Beacon Press, 1987), p. 301; *A Berlin Republic: Writings on Germany* (Lincoln: University of Nebraska Press, 1997), p. 60.

50. *The Protestant Ethic*, pp. 71–72.

51. *Lifeworld and System*, p. 302.

CHAPTER 2   WEBER AND WESTERN MARXISM

1. *Marxism and Class Theory: A Bourgeois Critique* (New York: Columbia University Press, 1979), p. 25.

2. *The Protestant Ethic and the Spirit of Capitalism* (New York: Charles Scribner's Sons, 1958), p. 183. See also Wolfgang J. Mommsen, "Capitalism and Socialism: Weber's Dialogue with Marx," in *A Weber–Marx Dialogue*, edited by Robert J. Antonio and Ronald M. Glassman (Lawrence: University Press of Kansas, 1985), pp. 234–261. Weber based his oft-quoted definition of the modern state as the monopoly of the legitimate use of force in a specific territory, without the word "legitimate," partly on a remark from Leon Trotsky: "Politics as a Vocation," in *From Max Weber: Essays in Sociology*, edited by H. H. Gerth and C. Wright Mills (New York: Oxford University Press, 1958), p. 78.

3. Cohen, G. A., *Karl Marx's Theory of History: A Defense* (Princeton, NJ: Princeton University Press, 1978), pp. 34–35, p. 32.

4. See Douglas Kellner, "Critical Theory, Max Weber, and the Dialectics of Domination," in Antonio and Glassman, op. cit., p. 90.

5. *History and Class Consciousness: Studies in Marxist Dialectics* (Cambridge, MA: MIT Press, 1971), p. 87.

6. Ibid., p. 100.

7. Ibid., pp. 165–166.

8. Ibid., p. 164.

9. Ibid., p. 169.

10. Ibid., p. 172.

11. Ibid., p. 330.

12. *The Philosophical Discourse of Modernity* (Cambridge, MA: MIT Press, 1990), p. 116.

13. Max Horkheimer and Theodor Adorno, *Dialectic of Enlightenment* (New York: The Continuum Publishing Company, 1989), p. xi.

14. See Mommsen, op. cit., pp. 242–243.

15. Max Horkheimer, *Eclipse of Reason* (New York: Seabury Press, 1974), p. 40. Contemporaneous with *Dialectic of Enlightenment*, *Eclipse of Reason* is generally regarded as a more accessible treatment of the principal arguments of *Dialectic of Enlightenment*. In *Eclipse of Reason*, p. vii, Horkheimer writes of his collaboration with Adorno: "It would be difficult to say which of the ideas originated in his mind and which in my own; our philosophy is one." Taking him at his word, I will more or less attribute arguments in either work to Horkheimer and Adorno together. However, it needs to be noted that in at least one place Habermas disputes the intellectual identification of Horkheimer and Adorno, even in writing the *Dialectic of Enlightenment*. See "Notes on the Developmental History of Horkheimer's Work," *Theory, Culture, and Society*, volume 10 (1993), pp. 61–77, especially p. 64.

16. *Eclipse of Reason*, p. 176; *Dialectic of Enlightenment*, p. 90.

17. *Eclipse of Reason*, p. 4.

18. *Eclipse of Reason*, chapter 1; *Dialectic of Enlightenment*, pp. 4–6.

19. *Dialectic of Enlightenment*, p. 83.

20. *Eclipse of Reason*, p. 110.

21. Ibid., pp. 95–96.
22. *Dialectic of Enlightenment*, p. 28.
23. Ibid., p. 38, p. 91.
24. Ibid., p. 54.
25. *Eclipse of Reason*, p. 93; Friedrich Nietzsche, *The Will to Power* (New York: Vintage Books, 1968), p. 3.
26. *Dialectic of Enlightenment*, p. 118. Also, subjective reason is not "more closely allied to morality than to immorality."
27. *Eclipse of Reason*, p. 31.
28. Ibid., p. 109.
29. Ibid., pp. 114–116, pp. 121–122.
30. Ibid., p. 175, p. 6.
31. *Natural Right and History* (Chicago: The University of Chicago Press, 1953), pp. 4–5.
32. Ibid., p. 4, pp. 7–8. Horkheimer and Adorno referred to "the enthronement of the means as an end, which under late capitalism is tantamount to open insanity...": *Dialectic of Enlightenment*, p. 54.
33. *Eclipse of Reason*, p. 62.
34. *Dialectic of Enlightenment*, p. xvi, p. xii, p. xiv, p. 15. Horkheimer speaks of a kind of "disease affecting reason": *Eclipse of Reason*, p. 176.
35. *The Theory of Communicative Action, volume 1: Reason and the Rationalization of Society* (Boston: Beacon Press, 1984), pp. 389–390.
36. Ibid., pp. 382–385; *The Postnational Constellation: Political Essays* (Cambridge, MA: MIT Press, 2001), p. 141.
37. *Eclipse of Reason*, p. 180.
38. Ibid., p. vi.
39. *Reason and the Rationalization of Society*, p. 384.
40. *Dialectic of Enlightenment*, p. 41.
41. *Eclipse of Reason*, p. 153.
42. "Psychic Thermidor and the Rebirth of Rebellious Subjectivity," in *Habermas and Modernity*, edited by Richard Bernstein (Cambridge, MA: MIT Press, 1985), p. 67.
43. *An Essay on Liberation* (Boston: Beacon Press, 1969), p. 11.
44. Ibid., pp. 10–11.
45. Ibid., p. 11.
46. Ibid., p. 6.
47. *Eros and Civilization: A Philosophical Inquiry into Freud* (New York: Vintage Books, 1962), p. 7.
48. Ibid., p. 24.
49. Ibid., p. 28.
50. *An Essay on Liberation*, p. 5.
51. *Eros and Civilization*, p. 40.
52. Ibid., pp. 23–24.
53. *Counterrevolution and Revolt* (Boston: Beacon Press, 1972), p. 17.
54. Ibid., p. 16.

55. *An Essay on Liberation*, p. 56.
56. Ibid., p. 14.
57. *The Postnational Constellation*, pp. 157–162.
58. Quoted in Martin Jay, *The Dialectical Imagination: A History of the Frankfurt School and the Institute of Social Research 1923–1950* (Boston: Little, Brown and Company, 1973), p. 296.
59. "Psychic Thermidor and the Rebirth of Rebellious Subjectivity," *Toward a Rational Society: Student Protest, Science, and Politics* (Boston: Beacon Press, 1970), p. 88.
60. *Toward a Rational Society*, p. 101.
61. Ibid., p. 104.
62. Ibid., p. 104.
63. Ibid., p. 113.
64. This interpretation is contestable. It is true that in the *Grundrisse: Foundations of the Critique of Political Economy* (New York: Vintage Books, 1973), especially pp. 700–701 and pp. 704–706, and in *Capital: A Critique of Political Economy*, volume 1 (New York: Vintage Books, 1977), p. 754, Marx says that science is a source of wealth, a productive force. In the service of capital it reduces the "value of labor" by increasing productivity. Whether it is therefore an independent source of "value," a technical term in Marxian economics, is unclear but the distinction is definitely blurred by Habermas. Marx does say that as technologically useful science advances it will become increasingly absurd to constrain the productive forces by the calculations of commodities embodying labor. Marcuse's interpretation is more careful: *Five Lectures: Psychoanalysis, Politics, and Utopia* (Boston: Beacon Press, 1970), p. 66.
65. *Toward a Rational Society*, p. 109.
66. Ibid., p. 110.
67. Ibid., pp. 103–104, p. 107.
68. Ibid., pp. 121–122. The thesis of the decay of the achievement principle was pursued contemporaneously by an associate of Habermas, Claus Offe, in *Industry and Inequality: The Achievement Principle in Work and Social Status* (New York: St. Martin's Press, 1977).
69. *Toward a Rational Society*, pp. 118–119.
70. *Reason and the Rationalization of Society*, p. xxxix.
71. *The Philosophical Discourse of Modernity*, p. 119.
72. His sentiment runs deep on this point. Regarding Horkheimer and Adorno's above comment about "murder," Habermas recently stated, "I have to admit that this remark irritates me now no less than it did almost four decades ago when I first read it." *Justification and Application: Remarks on Discourse Ethics* (Cambridge, MA: MIT Press, 1993), p. 134.
73. *The Philosophical Discourse of Modernity*, pp. 125–127.
74. Ibid., p. 119.
75. Ibid., pp. 128–129.
76. *The Philosophical Discourse of Modernity*, p. 111.

CHAPTER 3   RATIONALITY AND COMMUNICATIVE ACTION

1. *The Philosophical Discourse of Modernity: Twelve Lectures* (Cambridge, MA: MIT Press, 1990), pp. 297–298.
2. *The Theory of Communicative Action, volume 2, Lifeworld and System: A Critique of Functional Reason* (Boston: Beacon Press, 1987), p. 160; *The Theory of Communicative Action, volume 1, Reason and The Rationalization of Society* (Boston: Beacon Press, 1984), p. 10.
3. *Reason and The Rationalization of Society*, p. 12.
4. Ibid., pp. 170–174.
5. Ibid., p. 11.
6. Ibid., p. 12.
7. Ibid., p. 10.
8. *Postmetaphysical Thinking: Philosophical Essays* (Cambridge, MA: MIT Press, 1992), p. 77.
9. *Reason and the Rationalization of Society*, p. 15.
10. Ibid., p. 20.
11. Ibid., p. 17.
12. Ibid., p. 20.
13. "Remarks on the Concept of Communicative Action," in *Social Action*, edited by Gottfried Seebass and Raimo Tuomela (Boston: D. Reidel Publishing Company, 1985), p. 161; *The Philosophical Discourse of Modernity*, p. 313.
14. *The Philosophical Discourse of Modernity*, p. 313.
15. "Remarks on the Concept of Communicative Action," p. 162.
16. Ibid., pp. 162–163; *The Philosophical Discourse of Modernity*, p. 313.
17. *Postmetaphysical Thinking*, p. 75.
18. Ibid., p. 76; "Remarks on the Concept of Communicative Action," p. 162.
19. *Reason and the Rationalization of Society*, p. 306; Allen Wood, "Habermas's Defense of Rationalism," *New German Critique* number 35 (Spring/Summer 1985), p. 152; "A Reply," in *Communicative Action: Essays on Jürgen Habermas's The Theory of Communicative Action*, edited by Axel Honneth and Hans Joas (Cambridge, MA: MIT Press, 1991), p. 223. Although Habermas uses the phrases "insincere" and "untruthful," in order to avoid confusion I will only use the former.
20. *The Philosophical Discourse of Modernity*, p. 314, p. 315.
21. Ibid., p. 113.
22. *Reason and the Rationalization of Society*, p. 58. Winch cites Wittgenstein in "Understanding a Primitive Society," in *Rationality*, edited by Bryan R. Wilson (New York: Harper and Row, 1970), p. 90.
23. "A Reply," p. 227, pp. 221–222.
24. Winch, op. cit., p. 106; *Reason and the Rationalization of Society*, p. 59.
25. *Reason and the Rationalization of Society*, p. 45, p. 48, p. 50. See comments by the contributors to Wilson, op. cit., especially MacIntyre.

26. Op. cit., pp. x–xi. Habermas recounts MacIntyre's critique of Winch on the preconditions of learning.

27. "Rationality," in *Rationality and Relativism*, edited by Martin Hollis and Steve Lukes (Cambridge, MA: MIT Press, 1982), pp. 87–105. Taylor's argument seems to be that, leaving aside where their goals are similar, different cultures should be regarded as different research programs that can be evaluated on how well each accomplishes its internal goals.

28. *Reason and the Rationalization of Society*, pp. 68–69.

29. *Moral Consciousness and Communicative Action* (Cambridge, MA: MIT Press, 1990), p. 34.

30. *Whose Justice? Which Rationality?* (Notre Dame, IN: University of Notre Dame Press, 1988), pp. 79–80.

31. *Moral Consciousness and Communicative Action*, p. 33.

32. "Remarks on the Concept of Communicative Action," pp. 152–153.

33. *Between Facts and Norms: Contributions to a Discourse Theory of Law and Democracy* (Cambridge, MA: MIT Press, 1996), p. 27.

34. "A Reply," pp. 240–242.

35. *Reason and the Rationalization of Society*, p. 289.

36. "Remarks on the Concept of Communicative Action," p. 153.

37. *Postmetaphysical Thinking*, pp. 80–81.

38. Ibid., p. 82, p. 84.

39. "Remarks on the Concept of Communicative Action," p. 153. *Between Facts and Norms*, p. 18.

40. *Moral Consciousness and Communicative Action*, p. 30.

41. This concept of idealizations replaces the phrase "ideal speech situation" that Habermas previously employed because the latter suggests that it is possible to free discourse from interested positions and strategic behavior. The phrase also suggests an external yardstick by which we would measure existing practices. It sets up an ideal *separate* from existing practices. Idealizations, contrary to the previous phrase, are necessary to existing practices, therefore grounding an immanent critique (criticism that draws on the principles organizing social practice) rather than merely setting up an idle yardstick for measuring distortions that will never be overcome. For this reason Habermas now refers to the "ideal speech situation" as an unfortunate phrase. See Peter Dews, editor, *Autonomy and Solidarity: Interviews with Jürgen Habermas* (London: Verso, 1992), p. 260.

42. *Between Facts and Norms*, p. 19, pp. 18–20. Thomas McCarthy, "Philosophy and Social Practice: Avoiding the Ethnocentric Predicament," in *Philosophical Interventions in the Unfinished Project of Enlightenment*, edited by Axel Honneth, Thomas McCarthy, Claus Offe, and Albrecht Wellmer (Cambridge, MA: MIT Press, 1992), pp. 246–247, pp. 258–259.

43. *Between Facts and Norms*, p. 20.

44. McCarthy, "Philosophy and Social Practice," p. 251.

45. *Between Facts and Norms*, p. 20; "A Reply," p. 243.

46. *Postmetaphysical Thinking*, pp. 137–139.
47. Ibid., p. 103; *Between Facts and Norms*, pp. 14–15.
48. *Between Facts and Norms*, p. 14; *Postmetaphysical Thinking*, p. 104.
49. *Communication and the Evolution of Society* (Boston: Beacon Press, 1979), p. 105.
50. *Reason and the Rationalization of Society*, p. 159.
51. Ibid., pp. 177–178.
52. Ibid., pp. 162–163.
53. Ibid., p. 191.
54. Ibid., pp. 199–200.
55. Ibid., p. 223.
56. *Communication and the Evolution of Society*, p. 120.
57. *Reason and the Rationalization of Society*, p. 218.
58. Ibid., p. 241.

CHAPTER 4   SOCIETY AS LIFEWORLD AND SYSTEM

1. Dallmayr, "Life-World: Variations on a Theme," in *Lifeworld and Politics: Between Modernity and Postmodernity*, edited by Steven K. White (Notre Dame, IN: University of Notre Dame Press, 1989), pp. 25–65.
2. "Reply to Symposium Participants," in *Habermas on Law and Democracy: Critical Exchanges*, edited by Michel Rosenfeld and Andrew Arato (Berkeley: University of California Press, 1998), p. 423.
3. *Between Facts and Norms: Contributions to a Discourse Theory of Law and Democracy* (Cambridge, MA: MIT Press, 1996), p. 295.
4. *The Theory of Communicative Action, volume 1, Reason and The Rationalization of Society* (Boston: Beacon Press, 1984), pp. 285–286.
5. Ibid., pp. 336–337; *The Theory of Communicative Action, volume 2, Lifeworld and System: A Critique of Functionalist Reason* (Boston: Beacon Press, 1987), pp. 132–133.
6. *Lifeworld and System*, p. 132.
7. Ibid., pp. 122–123.
8. Ibid., pp. 136–137.
9. Ibid., pp. 131.
10. "Toward a Critique of the Theory of Meaning," in *Postmetaphysical Thinking: Philosophical Essays* (Cambridge, MA: MIT Press, 1992), pp. 57–87.
11. "Individuation through Socialization: On George Herbert Mead's Theory of Subjectivity," in *Postmetaphysical Thinking*, pp. 149–204.
12. *Lifeworld and System*, pp. 137–138.
13. *Between Facts and Norms*, p. 462; "Reply to Symposium Participants," p. 385.
14. *Between Facts and Norms*, p. 80.
15. *The Philosophical Discourse of Modernity: Twelve Lectures* (Cambridge, MA: MIT Press, 1990), p. 343.

16. *Lifeworld and System*, pp. 140–141.
17. Ibid., p. 141.
18. *Between Facts and Norms*, p. 25.
19. *Postmetaphysical Thinking*, p. 195.
20. *Lifeworld and System*, pp. 146–147.
21. Ibid., p. 135.
22. Ibid., p. 145.
23. Ibid., p. 89.
24. *Between Facts and Norms*, p. 22. In another place Habermas refers to "*massive* preunderstanding": "A Reply," in *Communicative Action: Essays on Jürgen Habermas's The Theory of Communicative Action*, edited by Axel Honneth and Hans Joas (Cambridge, MA: MIT Press, 1991), p. 244.
25. *Reason and the Rationalization of Society*, pp. 69–70.
26. *Lifeworld and System*, pp. 152–154.
27. Ibid., pp. 137–138.
28. "A Reply," p. 252.
29. *A Contribution to the Critique of Political Economy* (New York: International Publishers, 1970), pp. 30–31.
30. *Capital*, volume one (New York: Vintage Books, 1977), p. 135.
31. Georg Lukács, *History and Class Consciousness* (Cambridge, MA: MIT Press, 1971), pp. 83–222; I. I. Rubin, *Essays on Marx's Theory of Value* (Detroit: Black and Red, 1972), pp. 131–158; Moishe Postone, *Time, Labor, and Social Domination: A Reinterpretation of Marx's Critical Theory* (Cambridge: Cambridge University Press, 1993), p. 152.
32. *Legitimation Crisis* (Boston: Beacon Press, 1975), pp. 52–53; *Lifeworld and System*, pp. 338–343.
33. *Between Facts and Norms*, p. 39; Peter Dews, editor, *Autonomy and Solidarity: Interviews with Jürgen Habermas* (London: Verso Books, 1992), p. 262.
34. *Lifeworld and System*, pp. 339–340.
35. Ibid., p. 183.
36. F. A. Hayek, *The Fatal Conceit: The Errors of Socialism* (Chicago: The University of Chicago Press, 1988), pp. 86–88; Alec Nove, *The Economics of Feasible Socialism* (London: George Allen and Unwin, 1983), pp. 100–102. See also Robin Blackburn, "Fin de Siecle: Socialism After the Crash," in *After the Fall: The Failure of Communism and the Future of Socialism*, edited by Robin Blackburn (London: Verso Books, 1991), pp. 173–249.
37. *Lifeworld and System*, pp. 264–265.
38. *Between Facts and Norms*, pp. 117–118.
39. *Lifeworld and System*, p. 321.
40. Ibid., p. 322.
41. Ibid., p. 292.
42. Ibid., p. 347.
43. Ibid., p. 350.

44. Ibid., p. 232.
45. Ibid., pp. 171–172. But see where he doubts the phrase: "A Reply," p. 257.
46. *At Home in the Universe: The Search for Laws of Self-Organization and Complexity* (New York: Oxford University Press, 1995), pp. 49–50, p. 71.
47. Oxford: Blackwell Publishers, 1996. However Krugman criticizes those who assume that self-organization is necessarily a *good* thing: pp. 5–6. For a general discussion see M. Michell Waldrop, *Complexity: The Emerging Science on the Edge of Order and Chaos* (New York: Simon and Schuster, 1992).
48. *Lifeworld and System*, p. 348.
49. Ibid., pp. 348–350.
50. *The Past as Future* (Lincoln: University of Nebraska Press, 1994), p. 158; "What Does Socialism Mean Today? The Rectifying Revolution and the Need for New Thinking on the Left," *New Left Review*, number 183 (September/October 1990), p. 17.

CHAPTER 5   SOCIAL CONFLICT AND PROGRESSIVE POLITICS

1. *The Theory of Communicative Action, volume 2, Lifeworld and System: A Critique of Functionalist Reason* (Boston: Beacon Press, 1987), p. 322. Although Habermas's primary interest is contemporary capitalism, the overextension of power in state socialist societies is also a case in point: *The Past as Future* (Lincoln: University of Nebraska Press, 1994), pp. 88–89.
2. *Between Facts and Norms: Contributions to a Discourse Theory of Law and Democracy* (Cambridge, MA: MIT Press, 1996), p. 407, p. 416, p. 78.
3. "Reply to Symposium Participants," in *Habermas on Law and Democracy: Critical Exchanges*, edited by Michel Rosenfeld and Andrew Arato (Berkeley: University of California Press, 1998), p. 439.
4. *Between Facts and Norms*, p. 480.
5. "A Reply," in *Communicative Action: Essays on Jürgen Habermas's The Theory of Communicative Action* (Cambridge, MA: The MIT Press, 1991), pp. 255–256.
6. *Lifeworld and System*, p. 184.
7. Ibid., p. 351.
8. Ibid., p. 355.
9. Ibid., pp. 367–368.
10. Ibid., p. 395.
11. Ibid., p. 393.
12. Habermas, ibid., pp. 392–393; Offe, "New Social Movements: Challenging the Boundaries of Institutional Politics," *Social Research*, volume 52, number 4 (Winter 1985), pp. 830–831.
13. "A Reply," p. 225.
14. *Lifeworld and System*, pp. 385–386.

15. Ibid., p. 292.
16. Respectively: *Between Facts and Norms*, p. 350; *The Inclusion of the Other: Studies in Political Theory* (Cambridge, MA: MIT Press, 1998), p. 127, and *Between Facts and Norms*, p. xlii; *The Inclusion of the Other*, p. 123; *Between Facts and Norms*, p. 445; and ibid., p. xlii.
17. *The Inclusion of the Other*, p. 123.
18. *Lifeworld and System*, pp. 385–386.
19. *Between Facts and Norms*, p. 445.
20. *Eclipse of Reason* (New York: The Seabury Press, 1974), p. 34.
21. "Reply to Symposium Participants," p. 441.
22. *Between Facts and Norms*, p. 56, p. 354.
23. Ibid., p. 37.
24. Ibid., p. 40.
25. Ibid., p. 372. But see Habermas, "The European Nation-State and the Pressures of Globalization," *New Left Review*, number 235 (May/June 1999), p. 47.
26. *Between Facts and Norms*, p. 302.
27. Ibid., p. 372.
28. Ibid., p. 326, p. 80.
29. Ibid., p. 28.
30. Ibid., pp. 32–33.
31. Ibid., p. 462.
32. Ibid., p. 453.
33. Ibid., p. 107.
34. Ibid., p. 103.
35. Ibid., p. 108.
36. Ibid., p. 282. See also *Legitimation Crisis* (Boston: Beacon Press, 1975), p. 112.
37. *Between Facts and Norms*, pp. 166–167.
38. John Dryzek, *Discursive Democracy: Politics, Policy, and Political Science* (New York: Cambridge University Press, 1990); Jeffrey C. Isaac, *Democracy in Dark Times* (Ithaca, NY: Cornell University Press, 1998); James C. Scott, *Seeing Like a State: How Certain Schemes to Improve the Human Condition Have Failed* (New Haven, CT: Yale University Press, 1998).
39. "The New Obscurity," pp. 8–9. As Habermas argues regarding the former East Germany: *The Past as Future*, pp. 88–89.
40. Jean Cohen and Andrew Arato, *Civil Society and Political Theory* (Cambridge, MA: MIT Press, 1992), pp. 451–454.
41. "A Reply to My Critics," in *Habermas: Critical Debates*, edited by John B. Thompson and David Held (Cambridge, MA: MIT Press), p. 223; "Concluding Remarks," in *Habermas and the Public Sphere*, edited by Craig Calhoun (Cambridge, MA: MIT Press, 1992), p. 469; *Between Facts and Norms*, p. 57, p. 372.
42. *Between Facts and Norms*, p. 467.
43. Ibid., p. xli, p. 478.

44. Cambridge, MA: MIT Press, 1989. Originally published in 1962.
45. *Between Facts and Norms*, pp. 360–361.
46. Ibid., pp. 298–299.
47. Ibid., pp. 287–288.
48. Ibid., p. 287.
49. "Reply," p. 386.
50. *Between Facts and Norms*, pp. 300–301.
51. Ibid., p. 288.
52. Ibid., p. 299.
53. Cited in Hannah Arendt, *Between Past and Future: Eight Exercises in Political Thought* (New York: Penguin Books, 1968), p. 123.
54. *Lifeworld and System*, pp. 183–184, pp. 275–277; Talcott Parsons, *Sociological Theory and Modern Society* (New York: The Free Press, 1967), chapters 10 and 11.
55. *Between Facts and Norms*, p. 359.
56. Ibid., p. 372.
57. Ibid., p. 175.
58. Ibid., p. 308.
59. Ibid., p. 341.
60. Ibid., p. 364.
61. Ibid., p. 400, p. 404, p. 417.
62. Ibid., p. 352.
63. Ibid., p. 418. Hannah Arendt, *On Revolution* (New York: Penguin Books, 1977).
64. *Between Facts and Norms*, p. 440.
65. Ibid., p. 375.
66. "Further Reflections on the Public Sphere," in Calhoun, op. cit., p. 453.
67. *Between Facts and Norms*, p. 151.
68. Ibid., p. 95, pp. 98–99.
69. Ibid., pp. 445–446.
70. Ibid., p. 552, endnote 56. In other places Habermas reminds us of the reluctance of Marx and others to, as Lenin put it, "write recipes for the cookshops of the future." See *Autonomy and Solidarity: Interviews with Jürgen Habermas*, edited by Peter Dews (London: Verso, 1992), p. 145 and p. 207.
71. Dews, op. cit., p. 207.

CHAPTER 6   CONTESTED TERRAIN: LANGUAGE,
ART, AND GENDER

1. "A Reply," in *Communicative Action: Essays on Jürgen Habermas's The Theory of Communicative Action* (Cambridge, MA: MIT Press, 1991), p. 214. See also *The Theory of Communicative Action, volume 2, Lifeworld and System: A Critique of Functionalist Reason* (Boston: Beacon Press, 1987), p. 397. For example, Allen Wood concludes that Habermas does not really *argue* for the logical priority of reaching

understanding via validity claims, he more appears to assume its truth. For this reason, Wood states that the discussion often appears "simply question-begging." "Habermas's Defense of Rationalism," *New German Critique*, number 35 (Spring/Summer 1985), p. 161.

2. *The Postmodern Condition: A Report on Knowledge* (Minneapolis: University of Minnesota Press, 1984).

3. Ibid., p. 36, p. 40.

4. Ibid., p. xxiv.

5. Ibid., p. 60.

6. *The Postnational Constellation: Political Essays* (Cambridge, MA: MIT Press, 2001), p. 150.

7. *The Postmodern Condition*, p. 59.

8. Ibid., p. 4. It is possible the phrase was intended as a joke.

9. *The Postnational Constellation*, p. 149. It should also be recalled that Weber argues in "Science as a Vocation" that science cannot ground its own presupposition that it is a worthwhile endeavor.

10. *A Berlin Republic: Writings on Germany* (Lincoln: University of Nebraska Press, 1997), p. 59, p. 61; *The New Conservatism: Cultural Criticism and the Historians Debate* (Cambridge, MA: MIT Press, 1989), p. 201.

11. *The Postmodern Condition*, p. 72.

12. Peter Dews, *Autonomy and Solidarity: Interviews with Jürgen Habermas* (New York: Verso, 1992), pp. 21–22. The reference to games raises another possibility: Wittgenstein says that "games" are not indicated by the same word because they have one element in common. Instead, games have a "family resemblance" to each other. Do the modes of argumentation in different value spheres share a common element—raising validity claims—or do they only have a family resemblance to each other? The kind of claims raised in aesthetic evaluation suggests the possibility of the latter, but we must leave this for another occasion.

13. "A Reply," p. 221.

14. *The Postnational Constellation*, p. 151.

15. "A Reply," p. 222.

16. *The Postnational Constellation*, p. 147.

17. Marie Fleming points to a third expression as well, the aesthetic as one of three "complexes of knowledge": *Emancipation and Illusion: Rationality and Gender in Habermas's Theory of Modernity* (University Park: Pennsylvania State University Press, 1997), p. 195, footnote 28. See also Habermas, *Lifeworld and System*, p. 326.

18. "Questions and Counterquestions," in Richard J. Bernstein, *Habermas and Modernity* (Cambridge, MA: MIT Press, 1985), p. 199.

19. *The Theory of Communicative Action, volume 1, Reason and the Rationalization of Society* (Boston: Beacon Press, 1984), p. 240. Quoted by David Ingram, "Habermas on Aesthetics and Rationality: Completing the Project of Enlightenment," *New German Critique* 53 (1991), p. 78.

20. Ingram, op. cit., p. 79.

21. Ibid., pp. 84–85. Ingram argues that these "evaluative claims" will remain "nonuniversal." Habermas's position appears open to alternative interpretations. See *Reason and the Rationalization of Society*, p. 20.
22. "Questions and Counterquestions," p. 200.
23. Ibid., pp. 200–201. See also Habermas, *Moral Consciousness and Communicative Action* (Cambridge, MA: MIT Press, 1990), p. 17.
24. *The Philosophical Discourse of Modernity: Twelve Lectures* (Cambridge, MA: MIT Press, 1990), p. 314.
25. Arthur Danto, *Beyond the Brillo Box: The Visual Arts in Post-Historical Perspective* (New York: Farrar, Straus, Giroux, 1992), p. 4.
26. *The Philosophical Discourse of Modernity*, p. 203; "Questions and Counterquestions," p. 203.
27. "Questions and Counterquestions," p. 203; "A Reply," p. 227. Also see Ingram, op. cit., p. 87.
28. "Questions and Counterquestions," p. 209.
29. Ingram, op. cit., p. 91. Einstein once reportedly remarked that "imagination is more important than knowledge."
30. Danto, op. cit., p. 10. Art as the history of erasures once became literally true in regard to the artists Willem de Kooning and Robert Rauschenberg. De Kooning once gave Rauschenberg a drawing, which Rauschenberg then erased and hung on his wall with the title "Drawing by Willem de Kooning, Erased by Robert Rauschenberg."
31. *The Anxious Object* (Chicago: University of Chicago Press, 1983); *The De-definition of Art* (Chicago: University of Chicago Press, 1972).
32. *The De-Definition of Art*, p. 12.
33. *Moral Consciousness and Communicative Action*, p. 18.
34. "Critical Social Theory and Feminist Critiques: The Debate with Jürgen Habermas," in *Feminists Read Habermas: Gendering the Subject of Discourse*, edited by Johanna Meehan (New York: Routledge, 1995), p. 57.
35. Habermas, *Communication and the Evolution of Society* (Boston: Beacon Press, 1979), pp. 135–136.
36. Fleming, op.cit., pp. 127–129.
37. *Communication and the Evolution of Society*, p. 138.
38. Ricardo Blaug, *Democracy, Real and Ideal: Discourse Ethics and Radical Politics* (Albany: State University of New York Press, 1999), p. 91; cf. pp. 91–92.
39. Seyla Benhabib, "The Generalized and the Concrete Other: The Kohlberg–Gilligan Controversy and Feminist Theory," in *Feminism as Critique: On the Politics of Gender*, edited by Seyla Benhabib and Drucilla Cornell (Minneapolis: University of Minnesota Press, 1987), p. 78.
40. *Moral Consciousness and Communicative Action*, pp. 179–184. Seyla Benhabib, "The Debate Over Women and Moral Theory Revisited," in Meehan, op. cit., p. 186.
41. Benhabib, "The Debate Over Women and Moral Theory Revisited," pp. 190–191.

42. Ibid., pp. 191–192.
43. "The Generalized and Concrete Other," p. 81.
44. "The Debate Over Women and Moral Theory Revisited," p. 189.
45. Ibid., pp. 193–194 and pp. 196–197.
46. Iris Marion Young, "Impartiality and the Civic Public: Some Implications of Feminist Critiques of Moral and Political Theory," in Benhabib and Cornell, op. cit., p. 62.
47. Ibid., p. 61, p. 63.
48. Ibid., p. 63.
49. Ibid., p. 58.
50. Ibid., p. 68.
51. Ibid., p. 69.
52. Ibid., p. 69.
53. See Habermas's comments in "Psychic Thermidor and the Rebirth of Rebellious Subjectivity," in Bernstein, op. cit., p. 77, and in *The Inclusion of the Other: Studies in Political Theory* (Cambridge, MA: MIT Press, 1998), pp. 4–5.
54. Fredric Jameson, "Foreword" to Lyotard, *The Postmodern Condition*, p. xi. He is quoting Mallarmé.
55. Young, op. cit., pp. 70–73.
56. Ibid., pp. 75–76.
57. Benhabib, "The Generalized and the Concrete Other," p. 80.
58. Nancy Fraser, "What's Critical About Critical Theory?" in Meehan, op. cit., pp. 28–29.
59. Ibid., p. 29.
60. Young, op. cit., p. 66.
61. Fraser, op. cit., p. 35. Cohen, op. cit., p. 71.
62. Fraser, op. cit., pp. 40–41, pp. 36–37.
63. Ibid., p. 30.
64. Ibid., p.24.
65. Cohen, op. cit., p. 66 and p. 70. Fraser, op. cit., pp. 35–36.
66. Fraser, op. cit., pp. 45–46.
67. Cohen, op. cit., p. 76, pp. 76–77.
68. Ibid., p. 75.
69. Ibid., p. 72.
70. Fraser, op. cit., p. 42.
71. Cohen, op. cit., pp. 72–73.
72. "A Reply," p. 214; *The Postnational Constellation*, p. 125.
73. Habermas, *Between Facts and Norms: Contributions to a Discourse Theory of Law and Democracy* (Cambridge, MA: MIT Press, 1996), p. 423; "Struggles for Recognition in the Democratic Constitutional State," in *Multiculturalism: Examining the Politics of Recognition*, edited by Amy Gutmann (Princeton, NJ: Princeton University Press, 1994), p. 114.
74. *Between Facts and Norms*, p. 424.
75. *The Inclusion of the Other*, p. 262. See also *A Berlin Republic*, p. 74.

76. "Struggles for Recognition in the Democratic Constitutional State," p. 117.

77. *Between Facts and Norms*, p. 426.

CHAPTER 7   THE LIMITATIONS OF HABERMAS'S SOCIAL AND POLITICAL ARGUMENT

1. Moishe Postone, *Time, Labor, and Social Domination: A Reinterpretation of Marx's Critical Theory* (Cambridge: Cambridge University Press, 1993), p. 253, p. 251.

2. "A Reply," in *Communicative Action: Essays on Jürgen Habermas's The Theory of Communicative Action*, edited by Axel Honneth and Hans Joas (Cambridge, MA: MIT Press, 1991), p. 255.

3. Ibid., p. 257.

4. *The Theory of Communicative Action, volume 2, Lifeworld and System: A Critique of Functionalist Reason* (Boston: Beacon Press, 1987), p. 166.

5. Ibid., p. 266.

6. Ibid., p. 267; *The Theory of Communicative Action, volume 1, Reason and the Rationalization of Society* (Boston: Beacon Press, 1984), p. 342.

7. "A Reply," p. 256.

8. *Lifeworld and System*, p. 154.

9. Ibid., p. 165.

10. Ibid., p. 322.

11. *Reason and the Rationalization of Society*, p. 260.

12. *Between Facts and Norms: Contributions to a Discourse Theory of Law and Democracy* (Cambridge, MA: MIT Press, 1996), p. 360.

13. *Lifeworld and System*, p. 160.

14. Ibid., p. 306. "A Reply," p. 258; *Between Facts and Norms*, p. 481.

15. "A Reply," pp. 257–258.

16. *Lifeworld and System*, p. 117.

17. Ibid., p. 264.

18. Ibid., p. 369; *Between Facts and Norms*, pp. 26–27, p. 83, p. 118.

19. *Lifeworld and System*, p. 182.

20. Ibid., pp. 308–309.

21. Ibid., p. 308. Georg Lukács refers to this as "objectified performance": *History and Class Consciousness: Studies in Marxist Dialectics* (Cambridge, MA: MIT Press, 1971), p. 90.

22. *Lifeworld and System*, p. 306, p. 321.

23. Ibid., p. 335.

24. Ibid., p. 335. Claus Offe, *Contradictions of the Welfare State* (Cambridge, MA: MIT Press, 1984), p. 83, and *Disorganized Capitalism* (Cambridge, MA: MIT Press, 1985), pp. 56–57.

25. Offe, *Industry and Inequality: The Achievement Principle in Work and Social Status* (New York: St. Martin's Press, 1977), pp. 28–29, pp. 36–37, p. 54; Offe, *Disorganized Capitalism*, p. 126, p. 138, pp. 106–107. Cf. John F. Sitton, *Recent Marxian Theory: Class Formation and Social*

Conflict in Contemporary Capitalism (Albany: State University of New York Press, 1996), pp. 144–147; and David L. Harvey and Mike Reed, "The Limits of Synthesis: Some Comments on Habermas's Recent Sociological Writings," *International Journal of Politics, Culture, and Society*, volume 4, number 3 (1991), pp. 357.

26. *The System of Modern Societies* (Englewood Cliffs, NJ: Prentice-Hall, Inc., 1971), p. 105.
27. *Lifeworld and System*, p. 308.
28. Ibid., pp. 310–311. See related comments in *Postmetaphysical Thinking: Philosophical Essays* (Cambridge, MA: MIT Press, 1992), pp. 198–199.
29. *Lifeworld and System*, p. 356, p. 350.
30. Ibid., pp. 321–322.
31. "A Reply," p. 261; *Lifeworld and System*, p. 347; "A Philosophico-Political Profile," *New Left Review*, number 151 (May/June 1985), p. 103.
32. *Lifeworld and System*, p. 395.
33. Ibid., pp. 395–396.
34. *Autonomy and Solidarity: Interviews with Jürgen Habermas*, edited by Peter Dews (London: Verso, 1992), pp. 117–118.
35. For further criticism of Habermas's separation of politics and the economy, see: Thomas McCarthy, "Complexity and Democracy, or the Seducements of Systems Theory," *New German Critique*, number 35 (Spring/Summer 1985), pp. 27–53; Sitton, *Recent Marxian Theory*, chapter 6; William E. Forbath, "Short Circuit: A Critique of Habermas's Understanding of Law, Politics, and Economic Life," in *Habermas on Law and Democracy: Critical Exchanges*, edited by Michel Rosenfeld and Andrew Arato (Berkeley: University of California Press, 1998), pp. 272–286.
36. *Between Facts and Norms*, p. 442.
37. Habermas, *Justification and Application: Remarks on Discourse Ethics* (Cambridge, MA: MIT Press, 1993), p. 170.
38. Habermas, *The Structural Transformation of the Public Sphere: An Inquiry into a Category of Bourgeois Society* (Cambridge, MA: MIT Press, 1989), p. 82.
39. *Between Facts and Norms*, p. 359. In *The Inclusion of the Other: Studies in Social Theory* (Cambridge, MA: MIT Press, 1998), he states it as "the detection, identification, and interpretation of problems affecting society as a whole": p. 251.
40. *Between Facts and Norms*, p. 300.
41. Joshua Cohen, "Reflections on Habermas on Democracy," *Ratio Juris*, volume 12, number 4 (December 1999), pp. 389–390; Forbath, op. cit., p. 277.
42. Cohen, op. cit., p. 412 and p. 414.
43. Ibid., pp. 389–390; also p. 415.
44. *Between Facts and Norms*, p. 343 and p. 301.
45. Ibid., p. 350; also p. 351.

46. *Postmetaphysical Thinking*, p. 141.
47. For a summary of these difficulties, see John Dryzek, *Democracy in Capitalist Times: Ideals, Limits, Struggles* (New York: Oxford University Press, 1996), pp. 96–101.
48. James Bohman, *Public Deliberation: Pluralism, Complexity, and Democracy* (Cambridge, MA: MIT Press, 1996); John Dryzek, *Discursive Democracy: Politics, Policy, and Political Science* (Cambridge: Cambridge University Press, 1990) and *Democracy in Capitalist Times*; Cohen, op. cit.; *The Good Society: A PEGS Journal* (Committee on the Political Economy of the Good Society), volume 7, numbers 2 and 3 (1997), and volume 9, numbers 1 and 2 (1999).
49. *Public Deliberation*, p. 159. The comment occurs in a discussion of "hypercomplexity."
50. "What Does Socialism Mean Today? The Rectifying Revolution and the Need for New Thinking on the Left," *New Left Review*, number 183 (September/October 1990), pp. 16–17. See also "Jürgen Habermas: A Philosophico-Political Profile," *New Left Review*, number 151 (May/June 1985), p. 103.
51. Jean Cohen and Andrew Arato, *Civil Society and Political Theory* (Cambridge, MA: MIT Press, 1992), pp. 479–480.
52. *Between Facts and Norms*, pp. 440–441.
53. Michel Crozier, Samuel P. Huntington, and Joji Watanuki, *The Crisis of Democracy* (New York: New York University Press, 1975), pp. 113–115.
54. *Between Facts and Norms*, pp. 255–256.
55. Ibid., pp. 259–260. "Alleged" because Bernhard Schlink denies that the German court ever had a clear philosophy it was trying to advance: "The Dynamics of Constitutional Adjudication," in Rosenfeld and Arato, op. cit., pp. 374–375.
56. *Between Facts and Norms*, p. 254.
57. Ibid., p. 255.
58. Ibid., pp. 256–257.
59. Ibid., p. 255.
60. Two considerations should be noted here. First, Habermas may be overestimating the systematic character of law. Inescapable centrifugal effects from specific legal decisions and equally inescapable centripetal effects from the need for legal consistency will always make the "systematicity" of the legal system a work in progress. Second, the idea that one cannot be under contradictory obligations, that, following Kant, "ought implies can," is itself contestable. As for example Sartre's plays illustrate, we often find ourselves under contradictory obligations that do not by that fact lose their hold on us. That is where guilt and remorse come in. A tragic view of moral life, as one finds in existentialism and Weber's cultural reflections on politics as a vocation, could unfold this alternative perspective.
61. *Between Facts and Norms*, p. 260 and p. 259. All phrases in quotes are his own.

62. Ibid., p. 261 and p. 256. Further discussion of the distinction between norms and values occurs in Robert Alexy, "Jürgen Habermas's Theory of Legal Discourse," in Rosenfeld and Arato, op. cit., pp. 228–230, and Habermas, "Reply to Symposium Participants," in the same place, pp. 428–431.

63. He says the same about rights: "[A]s legal norms, basic rights are, like moral rules, modelled after obligatory norms of action—and not after attractive goods." *Between Facts and Norms*, p. 256.

64. *The Postnational Constellation: Political Essays* (Cambridge, MA: MIT Press, 2001), pp. 124–125.

65. Charles E. Lindblom, *Politics and Markets: The World's Political-Economic Systems* (New York: Basic Books, 1977), pp. 170–188. See also Dryzek, *Democracy in Capitalist Times*, pp. 25–28 and p. 72.

66. *Democracy in Capitalist Times*, p. 28.

67. John F. Sitton, op. cit., pp. 92–93, in a discussion of Adam Przeworski's analysis.

68. Offe, "Democracy Against the Welfare State? Structural Foundations of Neoconservative Political Opportunities," *Political Theory*, volume 15, number 4 (November 1987), pp. 501–537.

69. "Reply to Symposium Participants," p. 438.

70. *Between Facts and Norms*, p. 383.

71. James C. Scott, *Domination and the Arts of Resistance: Hidden Transcripts* (New Haven, CT: Yale University Press, 1990), p. 115, footnote 12.

72. Nicos Poulantzas, *State, Power, Socialism* (London: Verso, 1980); Panitch, "Rethinking the Role of the State," in *Globalization: Critical Reflections*, edited by James H. Mittelman (Boulder, CO: Lynne Rienner Publishers, 1996), pp. 83–113; Bohman, op. cit. Habermas's withdrawal of his earlier idea that the public sphere must "besiege" the political apparatus from the outside opens the door for expanding his recommendations for democratization of the apparatus itself: *Between Facts and Norms*, p. 440.

73. Quoted in William Greider, *Who Will Tell the People: The Betrayal of American Democracy* (New York: Simon and Schuster/Touchstone, 1992), p. 20.

CHAPTER 8   HABERMAS AND THE POLITICS OF THE
TWENTY-FIRST CENTURY

1. "Struggles for Recognition in the Democratic Constitutional State," in *Multiculturalism: Examining the Politics of Recognition*, edited by Amy Gutmann (Princeton, NJ: Princeton University Press, 1994), p. 108. See also *The Postnational Constellation: Political Essays* (Cambridge, MA: MIT Press, 2001), p. 87; *The Past as Future* (Lincoln: University of Nebraska Press, 1994), p. 67; *A Berlin Republic: Writings on Germany* (Lincoln: University of Nebraska Press, 1997), p. 62.

2. *The Inclusion of the Other: Studies in Political Theory* (Cambridge, MA: MIT Press, 1998), p. 122, p. 174; *The Postnational Constellation*, p. 69.
3. *The Postnational Constellation*, p. 105.
4. Ibid., p. 79; *The Past as Future*, pp. 77–78; "Citizenship and National Identity: Some Reflections on the Future of Europe," *Praxis International* 12:1 (1992), p. 9.
5. *The Past as Future*, p. 95.
6. *The Postnational Constellation*, p. 104; *The Inclusion of the Other*, pp. 251–252.
7. *The Inclusion of the Other*, p. 121, p. 151.
8. *The Past as Future*, p. 117. The word "pacemaker," although at odds with Habermas's much more frequent statement that moral-legal developments are the "pacemaker of social evolution," probably merely indicates that capitalism, once freed, creates the leading dynamic.
9. *The Inclusion of the Other*, p. 174; cf. *The New Conservatism: Cultural Criticism and the Historians' Debate* (Cambridge, MA: MIT Press, 1989), p. 257. Habermas even goes so far as to say that the "territorial state" itself is "washed up," in *The Past as Future*, p. 81.
10. *The Postnational Constellation*, p. 49, p. 51.
11. Ibid., p. 79, pp. 89–91; *A Berlin Republic*, p. 62.
12. *The Inclusion of the Other*, p. 123; *The New Conservatism*, pp. 61–62; *The Past as Future*, p. 56.
13. *The New Conservatism*, p. 62; *A Berlin Republic*, p. 98, p. 180.
14. "Citizenship and National Identity," p. 13; *The Past as Future*, p. 135.
15. *A Berlin Republic*, p. 98; *The Postnational Constellation*, p. xix, p. 72; *The New Conservatism*, p. 191. In *The New Conservatism* Habermas discusses the "social Darwinism of the two-thirds society."
16. *The New Conservatism*, p. 61.
17. Ibid., p. 201.
18. "Struggles for Recognition in the Democratic Constitutional State," p. 132.
19. Ibid., p. 127. Contentiously, Habermas even links the popularity of post-modernism with fundamentalism: "Here the counterpart to religious fundamentalism forms the skepticism of a self-destructive critique of reason, one that senses behind every universal validity claim the dogmatic will to domination of a cunningly concealed particularism": *The Past as Future*, p. 21.
20. *The Past as Future*, p. 9; *The Postnational Constellation*, p. 53.
21. *The Past as Future*, p. 19; *The Postnational Constellation*, p. 134.
22. *A Berlin Republic*, p. 63.
23. Ibid., p. 180.
24. *A Berlin Republic*, p. 157. In other places he refers to "collapse" or that the welfare state is "no longer obtaining." See *The Postnational Constellation*, p. 87, and *The Inclusion of the Other*, p. 119.
25. *The Postnational Constellation*, p. 52.

26. Rudolf Meidner, "Why Did the Swedish Model Fail?" in *Socialist Register 1993*, edited by Ralph Miliband and Leo Panitch (London: The Merlin Press, 1993), pp. 211–228.
27. *The Postnational Constellation*, pp. 50–51. Cf. ibid., p. 79, *A Berlin Republic*, p. 180, and *The Inclusion of the Other*, p. 123.
28. *The Postnational Constellation*, p. 61.
29. "Citizenship and National Identity," pp. 3–4.
30. *The Inclusion of the Other*, p. 111.
31. Ibid., p. 117.
32. "Citizenship and National Identity," p. 2.
33. *The Postnational Constellation*, p. 64.
34. *The New Conservatism*, pp. 256–257. The Basic Law is the title of Germany's constitution.
35. "Struggles for Recognition in the Democratic Constitutional State," p. 134; "Citizenship and National Identity," p. 7; *The Inclusion of the Other*, p. 118.
36. *The Inclusion of the Other*, p. 118.
37. "Struggles for Recognition in the Democratic Constitutional State," p. 139, p. 133. The phrase is that of John Rawls.
38. *The Postnational Constellation*, p. 76.
39. Ibid., p. 73.
40. *The Inclusion of the Other*, p. 161.
41. *The Postnational Constellation*, p.19; *The Inclusion of the Other*, p. 106.
42. *The Postnational Constellation*, p. 154.
43. Ibid., p. 83.
44. *The Inclusion of the Other*, p. 252; *A Berlin Republic*, p. 76.
45. *The Postnational Constellation*, p. 76.
46. Ibid., p. 52; *The Inclusion of the Other*, pp. 157–158.
47. *The Postnational Constellation*, p. 70; *A Berlin Republic*, p. 168; *The Past as Future*, p. 78.
48. *The Postnational Constellation*, p. 81, p. 53.
49. Ibid., p. 99.
50. "Citizenship and National Identity," p. 9.
51. *The Past as Future*, p. 12; "Struggles for Recognition in the Democratic Constitutional State," pp. 141.
52. *The Past as Future*, p. 22.
53. *The Inclusion of the Other*, pp. xxxvi–xxxvii, p. 147.
54. Ibid., p. 177, p. 127; *The Past as Future*, p. 92.
55. *The Postnational Constellation*, p. 55.
56. *The Inclusion of the Other*, p. 168; *The Postnational Constellation*, p. 56.
57. *The Inclusion of the Other*, p. 181.
58. *The Postnational Constellation*, p. 56.
59. Ibid., pp. 111–112, pp. 54–55.
60. Ibid., pp. 108–109, p. 56.
61. Ibid., p. 102.
62. Ibid., p. 49, pp. 108–110.

63. Karl Polanyi, *The Great Transformation: The Political and Economic Origins of Our Time* (Boston: Beacon Press, 1957), p. 139.

64. William G. Roy, *Socializing Capital: The Rise of the Large Industrial Corporation in America* (Princeton, NJ: Princeton University Press, 1997).

65. Paul Hirst, *On Law and Ideology* (Atlantic Highlands, NJ: Humanities Press, 1979), p. 56.

66. *The Theory of Communicative Action, volume 2, Lifeworld and System: A Critique of Functionalist Reason* (Boston: Beacon Press, 1987), pp. 383–384.

67. "Concluding Remarks," in *Habermas and the Public Sphere*, edited by Craig Calhoun (Cambridge, MA: MIT Press, 1992), p. 470; cf. Peter Dews (ed.), *Autonomy and Solidarity: Interviews with Jürgen Habermas* (London: Verso, 1992), p. 83.

68. "Marxist Century—American Century: The Making and Remaking of the World Labor Movement," in *Transforming the Revolution: Social Movements and the World-System*, Samir Amin, Giovanni Arrighi, Andre Gunder Frank, and Immanuel Wallerstein (New York: Monthly Review Press, 1990), p. 64.

69. Friedrich Hayek, *The Fatal Conceit: The Errors of Socialism* (Chicago: The University of Chicago Press, 1988), pp. 36–37. Habermas once briefly alludes to the importance for capitalists of maintaining property right: *The Postnational Constellation*, p. 105.

70. "What Does Socialism Mean Today? The Rectifying Revolution and the Need for New Thinking on the Left," *New Left Review* 183 (1990), p. 17; *Lifeworld and System*, pp. 348–350.

71. *Legitimation Crisis* (Boston: Beacon Press, 1975), pp. 37–38, p. 73, and p. 93; *Lifeworld and System*, p. 302, p. 303, p. 332, p. 364, pp. 391–392, p. 347.

72. Dews, op. cit., p. 69.

73. On Luhmann, *The Philosophical Discourse of Modernity: Twelve Lectures* (Cambridge, MA: MIT Press, 1987), pp. 354–355; on Parsons, *Lifeworld and System*, p. 285. And George Herbert Mead, *Lifeworld and System*, p. 110: "The material reproduction of society—securing its physical maintenance both externally and internally—is blended out of the picture of society understood as a communicatively structured lifeworld. The neglect of economics, warfare, and the struggle for polit-ical power, the disregard for dynamics in favor of the logic of societal development are detrimental, above all, to Mead's reflections on social evolution."

74. *The Past as Future*, p. 121.

75. *The Postnational Constellation*, p. 95; *The Past as Future*, p. 122.

76. *The Inclusion of the Other*, p. 183.

77. *The Past as Future*, p. 152.

78. James L. Marsh, "What's Critical About Critical Theory?" in *Perspectives on Habermas*, edited by Lewis Edwin Hahn (Chicago: Open Court

Press, 2000), p. 559. Or as Anthony Giddens put it once, "Too much Weber! Too little Marx!" "Reason Without Revolution? Habermas's *Theorie des communikativen Handelns*," in *Habermas and Modernity*, edited by Richard J. Bernstein (Cambridge, MA: MIT Press, 1985), p. 120.

WORKS CITED

Alexy, Robert. "Jürgen Habermas's Theory of Legal Discourse." In Michel Rosenfeld and Andrew Arato (eds.), *Habermas on Law and Democracy: Critical Exchanges*. Berkeley: University of California Press, 1998. Pp. 226–233.

Amin, Samir, Giovanni Arrighi, Andre Gunder Frank, and Immanuel Wallerstein. *Transforming the Revolution: Social Movements and the World-System*. New York: Monthly Review Press, 1990.

Antonio, Robert J., and Ronald M. Glassman (eds.). *A Weber–Marx Dialogue*. Lawrence: University Press of Kansas, 1985.

Arendt, Hannah. *Between Past and Future: Eight Exercises in Political Thought*. New York: Penguin Books, 1968.

———. *On Revolution*. New York: Penguin Books, 1977.

Arnason, Johann P. "Modernity as Project and as Field of Tensions." In Axel Honneth and Hans Joas (eds.), *Communicative Action: Essays on Jürgen Habermas's The Theory of Communicative Action*. Cambridge, MA: MIT Press, 1991. Pp. 181–213.

Arrighi, Giovanni. "Marxist Century—American Century: The Making and Remaking of the World Labor Movement." In Samir Amin, Giovanni Arrighi, Andre Gunder Frank, and Immanuel Wallerstein, *Transforming the Revolution: Social Movements and the World-System*. New York: Monthly Review Press, 1990. Pp. 54–95.

Bendix, Reinhard. *Max Weber: An Intellectual Portrait*. New York: Doubleday/Anchor Books, 1962.

Benhabib, Seyla. "The Generalized and the Concrete Other: The Kohlberg–Gilligan Controversy and Feminist Theory." In Seyla Benhabib and Drucilla Cornell (eds.), *Feminism as Critique: On the Politics of Gender*. Minneapolis: University of Minnesota Press, 1987. Pp. 77–95.

———. "The Debate Over Women in Moral Theory Revisited." In Johanna Meehan (ed.), *Feminists Read Habermas: Gendering the Subject of Discourse*. New York: Routledge, 1995. Pp. 181–203.

———, and Drucilla Cornell (eds.), *Feminism as Critique: On the Politics of Gender*. Minneapolis: University of Minnesota Press, 1987.

Berger, Johannes. "The Linguistification of the Sacred and the Delinguistification of the Economy." In Axel Honneth and Hans Joas (eds.), *Communicative Action: Essays on Jürgen Habermas's The Theory of Communicative Action*. Cambridge, MA: MIT Press, 1991. Pp. 165–180.

Bernstein, Richard J. (ed.). *Habermas and Modernity*. Cambridge, MA: MIT Press, 1985.

Blackburn, Robin (ed.). *After the Fall: The Failure of Communism and the Future of Socialism*. London: Verso, 1991.

——. "Fin de Siecle: Socialism after the Crash." In Robin Blackburn (ed.), *After the Fall: The Failure of Communism and the Future of Socialism*. London: Verso, 1991. Pp. 173–249.

Blaug, Ricardo. *Democracy, Real and Ideal: Discourse Ethics and Radical Politics*. Albany: State University of New York Press, 1999.

Bohman, James. *Public Deliberation: Pluralism, Complexity, and Democracy*. Cambridge, MA: MIT Press, 1996.

Calhoun, Craig (ed.). *Habermas and the Public Sphere*. Cambridge, MA: MIT Press, 1992.

Cohen, G. A. *Karl Marx's Theory of History: A Defense*. Princeton, NJ: Princeton University Press, 1978.

Cohen, Jean L. "Critical Social Theory and Feminist Critiques: The Debate with Jürgen Habermas." In Johanna Meehan (ed.), *Feminists Read Habermas: Gendering the Subject of Discourse*. New York: Routledge, 1995. Pp. 57–90.

——, and Andrew Arato. *Civil Society and Political Theory*. Cambridge, MA: MIT Press, 1992.

Cohen, Joshua. "Reflections on Habermas on Democracy." *Ratio Juris* 12:4 (1999). Pp. 385–416.

Crozier, Michel, Samuel P. Huntington, and Joji Watanuki. *The Crisis of Democracy*. New York: New York University Press, 1975.

Dallmayr, Fred R. "Life-World: Variations on a Theme." In Steven K. White (ed.), *Lifeworld and Politics: Between Modernity and Postmodernity*. Notre Dame, IN: University of Notre Dame Press, 1989. Pp. 25–65.

Danto, Arthur. *Beyond the Brillo Box: The Visual Arts in Post-Historical Perspective*. New York: Farrar, Straus, Giroux, 1992.

Dews, Peter. *Autonomy and Solidarity: Interviews with Jürgen Habermas*. London: Verso, 1992.

Dryzek, John S. *Discursive Democracy: Politics, Policy, and Political Science*. New York: Cambridge University Press, 1990.

——. *Democracy in Capitalist Times: Ideals, Limits, Struggles*. New York: Oxford University Press, 1996.

Fleming, Marie. *Emancipation and Illusion: Rationality and Gender in Habermas's Theory of Modernity*. University Park: Pennsylvania State University Press, 1997.

Forbath, William E. "Short Circuit: A Critique of Habermas's Understanding of Law, Politics, and Economic Life." In Michel Rosenfeld and Andrew Arato (eds.), *Habermas on Law and Democracy: Critical Exchanges*. Berkeley: University of California Press, 1998. Pp. 272–286.

Fraser, Nancy. "Rethinking the Public Sphere: A Contribution to the Critique of Actually Existing Democracy." In Craig Calhoun (ed.), *Habermas and the Public Sphere*. Cambridge, MA.: MIT Press, 1992. Pp. 109–142.

——. "What's Critical About Critical Theory?" In Johanna Meehan (ed.), *Feminists Read Habermas: Gendering the Subject of Discourse*. New York: Routledge, 1995. Pp. 21–55.

Gerth, H. H., and C. Wright Mills (eds.). *From Max Weber: Essays in Sociology*. New York: Oxford University Press, 1958.

Giddens, Anthony. "Reason Without Revolution? Habermas's *Theorie des kommunikativen Handelns*." In Richard J. Bernstein (ed.), *Habermas and Modernity*. Cambridge, MA: MIT Press, 1985. Pp. 95–121.

The Good Society: A PEGS Journal (Committee on the Political Economy of the Good Society), volume 7 (1997) and volume 9 (1999).

Greider, William. *Who Will Tell the People: The Betrayal of American Democracy*. New York: Simon and Schuster/Touchstone, 1992.

Gutmann, Amy (ed.). *Multiculturalism: Examining the Politics of Recognition*. Princeton, NJ: Princeton University Press, 1994.

Habermas, Jürgen. *Toward a Rational Society: Student Protest, Science, and Politics*. Boston: Beacon Press, 1970.

——. *Legitimation Crisis*. Boston: Beacon Press, 1975.

——. *Communication and the Evolution of Society*. Boston: Beacon Press, 1979

——. *The Theory of Communicative Action, volume 1, Reason and the Rationalization of Society*. Boston: Beacon Press, 1984.

——. *The Theory of Communicative Action, volume 2, Lifeworld and System: A Critique of Functionalist Reason*. Boston: Beacon Press, 1987.

——. *The New Conservatism: Cultural Criticism and the Historians' Debate*. Cambridge, MA: MIT Press, 1989.

——. *The Structural Transformation of the Public Sphere: An Inquiry into a Category of Bourgeois Society*. Cambridge, MA: MIT Press, 1989.

——. *Moral Consciousness and Communicative Action*. Cambridge, MA: MIT Press, 1990.

——. *The Philosophical Discourse of Modernity: Twelve Lectures*. Cambridge, MA: MIT Press, 1990.

——. *Postmetaphysical Thinking: Philosophical Essays*. Cambridge, MA: MIT Press, 1992.

——. *Justification and Application: Remarks on Discourse Ethics*. Cambridge, MA: MIT Press, 1993.

——. *The Past as Future*. Lincoln: University of Nebraska Press, 1994.

——. *Between Facts and Norms: Contributions to a Discourse Theory of Law and Democracy*. Cambridge, MA: MIT Press, 1996.

——. *A Berlin Republic: Writings on Germany*. Lincoln: University of Nebraska Press, 1997.

——. *The Inclusion of the Other: Studies in Political Theory*. Cambridge, MA: MIT Press, 1998.

Habermas, Jürgen. *The Postnational Constellation: Political Essays.* Cambridge, MA: MIT Press, 2001.

——. "A Reply to My Critics." In John B. Thompson and David Held (eds.), *Habermas: Critical Debates.* Cambridge, MA: MIT Press, 1982. Pp. 219–283.

——. "Remarks on the Concept of Communicative Action." In Gottfried Seebass and Raimo Tuomela (eds.), *Social Action.* Boston: D. Reidel Publishing Company, 1985. Pp. 151–178.

——. "A Philosophico-Political Profile." *New Left Review* 151 (1985). Pp. 75–105.

——. "Psychic Thermidor and the Rebirth of Rebellious Subjectivity." In Richard J. Bernstein (ed.), *Habermas and Modernity.* Cambridge, MA: MIT Press, 1985. Pp. 67–77.

——. "Questions and Counterquestions." In Richard J. Bernstein (ed.), *Habermas and Modernity.* Cambridge, MA: MIT Press, 1985.

——. "The New Obscurity: The Crisis of the Welfare State and the Exhaustion of Utopian Energies." *Philosophy and Social Criticism* 11 (1986). Pp. 1–17.

——. "What Does Socialism Mean Today? The Rectifying Revolution and the Need for New Thinking on the Left." *New Left Review* 183 (1990). Pp. 3–21.

——. "A Reply." In Axel Honneth and Hans Joas (eds.), *Communicative Action: Essays on Jürgen Habermas's The Theory of Communicative Action.* Cambridge, MA: MIT Press, 1991. Pp. 214–264.

——. "Citizenship and National Identity: Some Reflections on the Future of Europe." *Praxis International* 12:1 (1992). Pp. 1–19.

——. "Concluding Remarks." In Craig Calhoun (ed.), *Habermas and the Public Sphere.* Cambridge, MA: MIT Press, 1992. Pp. 462–479.

——. "Further Reflections on the Public Sphere." In Craig Calhoun (ed.), *Habermas and the Public Sphere.* Cambridge, MA: MIT Press, 1992. Pp. 421–461.

——. "Notes on the Developmental History of Horkheimer's Work." *Theory, Culture, and Society* 10 (1993). Pp. 61–77.

——. "Struggles for Recognition in the Democratic Constitutional State." In Amy Gutmann (ed.), *Multiculturalism: Examining the Politics of Recognition.* Princeton: Princeton University Press, 1994. Pp. 107–148.

——. "Reply to Symposium Participants, Benjamin W. Cardozo School of Law." In Michel Rosenfeld and Andrew Arato (eds.), *Habermas on Law and Democracy: Critical Exchanges.* Berkeley: University of California Press, 1998. Pp. 381–452.

——. "The European Nation-State and the Pressures of Globalization." *New Left Review* 235 (1999). Pp. 46–59.

Hahn, Lewis Edwin (ed.). *Perspectives on Habermas.* Chicago: Open Court Press, 2000.

Harvey, David L., and Mike Reed. "The Limits of Synthesis: Some Comments on Habermas's Recent Sociological Writings." *International Journal of Politics, Culture, and Society* 4:3 (1991). Pp. 345–370.

Hayek, F. A. *The Fatal Conceit: The Errors of Socialism.* Chicago: University of Chicago Press, 1988.

Hirst, Paul. *On Law and Ideology.* Atlantic Highlands, NJ: Humanities Press, 1979.

Hollis, Martin, and Steve Lukes (eds.). *Rationality and Relativism.* Cambridge, MA: MIT Press, 1982.

Honneth, Axel, Thomas McCarthy, Claus Offe, and Albrecht Wellmer (eds.). *Cultural-Political Interventions in the Unfinished Project of Enlightenment.* Cambridge, MA: MIT Press, 1992.

Horkheimer, Max. *Eclipse of Reason.* New York: Seabury Press, 1974.

——, and Theodor Adorno. *Dialectic of Enlightenment.* New York: The Continuum Publishing Company, 1989.

Ingram, David. "Habermas on Aesthetics and Rationality: Completing the Project of Enlightenment." *New German Critique* 53 (1991). Pp. 67–103.

Isaac, Jeffrey C. *Democracy in Dark Times.* Ithaca, NY: Cornell University Press, 1998.

Jameson, Fredric. "Foreword" to Jean-François Lyotard, *The Postmodern Condition: A Report on Knowledge.* Minneapolis: University of Minnesota Press, 1984. Pp. vii–xxi.

Jay, Martin. *The Dialectical Imagination: A History of the Frankfurt School and the Institute for Social Research 1923–1950.* Boston: Little, Brown, and Company, 1973.

Kauffman, Stuart. *At Home in the Universe: The Search for Laws of Self-Organization and Complexity.* New York: Oxford University Press, 1995.

Kellner, Douglas. "Critical Theory, Max Weber, and the Dialectics of Domination." In Robert J. Antonio and Ronald M. Glassman (eds.), *A Weber-Marx Dialogue.* Lawrence: University Press of Kansas, 1985. Pp. 89–116.

Krueger, Hans-Peter. "Communicative Action or the Mode of Communication for Society as a Whole." In Axel Honneth and Hans Joas (eds.), *Communicative Action: Essays on Jürgen Habermas's The Theory of Communicative Action.* Cambridge, MA: MIT Press, 1991. Pp. 140–164.

Krugman, Paul. *The Self-Organizing Economy.* Oxford: Blackwell Publishers, 1996.

Lindblom, Charles E. *Politics and Markets: The World's Political-Economic Systems.* New York: Basic Books, 1977.

Lukács, Georg. *History and Class Consciousness: Studies in Marxist Dialectics.* Cambridge, MA: MIT Press, 1971.

Lyotard, Jean-François. *The Postmodern Condition: A Report on Knowledge.* Minneapolis: University of Minnesota Press, 1984.

Marcuse, Herbert. *Eros and Civilization: A Philosophical Inquiry into Freud.* New York: Vintage Books, 1962.

——. *An Essay on Liberation.* Boston: Beacon Press, 1969.

——. *Five Lectures: Psychoanalysis, Politics, and Utopia.* Boston: Beacon Press, 1970.

——. *Counterrevolution and Revolt.* Boston: Beacon Press, 1972.

Marx, Karl. *A Contribution to the Critique of Political Economy.* New York: International Publishers, 1970.

———. *Grundrisse: Foundations of the Critique of Political Economy.* New York: Vintage Books, 1973.

———. *Capital: A Critique of Political Economy,* volume one. New York: Vintage Books, 1977.

MacIntyre, Alasdair. *A Short History of Ethics.* New York: The Macmillan Company, 1966.

———. *After Virtue: A Study in Moral Theory.* Notre Dame, IN: University of Notre Dame Press, 1984.

———. *Whose Justice? Which Rationality?* Notre Dame, IN: University of Notre Dame Press, 1988.

McCarthy, Thomas. "Complexity and Democracy, or the Seducements of Systems Theory." *New German Critique* 35 (1985). Pp. 27–53.

———. "Philosophy and Social Practice: Avoiding the Ethnocentric Predicament." In Axel Honneth, Thomas McCarthy, Claus Offe, and Albrecht Wellmer (eds.), *Philosophical Interventions in the Unfinished Project of Enlightenment.* Cambridge, MA: MIT Press, 1992. Pp. 241–260.

Marsh, James L. "What's Critical About Critical Theory?" In Lewis Edwin Hahn (ed.), *Perspectives on Habermas.* Chicago: Open Court Press, 2000. Pp. 555–567.

Meehan, Johanna (ed.). *Feminists Read Habermas: Gendering the Subject of Discourse.* New York: Routledge, 1995.

Meidner, Rudolf. "Why Did the Swedish Model Fail?" In Ralph Miliband and Leo Panitch (eds.), *Socialist Register 1993.* London: The Merlin Press, 1993. Pp. 211–228.

Mittelman, James H. (ed.). *Globalization: Critical Reflections.* Boulder, CO: Lynne Rienner Publishers, 1996.

Mommsen, Wolfgang. "Capitalism and Socialism: Weber's Dialogue with Marx." In Robert J. Antonio and Ronald M. Glassman (eds.), *A Weber–Marx Dialogue.* Lawrence: University Press of Kansas, 1985. Pp. 234–261.

Nietzsche, Friedrich. *The Will to Power.* New York: Vintage Books, 1968.

Nove, Alec. *The Economics of Feasible Socialism.* London: George Allen and Unwin, 1983.

Offe, Claus. *Industry and Inequality: The Achievement Principle in Work and Social Status.* New York: St. Martin's Press, 1977.

———. *Contradictions of the Welfare State.* Cambridge, MA.: MIT Press, 1984.

———. *Disorganized Capitalism.* Cambridge, MA.: MIT Press, 1985.

———. "New Social Movements: Challenging the Boundaries of Institutional Politics." *Social Research* 52:4 (1985). Pp. 817–868.

———. "Democracy Against the Welfare State? Structural Foundations of Neoconservative Political Opportunities." *Political Theory* 15:4 (1987). Pp. 501–537.

Panitch, Leo. "Rethinking the Role of the State." In James H. Mittelman (ed.), *Globalization: Critical Reflections.* Boulder, CO: Lynne Rienner Publishers, 1996. Pp. 83–113.

Parkin, Frank. *Marxism and Class Theory: A Bourgeois Critique*. New York: Columbia University Press, 1979.

Parsons, Talcott. *Sociological Theory and Modern Society*. New York: The Free Press, 1967.

———. *The System of Modern Societies*. Englewood Cliffs, NJ: Prentice-Hall, Inc., 1971.

Polanyi, Karl. *The Great Transformation: The Political and Economic Origins of Our Time*. Boston: Beacon Press, 1957.

Postone, Moishe. *Time, Labor, and Social Domination: A Reinterpretation of Marx's Critical Theory*. Cambridge: Cambridge University Press, 1993.

Poulantzas, Nicos. *State, Power, Socialism*. London: Verso, 1980.

Rosenberg, Harold. *The De-definition of Art*. Chicago: University of Chicago Press, 1972.

———. *The Anxious Object*. Chicago: University of Chicago Press, 1983.

Rosenfeld, Michel, and Andrew Arato (eds.). *Habermas on Law and Democracy: Critical Exchanges*. Berkeley: The University of California Press, 1998.

Roy, William G. *Socializing Capital: The Rise of the Large Industrial Corporation in America*. Princeton, NJ: Princeton University Press, 1997.

Rubin, Isaak Illich. *Essays on Marx's Theory of Value*. Detroit: Black and Red, 1972.

Schlink, Bernhard. "The Dynamics of Constitutional Adjudication." In Michel Rosenfeld and Andrew Arato (eds.), *Habermas on Law and Democracy: Critical Exchanges*. Berkeley: University of California Press, 1998. Pp. 371–378.

Scott, James C. *Domination and the Arts of Resistance: Hidden Transcripts*. New Haven, CT: Yale University Press, 1990.

———. *Seeing Like a State: How Certain Schemes to Improve the Human Condition Have Failed*. New Haven, CT: Yale University Press, 1998.

Seebass, Gottfried, and Raimo Tuomela (eds.). *Social Action*. Boston: D. Reidel Publishing Company, 1985.

Sitton, John F. *Recent Marxian Theory: Class Formation and Social Conflict in Contemporary Capitalism*. Albany: The State University of New York Press, 1996.

Strauss, Leo. *Natural Right and History*. Chicago: University of Chicago Press, 1953.

Taylor, Charles. "Rationality." In Martin Hollis and Steve Lukes (eds.), *Rationality and Relativism*. Cambridge, MA: MIT Press, 1982. Pp. 87–105.

Thompson, John B., and David Held (eds.). *Habermas: Critical Debates*. Cambridge, MA: MIT Press, 1982.

Thucydides. *The Peloponnesian War*.

Waldrop, M. Mitchell. *Complexity: The Emerging Science on the Edge of Order and Chaos*. New York: Simon and Schuster, 1992.

Weber, Max. *The Protestant Ethic and the Spirit of Capitalism*. New York: Charles Scribner's Sons, 1976.

Weber, Max. *Economy and Society: An Outline of Interpretive Sociology.* Two Volumes. Guenther Roth and Claus Wittich (eds.). Berkeley: University of California Press, 1978.

White, Stephen K. (ed.). *Lifeworld and Politics: Between Modernity and Postmodernity.* Notre Dame, IN: University of Notre Dame Press, 1989.

Wilson, Bryan R. (ed.). *Rationality.* New York: Harper and Row, 1970.

——. "A Sociologist's Introduction." In Bryan R. Wilson (ed.), *Rationality.* New York: Harper and Row, 1970. Pp. xii–xviii.

Winch, Peter. "Understanding a Primitive Society." In Bryan R. Wilson (ed.), *Rationality.* New York: Harper and Row, 1970. Pp. 78–111.

Wood, Allen W. "Habermas's Defense of Rationalism." *New German Critique* 35 (1985). Pp. 145–164.

Young, Iris Marion. "Impartiality and the Civic Public: Some Implications of Feminist Critiques of Moral and Political Theory." In Seyla Benhabib and Drucilla Cornell (eds.), *Feminism as Critique: On the Politics of Gender.* Minneapolis: University of Minnesota Press, 1987. Pp. 57–76.

INDEX